WORSHIP ACROSS CULTURES

WORSHIP ACROSS CULTURES

A Handbook

Kathy Black

ABINGDON PRESS
Nashville

WORSHIP ACROSS CULTURES
A HANDBOOK

Copyright © 1998 by Abingdon Press

All rights reserved.

This book is printed on acid-free, recycled paper.

Library of Congress Cataloging-in-Publication Data
Black, Kathy, 1956-
   Worship across cultures : a handbook / Kathy Black
      p. cm.
   ISBN 0-687-05652-7
   1. United Methodist Church (U.S.)—Liturgy   2. Ethnic-ity—Religious aspects—Methodist Church.   I. Title.
BX8337.B62   1998
264 ′.076—dc21

Unless otherwise noted, all scripture quotations are from The New Re-vised Standard Version Bible, copyright © 1989 by the Division of Christian Education of the National Council of the Churches of Christ in the USA. Used by permission.

98 99 00 01 02 03 04 05 06 07 — 10 9 8 7 6 5 4 3 2 1

to my nephew
Jeremy Raúl Andrade
who in his being represents our increasingly
multicultural world

CONTENTS

ACKNOWLEDGMENTS

This book would not be possible without the knowledge and experience of many seminary students, clergy, and laity of various cultures from all over the United States. There is no way I can thank the one hundred and fifty clergy who took time out of their busy schedules to fill out a very lengthy questionnaire. They represent six denominations and twenty-one cultures.

I do, however, want to thank those who have been my invaluable colleagues, co-authors, and editors: Rev. Marv Abrams (Native American), Rev. Samuel Arhin (Ghanaian), Rev. Sony Augustin (Haitian), Rev. Yvonne Williams Boyd (African-American), Rev. Dr. Seog Wan Cho (Korean), Rev. Samuel Chow (Chinese), John David (Pakistani), Rev. Dr. Ronald Dunk (Euro-American), Rev. Myriam Escorcia (Hispanic), Rev. Niponi Finau (Tongan), Rev. Dr. Daniel Gueh (Liberian), Rev. Keith Inouye (Japanese), Rev. Dr. Winson Josiah (Indian), Saimone Kete (Fijian), Rev. Mamie Ko (Chinese), Rev. Dr. John Kounthapanya (Laotian), Rev. Dr. Richard Kuyama (Japanese), Pitou Lao (Cambodian), Rev. Pita Lauti (Samoan), Rev. Dr. David Marcelo (Filipino), Rev. Cam Phu Nguyen (Vietnamese), Rev. Andrew Robinson-Gaither (African-American), Rev. Dr. Luat Trong Tran (Vietnamese), Rev. Frank Yang (Formosan), and Rev. Kham Dy Yang (Hmong). Each one graciously answered my questions and shared with me their rich cultures and worship practices. Their congregations welcomed me warmly as I worshiped among them.

I would also like to thank those who provided additional information on 1.5 and second generation worship practices as well as those who offered insights into various religious, linguistic, and cultural practices of the communities represented in the book: Rev. Jocelyn Jean-Baptiste Adhemar (Haitian), Rev. Keith Hwang (Korean), Lamuel Jacob (Indian), Rev. Gail Messner (Japanese-Hawaiian), Hao Hong and Ahn Tran Nguyen (Vietnamese), Rev. Homer Noley (Native American), Rev. John Parker (Korean), Rev. Gloria Yahng (Korean), and Rev. Michael Yahng (Korean).

While this book focuses on United Methodist worship practices, it began as a study of the cultural practices of six denominations. The information received from these additional denominations would not have been possible without the help of Rev. Don Reisinger (Christian Church, Disciples of Christ), Rev. Dr. Mary June Nestler (Episcopal

Church), Rev. Roger Rogahn (Evangelical Lutheran Church of America), Rev. Bear Scott (Presbyterian Church USA), and Rev. Dr. Jane Heckles (United Church of Christ).

Special thanks to Marjorie Suchocki for reading early versions of the manuscript and providing valuable editorial comments.

INTRODUCTION

Kalatini was born and raised in Tonga. He did his theological education at the Claremont School of Theology and his field education in a Tongan church. Upon graduation, he was appointed to a Euro-American congregation.

Gloria and Michael are a clergy couple. They were both born in Korea. They moved to the United States with their respective parents and finished their primary education here. Their theological training was likewise completed at the Claremont School of Theology. Their Christian worship experiences growing up were in Korean churches (Korean language ministries in the U.S.), and during their seminary education they undertook their field education in Korean-American churches (English language ministries). Upon graduation, Gloria was appointed by her local United Methodist bishop as sole pastor of a congregation that was two-thirds Euro-American and one-third Fili-pino-American. Michael was appointed as sole pastor to a congregation that was comprised of Euro-American and African-American members.

Sally, a Euro-American, is pastor of a multicultural congregation. When the mother of a Vietnamese parishioner in her church died, she knew nothing about the evening service customarily held between the death of a Vietnamese person and the final funeral, nor was she aware of the need to allow time in the service for the distribution of the mourning bands.

Bob, a Euro-American pastor of a multicultural congregation, was waiting at the church to lead a funeral for the father of an African-American member of the church. The family however, was waiting at their home for the pastor to arrive and pray with them before escorting them to the church for the funeral. Neither was aware of the expecta-tions of the other.

Numerous Euro-American pastors serve multicultural congrega-tions, and many clergy of various ethnicities occupy cross-cultural pastoral positions. Issues such as those experienced by the clergy mentioned above often arise when the assumed worship practices of the pastor are those of a different cultural orientation than those of the congregation. In such situations, ministry is hindered.

I teach a course at Claremont called "United Methodist Worship Practicum" in which we use the United Methodist *Book of Worship* as a major resource. It is not uncommon for one-third to one-half of the class to be non Euro-American. Many of these students do not use the UM *Book of Worship* in their local churches. Some of their churches use books of liturgies that come from their native country (Korea, India, Pakistan, China, Tonga, Haiti) and others pray, lead the congregation in Holy Communion, baptize, marry, and lead funerals extemporaneously, without any preprinted texts.

I also function as a faculty advisor to the worship coordinators who plan weekly worship at Claremont. "How is it possible," I find myself asking, "for us to be as inclusive as possible when we do not know the worship practices of many within our community?"

It is these contexts, situations, and questions that led me in search of basic knowledge about the way persons from other cultures worship. At the outset of this study I started with two basic hypotheses: (1) That baptism and communion practices would be determined more by one's denominational practices; and (2) That wedding and funeral practices would be determined more by one's cultural traditions.

After gathering all the data, I have modified my first hypothesis: Baptism and communion practices are often determined by the denomination that first missionized the home country, or by the denomination that is strongest in the home country, rather than by what denomination the American congregation is affiliated with in the United States today. For example, Vietnamese, Cambodian, Hmong, and Lao congregations are more apt to follow worship practices of the Christian Missionary Alliance denomination, which was the first to missionize Vietnam and other southeast Asian countries, and is still the strongest presence there today. Consequently, Vietnamese United Methodists often prefer baptism of adults through immersion and passing the communion elements to the people in the pews rather than the more traditional United Methodist practices.

In other countries, mainline protestant denominations merged to form the Church of Pakistan or the United Church of Japan or the Church of South India. Whether pastors are currently Presbyterian, United Church of Christ, or United Methodist in America, the worship resources and practices come from these united denominations in the native country. The United Church of Japan's worship, for example, is highly influenced by Presbyterian missionaries. The worship practices of The Church of Pakistan is based on an Anglican model.

Methodology

I began by identifying the cultures represented in the Los Angeles basin within six Protestant denominations: Christian Church (Disciples of Christ), Episcopalian, Evangelical Lutheran Church of America, Presbyterian Church USA, United Church of Christ, and United Methodist. Thirteen different cultures were identified with churches pastored by someone from the culture with worship services in the native language(s) of the people.

I then designed a questionnaire that asked as many questions as I could think of regarding general worship practices, the sacramental practices of communion and baptism, and the rituals surrounding the rites of passage of marriages and funerals. This questionnaire was used as a basic tool for interviews.

As the project grew, I eventually identified about twenty-five United Methodist clergy from twenty-one different cultures who were willing to work with me on this project.[1] A few I knew from the Los Angeles area, but most were strangers to me when I began. They are from New York, Seattle, San Francisco, New Jersey, Nebraska, Minnesota, and Southern California. They represent those cultures and languages long existent on the American soil—Native Americans, Euro-Americans, Hispanic-Americans, and African-Americans—as well as the later immigrants from Cambodia, China, Fiji, Ghana, Haiti, Hong Kong, India, Japan, Korea, Laos, Liberia, Pakistan, Philippines, Samoa, Taiwan (Formosa), Tonga, and Vietnam.

For some cultures, I interviewed more than one clergyperson because of the tremendous diversity of worship practices (as in the African-American churches) or because of generational differences (as in Korean, Japanese, Chinese, and Vietnamese congregations).

While I thought the original questionnaire was detailed, I was well aware that coming from my own cultural biases, I, too, did not know all the questions to ask. The original questionnaire was thus adapted and expanded after each interview. Each interview lasted a couple of hours. I then typed up the information the clergy had given to me and sent it to them for their additions and corrections.

Next, I designed individual questionnaires for each of the twenty-one cultures based on the specific information I had received from the clergy person(s) interviewed. Those individual questionnaires were sent to selected clergy of that culture serving churches of that culture throughout the United States. By restricting the questionnaires to

13

pastors and churches of the same culture, I avoided the problem of data from churches whose multicultural context had already begun the process of worship adaptation.[2] While I collected data from six denominations, I decided to limit the research to United Methodist churches for several reasons. First, this creates a uniform basis for case study, eliminating some of the variables of denominational differences. Second, The United Methodist Church has the greatest diversity of ethnicities, and thus provides data for twenty-one different cultures. Third, the appointive system within The United Methodist Church brings the issue of cross-cultural ministry to the fore in ways only beginning to be experienced by the other denominations.

I do believe, however, that the information gathered here will be valuable for a variety of denominations because, for example, such rites as weddings and funerals are more culturally determined. In the same way the research on baptism and communion is similar across denominations that are flexible in the use of denominational worship resources. It should be noted, however, that the *Book of Common Prayer* and the Lutheran *Book of Worship* tend to function as a unifying factor across cultures for the rites of baptism and communion.

Complicating Factors

1. Multicultural and Multilingual Congregations

While on the surface many ethnic minority local churches appear to be homogeneous, in reality some congregations are multicultural and monolingual while others are monocultural but bilingual. Still others are multicultural and multilingual. For example, there are a few Hispanic churches whose members come almost solely from Mexico or Cuba or Puerto Rico, but most Hispanic churches are comprised of members from several different countries: El Salvador, Guatemala, Puerto Rico, Nicaragua, Cuba, Brazil, Mexico. The various cultures are linked together through the common language—Spanish.

The members of Formosan-American churches are unified by their common language of Fukienese, yet they come from the island of Taiwan, the Fukien (now called Fujian) province of China, and immigrants who also lived in the Philippines before moving to the United States. Twi and Fanti are languages commonly used in Ghanaian-Ameri-

14

can churches while Liberian churches may communicate in Bassa, Kru, or Kpelle, or Kissi.

Some Chinese-American churches are bilingual, incorporating the primary languages of mainline China (Mandarin—now called Putonghua) and of Hong Kong (Cantonese). The country of the Philippines is made up of thousands of islands and many different languages and dialects. Tagalog and Ilacano are commonly used during worship services in America. Those from different islands may have different cultural practices, especially in regard to funerals.

There are some Native American churches originally established to be in ministry with a particular tribe such as Choctaw, Creek, or Navajo, but most Native American congregations are a mixture of people from a wide variety of tribes. Any number of tribal languages as well as English may be used.

India has fifteen regional languages. In Indian-American congregations (sometimes called South Asian congregations), Hindi, Urdu, Gujarati, Tamil, Telugu, and/or Malayalam may be used. Years ago India sent citizens to the South Pacific island of Fiji to work in the sugarcane fields. Consequently, Fijian-American communities also have many members with Indian descent who may speak one of the languages of India as well as the language of Fiji.

2. Generational Gap

Another issue with a project such as this is generational differences. Some cultures have been on the American soil for numerous generations. Native Americans were obviously here long before the Europeans arrived, and persons of Mexican ancestry lived in what is now the United States before the arrival of Europeans as well. African-Americans were brought from Africa at the very beginning of the European occupation of the colonies, and Chinese persons were present in large numbers for the building of the railroads in the nineteenth century. The Japanese have also been citizens of the United States for many generations. And, there are persons from various cultures that are more recent arrivals in the United States: Cambodians, Vietnamese, Hmong, Lao, Haitians, Ghanaians, Liberians, and Pacific Islanders. While each person's heritage is rooted in a particular culture, those who were born, raised, and educated in the United States are also influenced by the American culture that is largely determined by the Euro-American population.

The result of this history is that the more generations existing within a particular culture, and the greater the population size of that culture, the greater the diversity of their worship practice. Persons representing cultures that are more recent immigrants to the United States tend to have more similar worship practices than those long established in this land.

There are also generational differences that exist within congregations. In order for churches of a particular culture to include first, 1.5 (those born in the home country, yet who have lived outside it since they were children or adolescents), and second generations, both native language ministries and English language ministries may be offered. This is a prominent practice in Korean, Chinese, and Japanese churches. However, the English language worship services often differ from the native language services. Some of the differences stem from an attempt to assimilate Euro-American practices (e.g. having confirmation when that is not a traditional custom within the culture). Other differences result from a pastor who has been theologically trained in the United States rather than in the country of ancestral origin (e.g. using a loaf of bread rather than wafers for second generation Chinese-American communion). And some differences may be in opposition to the parents' practice of worship (e.g. preaching shorter sermons, keeping services to one hour in the English language ministries of Korean communities).

Another difference that arises between generations is the search of subsequent generations to reclaim aspects of their ancestors' culture. Growing up in America, second and third generations often want to reclaim their cultural roots by including various cultural aspects from their native land in worship: use of traditional instruments, use of native cloth on the altar, etc. But the first generation denounced many cultural practices in order to define themselves as Christian. In many Asian countries where Christianity is not the dominant religion of the culture, persons who chose to become Christian denounced certain practices as Buddhist (i.e.: bowing three times as a sign of paying respect to the deceased). Bowing to the deceased was eliminated from most Christian funerals but subsequent generations allow this practice in an attempt to reclaim their cultural heritage.

Another example is found in the African-American tradition. While there are many generations between the ancestors who were stolen from Africa to be slaves and African-Americans today, some African-Americans are trying to reclaim their African heritage and roots by

16

becoming more Afro-centric. One practice that has emerged in some African-American congregations is the pouring of libation in honor of the ancestors that is found in some African-American weddings, occasionally on All Saints Day, during Black History Month, or for the celebration of Kwanzaa. More recent immigrants from Africa (Ghana, for example), choose *not* to use the pouring of the *libation* because it is associated with ancestor worship in the traditional religions of Africa. In order to identify themselves as Christian in the African context, the pouring of the libation was eliminated from Christian worship. But in reclaiming their African roots, African-Americans are reintroducing this practice.

3. Location

As with congregations of every culture, geographical and social locations contribute to the worship practices of a local faith community. The educational background and economic status of the members, as well as the geographical location and size of the congregation, make each congregation unique. The theology of both the congregation and the pastor, as well as the pastor's theological training and personal gifts for ministry, also affect the various worship practices of the congregation.

4. Philosophical Worldviews

Western society has been strongly influenced in the last centuries by the philosophical worldview of Modernism and more recently, Postmodernism. Modernism began with the Enlightenment. Truth, for the empiricists, was what could be empirically identified through the five senses. Science and logic became the hallmarks of objective knowledge that was valid for every time and place.

Today, however, Postmodernism is changing the way people view the world. Truth is relative because it is now recognized that all perception involves interpretation to some degree depending upon one's race, gender, class, educational level, culture, political and religious affiliations. Cultures that have not adopted Modernism and/or Postmodernism have other philosophical or religious constructs by which they organize the world: Confucianism, Buddhism, Hinduism, etc. For Christianity, these various worldviews have major influence on one's relationship with others, one's interpretation of the Bible, understanding ultimate truth, and authority.

Difficulties arise when persons from the Euro-American culture assume a Postmodern worldview when persons from other cultures never adhered to either Western philosophical worldview. Likewise, Euro-Americans have a difficult time understanding Christians from some Asian cultures who view the world from a Confucian notion of order, status, and authority.

Since these various worldviews greatly influence who we are and what we do, several aspects of the life of the church and its worship are affected: the role of laity in worship, the congregation's understanding of scripture, the authority of the pastor, and the role of preaching in the life of the church.

Similarities and Differences

Every cultural tradition gathers weekly for worship, and many gather two or three times each week to praise God in the bond of community. Several Korean churches have prayer and Bible study each morning around 6:00 a.m. All churches, of whatever ethnicity, celebrate the sacraments of Baptism and Holy Communion and have rituals of passage for marriage and death. Within the Sunday worship experience there are many elements common to all cultures: the recitation of the Lord's Prayer, singing hymns, offering our gifts to God, the reading and preaching of God's word, and closing with a benediction. But many cultures also have unique aspects in their forms of prayer (Tong Song Kido prayer in Korean-American congregations), postures of prayer (standing for all prayer in Vietnamese-American congregations), in the instruments used to accompany music or preference for no instruments at all (Tongan-American churches), and in their dance of life as they offer their gifts to God (Ghanaian-American churches).

Weddings are a joyous occasion in every culture. Western-style weddings (brought to many cultures by missionaries) have been adopted by many cultures as a "Christian" wedding form. Some cultures also developed a Christian ritual surrounding their cultural celebration of announcing one's engagement.

During the wedding itself, some cultures symbolize the union of the couple with the jumping of the broomstick (African-American and Ghanaian-American weddings), or with a lasso that binds the two together (Hispanic weddings), or with a unity candle that symbolizes the two becoming one (Euro-American weddings), or with a veil that

18

covers the bridal couple with the presence of God (Filipino-American weddings), or with the sharing of a kola nut (Liberian-American weddings), or with symbols of an umbrella and a blanket (Hmong-American weddings). In Fijian-American weddings, the pastor stands on a pile of fine mats and tapa cloth to conduct the ceremony.

It is not surprising that the funeral rites of various cultures are the most diverse of all the rituals of the church. The expectations people have at the time of death emerge from the depths of their cultural heritage, from traditions passed down from generation to generation throughout the many ages. In the Tongan-American culture, an all-night "Awakening" service precedes the burial, which takes place the morning after death. In the Ghanaian-American community however, a quick burial is seen as dishonoring the deceased. The body is held for a month before the burial takes place. Samoans have three funeral services: Saturday, Sunday, and Monday. Korean-Americans prefer to bury their dead on the third or fifth day after death since the number four is considered an unlucky number (similar to number thirteen in the Euro-American culture). Hmong Christians hold three funeral services everyday for six days with burial on the seventh day. Every culture honors their dead but the ritual practices vary.

In the descriptions of all the aspects of worship—from Sunday services and sacramental practices to the rites of passage—one must keep in mind that each congregation is unique. Everything described in these chapters will not be present in all congregations of any particular culture because of variable ways of adapting to the United States. What is offered here are general practices that can serve as a guide to a basic understanding of each culture's ways of worship and ritual. Hopefully the information provided will at least give clergy some of the questions to ask in dealing cross-culturally.

The chapters that follow are organized by culture. Each chapter has the same format. They begin with various elements of the Service of the Word, followed by descriptions of the sacramental practices of baptism and communion. Each chapter concludes with the rites of passage: weddings and funerals. Definitions of words and phrases that appear in italics in the text can be found in the glossary.

Despite the difficulties and variables involved in identifying specific worship practices of a particular culture or multicultural context, much that is extremely valuable can be gained. Knowing even the generalities of the different worship practices is essential for clergy who increasingly are called to minister in a multicultural context. Appreciation for one another's worship practices deeply enhances our sense of the great diversity involved in the praise of God.

Notes

1. As far as I was able to determine, these are all the cultures represented in The United Methodist Church—not the cultures represented by the various members within the denomination but rather those cultures that have established churches pastored by clergy of that culture in the native language(s). If I have missed any congregation that represents a culture other than the twenty-one included, I apologize and would greatly appreciate knowing what culture(s) have been omitted.

2. I recognize the presence of the Deaf Culture within the UMC, but I did not include them in this book because to date, there is no deaf church pastored by a culturally deaf person. This cross-cultural mix has already led to worship adaptation.

AFRICAN-AMERICAN WORSHIP PRACTICES

with Rev. Yvonne Williams Boyd
and Rev. M. Andrew Robinson-Gaither

The Service of the Word

The Language of the Liturgy

African-American services are conducted in the English language. In those congregations that are more Afro-centric, words from various African languages may also be used.

The Liturgical Space

The liturgical space in many African-American churches is devoid of overt symbols of the African-American culture (except for the wearing of *Kente* cloth stoles). There are some churches, however, whose worshiping space has a variety of symbols identifying the community as African-American and/or Afro-centric.

The Black Liberation flag may be present along with the American and Christian flags. The cover of the Sunday worship bulletin may portray African symbols and images. Black Christ or Black Messiah images may be in sculpture, painting, or stained glass. African-American cultural images may also be found on banners hanging in the sanctuary. A flask of oil may be present on the altar for the purpose of anointing. Kente cloth is often used as an altar cloth, as well as made into stoles for the pastor, vests for the junior ushers, and vestments for the choir.

Liturgical Time

Most worship services in the African-American context last between one and two hours.

Liturgical Garb

While many African-American clergy wear a black pulpit robe, some now wear a white alb, or various forms of *grambuba* (African dress) when leading worship. Clergy may also wear stoles made from kente cloth, or, for men, a kente cloth tie with a suit. In those churches that are Afro-centric, the *anke* (an African symbol of life) may be worn in place of a cross.

Liturgical Seasons and Days

All the seasons of the church year are celebrated by most African-American churches. In addition to Advent, Christmas, Epiphany, Lent, Easter, and Pentecost, some churches also celebrate Kingdomtide. Holy Thursday and Good Friday services mark Holy Week. Mother's Day, Father's Day, and All Saints Day highlight various members of the community both past and present. Thanksgiving Eve services are also held in many congregations. Some churches, however, choose to substitute *Umoja Karamu* (Unity Feast) in place of the American Thanksgiving service.

Umoja Karamu is a "ritual of solidarity for the Black family"[1] The ritual is divided into five parts or periods "which depict different kinds of experiences that have served to decimate, divide, and fragment the Black Family": (1) The Black African Family in the Mother Country, (2) Slavery Horror, (3) The Period of the Emancipation Fight, (4) The Liberation Struggle, and (5) The Black Family Looks at the Future.[2] Each period is accompanied by a symbolic color (black, white, red, green, and orange or gold) and symbolic foods (black-eyed peas, rice, wine, collard greens or other green leafy vegetable, and sweet potato bread or cornbread).[3]

Most African-American churches celebrate Black History Month in February and observe Martin Luther King, Jr. Day on the Sunday nearest January 15. Some churches also observe Malcolm X Day (May 19), "Juneteenth" (June 19, 1862) which celebrates freedom from slavery in America, Children's Sabbath in October, and *Kwanzaa* which begins December 26 and ends January 1.

Kwanzaa is an African-American holiday celebrated in the United States, the Caribbean, Europe, South America, and Africa. It was created by Dr. Maulana Karenga, chairman of the "US" Cultural organization in 1966. "Kwanzaa derives its name from the Kiswahili language of East and Central Africa. Kwanzaa means 'the celebration of the First Fruits: the fruits of love and labor of our life's struggle and existence.' "[4] Each of the seven days of *Kwanzaa* is reflective of one of the *Nguzo Saba* (Seven Principles): *Umoja* (Unity), *Kujichagulia* (Self-

Determination), *Ujima* (Collective Work and Responsibility), *Ujamaa* (Familyhood and Cooperative Economics), *Nia* (Purpose), *Kuumba* (Creativity), and *Imani* (Faith). These seven principles are described as a "moral minimum" of a value system, regardless of one's religious tradition.

During *Kwanzaa*, the home may be decorated with the colors and symbols of the holiday. The main color theme is the Red, Black, and Green of the African Liberation Flag. The symbols of Kwanzaa are set upon the *Mkeka*, a straw mat, which is abundantly bestowed with fruits (*Mitunda*), nuts and vegetables representing the collective fruits and blessings we have received over the year. On the *mkeka* sits the *Kinara*, or candle holder, which represents the first stalk, or ancestor in our African family tree. On the *Kinara* are seven candles (*Mishuma*) representing each of the *Nguzo Saba*. One new candle is lit each day of *Kwanzaa*. The *Kikombe Cha Umoja* (unity cup) holds the *libation* (usually water) and represents unity between us and our ancestors. The corn (*Mihindi*) represents our present children, and our hope for the children through whom we live on. The gifts of *Kwanzaa* are called *Zawadi*, and are presented to the children on the last day of *Kwanzaa* as a reward for their hard work over the year.

It has become a part of the Christian tradition in celebrating *Kwanzaa* to light the Christ candle after the pouring of the libation. The Christ candle represents Jesus' presence in all that we do. We light all the other candles with the Christ candle to represent our faith that all of our values and principles find true meaning in the light of Jesus, who is the Word of God and the Light of the World.[5]

Some churches have assigned scripture texts to the seven principles of *Kwanzaa*. One example is:

- Unity (*Umoja*): Acts 2:44, "And all that believed were together and had all things in common."
- Self-Determination (*Kujichagulia*): 2 Corinthians 4:8–9, "We are troubled on every side, yet not distressed; we are perplexed, but not in despair; persecuted, but not forsaken; cast down, but not destroyed."
- Collective Work and Responsibility (*Ujima*): Nehemiah 4:6, "So built we the wall; and all the wall was joined together unto the half thereof for the people had a mind to work."
- Familyhood and Cooperative Economics (*Ujamaa*): Exodus 31:3-4, "And I have filled him with the Spirit of God, in wisdom, and in understanding, and in knowledge, and in all

23

manner of workmanship, to devise cunning works, to work in gold, and in silver, and in brass."

- Purpose (*Nia*): Ecclesiastes 3:1, "To everything there is a season, and a time to every purpose under heaven."
- Creativity (*Kuumba*): Genesis 1:2, "And the earth was without form, and void; and darkness was upon the face of the deep. And the Spirit of God moved upon the face of the waters."
- Faith (*Imani*): Hebrews 11:1, "Now faith is the substance of things hoped for, the evidence of things not seen."[6]

Beginning Our Praise to God

Many African-American worship services begin with both an opening prayer or invocation and a responsive call to worship that is scripturally based.

Prayer Forms

Prayer forms may include an opening prayer or invocation, the Lord's Prayer, a corporate prayer of confession, extemporaneous prayers by the pastor or laypersons, prayer of illumination before the scriptures are read or before the pastor preaches, and prayer requests made aloud by individual members of the congregation, which may then be incorporated into the pastoral prayer. The prayer before the sermon is sometimes offered by a layperson on behalf of the preacher for the morning.

The posture of prayer is primarily sitting, although kneeling is also practiced.

Various forms of altar calls are common in the African-American tradition. In most churches, people come and kneel at the altar during the pastoral prayer. The pastor usually decides where the altar call will take place in the liturgy, and in what form—praying silently, pastor praying collectively for the group kneeling at the altar, pastor praying with individuals upon request, or anointing with oil. Sometimes the altar call or anointing with oil is designed into the service. At other times, these elements occur spontaneously as the Spirit moves.

Often there is also an "invitation to Christian discipleship" that takes place immediately following the sermon. The pastor invites persons who wish to commit their lives to Jesus Christ or to join the church to come forward during the closing hymn. This is sometimes called "opening the doors of the church."

In some churches prayer may also take the form of ecstatic praise. This can involve raising the hands in the air, standing and swaying back and forth, jumping up and down, or calling out words of praise and response.

Creeds

The recitation of a creed during Sunday worship varies in the African-American context. Some use a creed on a weekly basis, while others may include a creed on Communion Sundays and/or other special occasions in the church year.

Music

The hymnals most commonly used in African-American churches are *The United Methodist Hymnal* and *Songs of Zion*. A few churches also use hymnals such as *Gospel Pearls* or other resources from traditional black denominations. Most churches sing from three to nine hymns and/or gospel songs on Sunday morning. The hymns are usually sung in unison by the congregation while the choir provides harmony when appropriate. The organ and/or piano accompany the hymns. Some churches also use guitars, drums, saxophones, and tambourines.

In addition to music, other art forms such as drama, liturgical dance, and cultural dance forms are also acceptable in many worship settings. Silence, clapping, saying "Amen!" are all common responses to the various artists sharing their gifts with the congregation.

One unique aspect in the African-American church is that organ music (usually a Hammond organ) plays background music undergirding much of the liturgy. This music reflects the various moods of worship from prayerful meditation to ecstatic jubilation.

Scripture Readings

The number of scripture passages read each week in worship varies. In some congregations only one text is read, while in others, two or three readings are included. While most churches use the Revised Standard or the New Revised Standard Versions of the Bible, there are some churches who use the African Heritage Bible, which is based on the King James Version.

The texts are either read by the pastor or lay liturgist, or, the text is read responsively verse by verse between the worship leader and the congregation. Occasionally the scripture is in the form of a song with added interpretation.

Preaching

Sermons in the African-American context usually last between twenty and forty-five minutes. The sermon is considered to be the most important part of the liturgy. Sermon structures and preaching styles vary. Topical, exegetical, and expository preaching are all possible. Many pastors consult the lectionary as they decide which text(s) to use as a basis for the sermon. Some however, pick a topic first, use texts that are being discussed in Bible study, or pick a text as they feel led by the Holy Spirit.

Some congregations expect the sermon to have a tight conclusion, ending in celebration and praise of what God has done through Jesus Christ. In other congregations, sermons can end in a wide variety of ways. Each church has its own expectations regarding the tools a pastor uses in delivering a sermon. Some congregations prefer the pastor to use a manuscript or notes as a sign of good preparation, while others prefer the pastor to preach extemporaneously as a sign of being inspired by the Holy Spirit. Likewise, some congregations prefer the pastor to preach from the pulpit while others want the pastor to move away from the pulpit.

The "call and response" form of preaching is common in much African-American or Black preaching.[7] During the sermon, members of the congregation often call out words of encouragement and praise to the preacher. Evans Crawford in *The Hum* identifies five common phrases used intentionally by the congregation: "Help 'em Lord!", "Well?", "That's all right!", "Amen!", and "Glory Hallelujah!" These phrases "are in fact the prayers of the human heart for help, guidance, and praise, enacted in the environment of worship and proclamation."[8]

"Help 'em Lord!" is used when the people are trying to make connections with what the pastor is saying and their own needs. It confirms that we all start out in need of prayer. "Well?" is used when the people are aware that the pastor is hinting to the gospel witness by using a repetitive phrase or chantable refrain called a "riff." "That's all right!" affirms the good news and gospel possibilities the individual is receiving from the sermon. When "That's all right!" is heard, the sermon is becoming persuasive to the hearts and minds of the congregation. "Amen!" is often sounded when the people agree that the message the preacher is proclaiming is true for them and consistent with the scripture witness. "Glory Hallelujah!" offers the loudest praise, the highest joy, the greatest praise to God.[9]

Passing of the Peace

The Passing of the Peace is common in the African-American context. In some congregations it is called the Ritual of Friendship.

Benediction

The benediction is usually given by clergy unless special dignitaries are in attendance. On these occasions, the honored guests, whether clergy or not, may be asked to pronounce the benediction. The benediction is usually offered with eyes open and two hands raised in a gesture of blessing (occasionally only one hand is used). The congregation often stands with their eyes open to receive the blessing.

Ushers' Guild

One unique aspect in the African-American tradition is the vital presence of the ushers within the congregation. While in many churches today the ushers can be both men and women of any age wearing no particular uniform, there are still some congregations whose ushers are comprised of older women who are considered the "saints" of the church. Some ushers' guilds dress in white uniforms, wear white gloves, assume particular postures (for example, one arm behind the back), and position themselves in various places throughout the congregation. In other churches, the ushers are identified by a particular kente cloth accessory on their clothing.

The job of the ushers' guild is not only to provide hospitality to those who attend worship, they are also responsible for keeping the pastor informed of any issues that arise during worship. Many ushers' guilds are trained on a national level. They learn hand signs that clue the pastor when issues of safety arise. In some churches, youth ushers may use the "ushers' strut"—a particular walk where they demonstrate the hand signs they've learned and display their camaraderie.

Sacramental Practices

Sacrament of Baptism

Infants, adolescents, and adults are all baptized in the African-American community. Baptisms are almost always held during worship after the sermon in the "Response" section of the liturgy. However, they may also occur on other days of the week when the community gathers outside the church for baptism by immersion. Baptisms take place whenever the need arises but some churches reserve one Sunday of the month for this sacrament.

The pastor meets with the family (or adult being baptized) at least once before the baptism. If parents choose godparents for their child, the godparents may be requested to attend a counseling session as well. While most pastors prefer godparents to be Christian, some clergy leave that decision up to the family.

Infants baptized in the African-American community often wear white clothing. The liturgy surrounding baptism is either a formal liturgy or predetermined questions and extemporaneous prayers. Whether formal or extemporaneous, many pastors include a blessing or thanksgiving over the water.

While sprinkling is the most common method of baptism, pouring and immersion are also practiced. When baptism takes place through immersion, family and members of the church community gather at a river, pool, lake, or the ocean. The person is immersed once. When baptism takes place by sprinkling or pouring, it is up to the pastor whether the water is administered once or three times for each person of the Trinity.

The person is baptized with either the *traditional baptismal formula* or with words similar to "In the name of God, our Creator; Jesus Christ, our Savior; and the Holy Spirit, our Comforter." A few pastors also make the sign of the cross on the person's forehead with the baptismal water.

A baptismal certificate is given to the one baptized. There are no expectations that the one baptized will give a gift to the church. The pastor may simply have the baptismal party turn and be welcomed by the congregation, or the pastor may walk down the aisle while holding the infant as a means of introducing the child to the community. In families that are strongly Afro-centric, the infant may be raised and "offered up" in the ancient African tradition.[10]

After a baptism, the family often invites persons for a celebratory meal at their home. Clergy are often expected to attend and offer prayer before the meal is served.

Confirmation

Confirmation for youth ages twelve to thirteen is a common ritual in the life of the African-American community. The period of preparation ranges from four to eighteen weeks. Some congregations have no set liturgical day for confirmation while others confirm on Palm Sunday or Pentecost.

Sacrament of Holy Communion

Various terms are used to refer to this sacrament in the African-American church: "Communion," "Holy Communion," "Lord's Supper," "Sacrament of the Lord's Supper," and "Eucharist." Holy Communion is celebrated on the first Sunday of every month. Some churches also serve communion on special liturgical days such as Christmas Eve, New Year's Eve, New Year's Day, Ash Wednesday, and Easter Sunday.

The elements traditionally used are wafers and individual cups of grape juice. Occasionally a loaf of bread, or unleavened bread, and one chalice are used. The elements are understood by the community to be the real presence of Jesus Christ, or symbols of Christ's presence and grace. The bread and grape juice are covered with white cloths until the appropriate time in the liturgy.

The communion liturgy usually consists of some version of a Great Prayer of Thanksgiving, often with responses by the laity. While most pastors break the bread during the *Words of Institution*, some pastors break the bread at the end of the Great Thanksgiving. Only clergy are permitted to celebrate the Sacrament of the Lord's Supper in the African-American context, although laypersons usually assist in distributing the elements. Pastors and lay servers traditionally partake before they serve the congregation.

In most congregations, the elements are distributed to the people as they kneel at the altar rail. In smaller churches, however, the congregation may stand in a circle around the altar and commune with one loaf and one cup through the method of *intinction*. The words used in distributing the elements vary from congregation to congregation: "This is the body and blood of our Lord Jesus Christ," "This is the Bread of the Covenant (or the Bread of Life), and the Cup of Salvation," or "This is the bread, take, eat. This is the cup, drink ye all of it." During the distribution of the elements, familiar music memorized over years of worshiping God is often sung.

Communion stewards are highly respected women (usually older women) within the church community. They often wear white dress uniforms and serve in the preparation of the elements: covering them before the service begins and uncovering them at the beginning of the communion liturgy, refilling the cups when necessary, and cleaning up afterwards.

The communion table is open to all regardless of whether one has been baptized. The parents usually decide at what age their children will begin to partake.

Rituals of Passage

Weddings

The night before the wedding in the African-American community, a wedding rehearsal and rehearsal dinner take place. In some African-American traditions, the bride may feel that it is bad luck to participate in the rehearsal. However, most pastors insist that she rehearse along with the others. The bride may come to the rehearsal wearing a "veil of ribbons." This "veil" or hat consists of bows and ribbons from presents given to the bride by female family and friends at a bridal shower. The bows and ribbons are attached to a paper plate and two of the ribbons tie the hat or "veil" to the bride's head.

The pastor is often expected to attend the rehearsal dinner which is hosted by the groom's parents. During the dinner, prayers and words of congratulations are offered for the couple.

While active church members usually hold their wedding in the church, weddings can take place anywhere. Before the wedding takes place, however, most pastors require premarital counseling sessions. The number of these sessions varies according to the needs of the couple. There is no stigma in the African-American community associated with marrying someone who is divorced.

While African-American weddings have assimilated to Western practices over the years, there are some couples in the community today who are including African elements in their ceremonies. The couples that are more Afro-centric may wear African garb and the altar may be stripped of Euro-centric symbols and covered with African kente cloth and African symbols. In many African-American weddings however, the bride is dressed in a white wedding gown, the groom in a tuxedo.

Regardless of dress, bridesmaids, ushers, flower girl, and ring bearer often serve as attendants to the couple. If altar candles or candelabras are used, they are lit by acolytes or representatives of the two families. The groom and ushers usually enter from the side at the front of the sanctuary. The bridesmaids, flower girl, and ring bearer process down the aisle, followed by the bride who is escorted by her father. Hymns or Western style music often accompany the procession, although African music may also be used.

During the wedding, scripture is read, a short sermon is preached, songs are sung, vows are made, rings are exchanged, and the couple is blessed in prayer.

At the beginning of the liturgy, there has traditionally been a question asked of the father of the bride: "Who gives this woman to be married to this man?" In many African-American weddings today the mother and the father of the bride as well as the mother and father of the groom are asked, "Who gives (name of bride) to be married to (name of groom)?" Parents of both the bride and the groom then respond "we do."

Some couples also choose to include in the wedding a time where they pay respect to their parents by honoring them with a kiss or presenting them with a rose.

The lighting of the Unity Candle is common in many African-American weddings. The outer candles are lit by the bride and groom, by mothers of the bride and groom, or by representatives from each family.

In addition, there are two unique practices that may take place in African-American weddings: pouring the *libation*, and "jumping the broomstick."

The pouring of *libation* is an African tradition and is occasionally included in African-American weddings. When used, it usually takes place at the beginning of the wedding liturgy, after the welcome. It is a time of prayer and remembrance, inviting the ancestors of the couple to be spiritually present at the wedding. The couple gives the pastor a list of their deceased ancestors' names that are to be read during the service. For each ancestor's name that the pastor reads, water is poured (by the bride and groom, or someone chosen by the couple) from a

31

gourd into a plant. If it is a large plant, it is placed on the floor; if a small plant, it may be placed on the altar.

Jumping the broomstick is another ritual found in African-American weddings. During the early years in this country when Euro-Americans owned slaves, African-Americans were forbidden to be legally married. Though not recognized by the laws of America, or the Euro-American community, African-American couples "jumped the broomstick" in their own weddings to symbolize their joining together in married life. In weddings today, after the pronouncement that the two are now husband and wife, the pastor lays a broomstick on the floor and the couple join hands, and jump over it together.

After the wedding, the entire bridal party, accompanied by the parents of the bride and groom greet their guests either in a receiving line at the back of the church or at the reception location.

A reception is held after the wedding at a hall or restaurant. There is usually a sit-down meal, music and dancing. Family and friends toast the couple with wishes for health and happiness in their marriage. The bride throws her bouquet over her shoulder to unmarried women, the groom throws the bride's garter over his shoulder to unmarried men, and the couple cuts the wedding cake.

Depending on the couple, clergy may be asked to be present at the reception and offer a prayer before the meal is served.

Funerals

In some African-American communities, a *wake* takes place the night before the funeral service. Usually held at the funeral home, a *wake* includes singing, praying, and testimonies about the life of the deceased. Occasionally a short sermon is also preached. The casket is open during the *wake* and a viewing of the body takes place before and after the *wake*. In addition to a *wake* or in place of a *wake*, viewings may be held at the funeral home on the evenings prior to the funeral.

The casket is surrounded by flowers, picture(s) of the deceased, and an American flag if the deceased was associated with the military. The family decides whether items of importance to the deceased are placed in the coffin. Both black and white are symbolic colors for funerals. Black represents mourning; white represents resurrection.

Most funerals take place at the church, although some families may hold the service at the funeral home. When the funeral service is at the church, it is often called the Service of Death and Resurrection. If the deceased was affiliated with other churches in the community, it is appropriate to invite those clergy to participate in the funeral.

On the morning of the funeral service, some families expect the pastor to pray with them at their home. Other families may ask active members of the congregation to come and pray with them before the funeral.

The casket may be placed at the front of the sanctuary before the service begins or there may be a procession from the back of the church to the front. The procession is led by the pastor, followed by the pallbearers carrying the casket (and honorary pallbearers if chosen), then the family. If the choir processes, they often follow the pastor.

The funeral service includes scripture reading, prayers, a sermon, and singing. Some families select a few persons to give testimony about the life of the deceased before the sermon. Occasionally, after the sermon, the pastor may invite anyone in the congregation to share briefly their memories about the one who died.

At the end of the service, the ushers carry all the flower arrangements to the rear of the church and create a "corridor of flowers." The pastor processes out through the flowers followed by the pallbearers carrying the casket (and honorary pallbearers if used), and then the family. The pallbearers place the casket in the hearse, and the ushers then lay the flowers around the coffin.

The hearse leads a procession of cars to the cemetery. At the cemetery, the pastor leads the procession to the grave site. The service at the grave site includes prayers, scripture reading, the Lord's Prayer, and a committal of the body. At the point in the liturgy where the pastor recites the biblical passage "ashes to ashes, dust to dust," the pastor may throw dirt on the casket, or the pastor or funeral director may place a flower on the casket. After the service, the family may choose to place flowers on the casket as well.

Following the committal service, there is often a reception back at the church for family and guests.

While there are no services that mark the anniversary of a person's death, the lives of those who have died throughout the year may be remembered during worship on the Sunday closest to All Saints Day (November 1), during the celebration of Kwanzaa, or during Black History month. The family may also provide the altar flowers for the Sunday service closest to the anniversary of death in memory of the deceased. Memorial flowers may also be given in the form of poinsettias at Christmas and lilies at Easter.

Notes

1. Edward Sims, , Jr. *Umoja Karamu: A Ritual for the Black Family* (New York: Urban Church Education of the United Church of Christ Board for Homeland Ministries, 1971.)

2. Ibid., p. 1.

3. For a copy of an *Umoja Karamu* ritual, see Sims, *Umoja Karamu.*

4. Rev. M. Andrew Robinson-Gaither, *See Christ in Kwanzaa.* A worship bulletin from Faith United Methodist Church, Los Angeles, on Tuesday, December 28, 1993.

5. Ibid., p. 6.

6. Rev. M. Andrew Robinson-Gaither, Faith United Methodist Church 1995 Annual Charge Conference Report, p. 17.

7. See Henry Mitchell's *Black Preaching* (New York: Harper and Row, 1979), *Black Preaching: The Recovery of a Powerful Art* (Nashville: Abingdon, 1990), *Celebration and Experience in Preaching* (Nashville: Abingdon, 1990); Evans Crawford's *The Hum: Call and Response in African-American Preaching* (Nashville: Abingdon, 1995), Warren H. Stewart, Sr.'s *Interpreting God's Word in Black Preaching* (Valley Forge: Judson Press, 1984), Samuel Proctor's *Sermons from the Black Pulpit* (Valley Forge: Judson Press, 1984) and *How Shall They Hear?* (Valley Forge: Judson Press, 1992); and Kenneth L. Walter's *Afrocentric Sermons* (Valley Forge: Judson Press, 1993)

8. Evans, *The Hum: Call and Response in African-American Preaching*, p. 21.

9. Ibid., p. 13.

10. For more information on this African ritual, see the section on Baptism in the chapter on Ghanaian-American Worship Practices.

CAMBODIAN-AMERICAN WORSHIP PRACTICES

with Pitou Lao

The Service of the Word

The Language of the Liturgy

Cambodian-American churches primarily use the Cambodian language in conducting their worship services. The sermon, however, may be translated into English.

The Liturgical Space

Since most Cambodian-American congregations share the worship space of another church, there are few cultural symbols visible in worship. A free standing banner with Cambodian writing and/or images may be brought in each week to claim the space as their own.

Liturgical Time

Worship services last approximately one hour.

Liturgical Garb

Most clergy do not wear any specific liturgical garb when conducting worship.

Liturgical Seasons and Days

Christmas and Easter are the two seasons of the church year that are celebrated in Cambodian-American churches. Services may also be held during Holy Week. During the Christmas Eve service, the Cambodian Blessing Dance may be performed. In addition, Mother's Day and Thanksgiving are honored liturgically. On April 13 (except for every fourth year when it falls on April 14), the Cambodian New Year is celebrated within the church and Cambodian community.

Beginning Our Praise to God

Worship is often begun with a prayer and an opening hymn, followed by the entire congregation reading a Psalm text in unison.

Prayer Forms

Prayer forms common in Cambodian-American worship every week are extemporaneous prayers by the pastor and lay worship leaders and a pastoral prayer. When lay people offer a prayer for the community, they often remain in their seat rather than coming to the lectern or pulpit. Some churches also include the Lord's Prayer on a weekly basis while others recite the prayer occasionally. Prayers of joys and concerns are sometimes offered aloud from individual members of the congregation. These intercessions and thanksgivings may be included in the pastoral prayer. Corporate prayers are rare since bulletins are not common. The Cambodian language is not easily accessible by typewriter or computer so bulletins need to be hand written.

At the end of every prayer, the congregation responds "Amen." The posture of prayer for Methodists in Cambodia is standing (the practice of the Christian Missionary Alliance Church which has the greatest influence in Cambodia). In America, some churches continue to stand for prayer while others have adopted the posture of sitting with heads bowed.

Creeds

Reciting a creed is not traditional in Cambodian-American worship. When churches do include a creed, it is usually the Apostles' Creed.

Music

Two to four hymns are usually sung during Sunday morning worship. Churches use a Cambodian hymnal (published by the Christian Missionary Alliance Church) and the United Methodist Hymnal. In addition to the hymns, songs written by Cambodian Christians to common Cambodian tunes may also be sung.

The piano is the most common instrument to accompany the hymns. The guitar and modern drums may also be used to accompany the Cambodian songs. Cambodian instruments may be used on special occasions: *tro* (a stringed instrument played with a bow), *khloy* (a bamboo flute), and *pey* (a reed instrument).

Clapping is an appropriate response to solos, choir anthems, and other special performances.

Scripture Readings

Two scripture readings are often read during worship. One of these texts is usually taken from the Psalms. These texts are either read by the pastor or lay liturgist while the people read along silently in their own Bibles, or, the text is read responsively verse by verse between the worship leader and the congregation.

Preaching

Sermons usually last between twenty and thirty minutes. Whether the sermon is placed in the middle of the service or at the end varies, but most congregations view the sermon as the most important part of the liturgy.

Most sermons are topical in nature. Some clergy however, base their sermon on the text that was used during Bible study the week before.

Humor is acceptable in preaching. Most congregations have no expectations regarding the ending of a sermon; tight conclusions and open-ended sermons are both appropriate. Most pastors use illustrations and stories from Cambodian resources. During the sermon, the pastor may ask the congregation to turn in their Bibles to a particular text and read it aloud.

Passing of the Peace

This ritual is acceptable but not traditional in most Cambodian-American churches.

Benediction

In some Cambodian-American churches, only clergy can offer the benediction. In other churches, it is acceptable for lay leaders to give the benediction. The benediction may be accompanied by both hands raised in a gesture of blessing. In most churches, everyone is standing during the benediction with their eyes closed.

37

Sacramental Practices

Sacrament of Baptism

The baptism of infants is not usually practiced within Cambodian-American churches. Adult baptism (the practice of the Christian Missionary Alliance Church) is the most common. Many pastors require four preparation classes before an adolescent or adult is baptized.

When sprinkling is the method used for the baptism, baptisms take place during any Sunday worship. However, since most baptisms take place through immersion, baptisms usually occur during the summer when the congregation can gather at the ocean, lake, or river.

A full worship service is conducted by the water's edge with singing, the reading of scripture, and a sermon following the baptism. The person(s) being baptized may also share their experience of faith.

The liturgy surrounding the baptism varies. Some use the liturgy printed in the United Methodist *Book of Worship*. Other pastors use only a printed set of questions for the candidate(s) while others conduct the sacrament entirely extemporaneously.

The *traditional baptismal formula* is recited and the person is immersed once. A baptismal certificate is given to those who are baptized. In some churches, it is expected that the person(s) being baptized will give something back to the church (usually money and time).

Confirmation

Since persons are usually baptized as adolescents or adults, there is no need for confirmation. Around the age of twelve there is a four-week preparation period for those who will be baptized.

Sacrament of Holy Communion

The most common terms used to refer to this sacrament are "Lord's Supper" and "Communion." It is celebrated once a month after the sermon. While it is most common for people to begin taking communion after they have been baptized (age twelve and above), the unbaptized are not explicitly rejected from the table.

Most congregations use small cubes of bread and individual cups of grape juice. Occasionally, a loaf of bread is used. The elements are covered until the appropriate time in the liturgy. Some members believe

38

in the doctrine of *consubstantiation* while others believe that the elements are symbols of Christ's presence and grace.

The liturgy surrounding communion is extemporaneously given by the pastor (occasionally by a lay leader). Some clergy bless the elements before reading the *Words of Institution* from the Bible (1 Corinthians 11:23-26) and break the bread at this time.

The elements are distributed to the people as they come forward and gather around or near the altar, or, they are passed to the people sitting in the pews. When the people come to the altar, most clergy and lay assistants partake before the congregation communes. When the elements are passed to the people in the pews, the clergy and lay servers partake simultaneously with the congregation. The elements are distributed with the words "This is the body and blood of our Lord Jesus Christ given for you."

Rituals of Passage

Weddings

In Cambodia, arranged marriages are still practiced. In America, it depends on the family. Some parents prefer to choose the spouse for their son or daughter, or the adult child requests the parents to choose their marriage partner for him or her. For those young adults who have lived in the United States for a long time, they may want to choose their own partner.

The formal agreement of the bond between the two families takes place at an engagement ritual held a couple of months before the wedding. The groom and his family gather at the house of the bride's parents. The groom's parents present gifts to the parents of the bride: drink, fruit, and the engagement ring (sometimes rice cakes, tea, and other gold jewelry as well). The minister presides over this religious ritual offering words of advice for the couple, prayers, scripture verses, and sometimes a sermon. After the ritual, there is a party with food and drink served to the guests to celebrate the engagement.

Between the engagement ritual and the wedding, the pastor has three to four premarital counseling sessions with the couple. If a person requesting to be married is divorced, the pastor may perform the ceremony, but it is often frowned upon.

The wedding may take place at the church or at the bride's parents' home. If the wedding is at the bride's home, usually the bride and groom wear traditional Cambodian wedding attire. If the wedding is held at the church, the bride may wear a white wedding gown and the groom a tuxedo or suit instead of the traditional clothing.

If a church wedding is planned, the altar candles are often lit by the mothers of the bride and groom. In some weddings they may be lit by other representatives of each family or by acolytes.

Bridesmaids, ushers, flower girl, and ring bearer, along with friends and relatives serve as attendants for the bride and groom. The groom and his attendants enter from the side of the church at the front. The bride's attendants process down the aisle followed by the bride who is escorted by her father. The processional music may be the "Wedding March" or Cambodian music. During the wedding, Cambodian hymns are sung, scripture is read, prayers are offered, a sermon is preached, vows and rings are exchanged, and the couple is pronounced husband and wife. If the Unity Candle is used, the bride and groom often light the outer candles. In some weddings, there is a place for the parents to give their blessing to the couple and a time when the couple bows to their parents as a sign of love and respect.

At the end of the wedding, the father of the bride often stands, thanks the people for coming and invites them to the reception. The couple may greet their guests formally in a receiving line at the back of the church or at the reception.

A reception follows at a restaurant or occasionally in the church hall. The bride usually changes into Cambodian dress for the reception; often changing outfits more than once. The pastor is usually asked to pray before the meal is served. During the reception there may be music, dancing, toasting the couple with words of health and happiness, and a ritual of cutting the wedding cake.

Traditionally, the couple goes to the bride's family's home after the reception. At this time, the bride and groom serve tea to their parents and grandparents. The couple kneel and bow to the floor three times before each relative with their hands in a prayerful position. In Cambodia, the couple spends their first married night at the home of the bride's parents. In America however, the couple often goes off on a honeymoon. The bride and groom may decide to pay respect to their elders by bowing to them at another time before the wedding or after the honeymoon.

Funerals

On an evening soon after a death, there is often a gathering of family and friends at the deceased's family home. The minister is expected to officiate at this prayer service. It may be a simple service of scripture reading and prayer or it may be more elaborate, including hymns, a sermon, and testimonies about the life of the deceased. The body is not present at this time. Between the day of death and the day of burial, there may be other prayer meetings and/or a viewing of the body at the funeral home. The body is dressed in special clothes and placed in a casket surrounded by flowers and a picture of the deceased.

If the family was associated with other Cambodian-American churches (even churches from other denominations), it is common for the pastor to invite clergy from these other churches to participate in the funeral.

On the day of the funeral, the pastor is expected to go to the family's home and accompany them to the place of the funeral. In America, the funeral service often takes place at the funeral home but it may be held at the church. The casket is already in place as the people gather. The family decides whether the casket is open or closed during the service.

The funeral usually lasts about an hour and includes the reading of scripture, prayers, Cambodian hymns, and a sermon. The family often selects someone to speak about the life of the deceased.

After the funeral, there is usually a procession of cars from the place of the funeral to the cemetery. Once at the cemetery, there may be a procession to the grave site led by the pastor, followed by the pallbearers carrying the casket, the family, and guests.

The grave site service includes scripture, prayers, and sometimes a sermon. Everyone throws dirt on the casket at the time when the pastor cites the scriptural passage, "ashes to ashes, dust to dust." After the service, everyone present places a flower on the casket. Usually the family and guests stay until the casket is lowered and the grave is completely filled in.

Memorial services are often held in the United States for family who have died in Cambodia.

Recent immigrants or those who have recently become Christian may mark the anniversary of the death of a loved one on the seventh day and one hundredth day after death as well as each yearly anniversary. This is a cultural practice influenced by Buddhism. Some Christians denounce this practice because of its Buddhist association.

CHINESE-AMERICAN WORSHIP PRACTICES

with Rev. Samuel Chow and Rev. Mamie Ko

The Service of the Word

The Language of the Liturgy

Although there are many dialects spoken in China, *Mandarin* is the spoken dialect officially adopted by the government. However, since the Cultural Revolution, the name of this dialect changed from *Mandarin* to *Putonghua*, meaning "the common language." *Putonghua* is now taught all over China in an attempt to unify the country under one spoken language.

The traditional spoken dialect of Hong Kong was *Cantonese* although with Hong Kong reverting back to China and the influx of mainland Chinese into Hong Kong, that too is changing to *Putonghua*. The written language, Chinese, is based on *Mandarin/Putonghua*, and is the same for the various spoken dialects.

In Chinese-American churches in the United States, the term "Mandarin" is still used although future generations of immigrants may prefer the term *Putonghua*. Most of these churches use *Mandarin/Putonghua* in worship, although there are some whose services are in *Cantonese*. Churches may offer bilingual services in both *Cantonese* and *Mandarin/Putonghua* to accommodate the diversity of members within the congregation. The bilingual nature of these services varies. Some may only translate the sermon into the other language while others may also translate various aspects of the liturgy.

Some Chinese-American churches have English language services for the children of the church as well as for any adults born and raised in the United States who feel more comfortable communicating in English. Other churches translate *Cantonese* or *Mandarin/Putonghua* into English during parts or all of their worship.

The Liturgical Space

While some Chinese-American churches have banners hanging in the sanctuary that contain Chinese characters (written script), for the most part Chinese-American churches have little within the sanctuary that identifies them as Chinese. There is a Chinese-American United Methodist church in downtown Los Angeles, however, where the very architecture of the building is Chinese in nature. There is no doubt looking at the outside of the building that it is both Chinese and a house of worship. It fits in very well in the midst of Los Angeles's Chinatown.

Liturgical Time

Worship in the Chinese-American tradition usually lasts between one and one and a half hours.

Liturgical Garb

No single item of liturgical garb is common among Chinese-American pastors. Some wear albs or a robe, while others wear regular street clothes. Some clergy may wear stoles with Chinese characters embroidered on them.

Liturgical Seasons and Days

Most of the liturgical seasons of the church year are followed except Epiphany. As in most cultures, Christmas and Easter are the most celebrated seasons, with Pentecost also a special day in the life of the church. Advent and Lent are recognized by some Chinese-American churches but not all.

For most Chinese-American churches, another important day celebrated liturgically is Chinese New Year. The date of the Chinese New Year varies according to the lunar calendar but is usually in February. Special worship services are held and often the various language ministries join together for this occasion.

Beginning Our Praise to God

The service is opened with a Call to Worship based on scripture and led by a lay liturgist.

Prayer Forms

Prayers within Chinese-American churches include the Lord's Prayer and extemporaneous prayers offered by the pastor and/or lay liturgist. Sometimes a pastoral prayer is given or prayers of intercession are offered. Prayers of confession are rare although they are sometimes included on Communion Sundays.

In the Chinese culture, formal events such as worship, call for a more formal, reserved posture and tone. It is therefore rare that individual members of the congregation would offer their individual prayers of joys or concerns aloud. In the English-language services, the people in the congregation feel more comfortable voicing their prayer requests aloud.

Sitting and standing are both acceptable postures for prayer.

Creeds

In most Chinese-American churches, the Apostles' Creed is recited while the congregation is standing facing the altar.

Music

The most common instruments to accompany the music in Chinese-American worship services are the piano and organ. Some Chinese-American churches are beginning to incorporate praise songs into the liturgy in addition to hymns. These songs may be accompanied by guitars and tambourines rather than the piano. Praise songs are more common in the English-language ministries than the *Cantonese* or *Mandarin/Putonghua* language ministries.

Occasionally, someone sings a solo in *Cantonese*-style music or the choir sings hymns by Chinese composers. More and more religious music is being composed in Hong Kong today, and sung in the English-language ministries of the Chinese-American church.

Cantonese and *Mandarin/Putonghua* congregations give no overt expressions such as clapping or verbal responses to musical presentations. However, English language ministries seem to be more comfortable with these more overt expressions of affirmation.

Scripture Readings

While some Chinese-American churches may read two or three scripture texts, often only one scripture passage is read during weekly

Sunday worship. The text is read by the pastor or lay liturgist. Occasionally, the text is read responsively verse by verse between the worship leader and the congregation.

Preaching

Sermons usually last twenty to thirty minutes in Chinese-American churches, or longer if the sermon is simultaneously translated into another language. The sermon is placed in the middle of the service and is seen by the laity as the most important part of the liturgy.

Humor and storytelling are both acceptable elements of a sermon. It is important that illustrations come from the daily lives of the community or from folktales, historical figures, and issues that are familiar to the members of the congregation.

Some Chinese-American churches utilize a variety of methods in preaching that facilitate the participation of the laity. The pastor may ask the congregation to turn in their Bibles to a particular text and read it aloud,

or the pastor may intentionally ask a question that requires a short, verbal response from the congregation.

Other churches have Bible study groups prior to the Sunday on which the sermon will be preached to discuss the text for the sermon. In English-language services, members of the congregation may offer words of affirmation during a sermon by saying "Amen" or other terms of encouragement.

Passing of the Peace

It is rare for Chinese-American congregations to include this ritual in their liturgy. If it is included, people may say words of greeting to one another or shake hands, but hugging is not acceptable. In the English language ministries of Chinese-American congregations, it is becoming more common to include the Passing of the Peace during worship, and hugging is more acceptable.

Benediction

Only ordained clergy are authorized to give the benediction in Chinese-American churches. The pastor's eyes are closed and a gesture of blessing (one or both hands raised) accompanies the benediction. The congregation stands with their eyes closed to receive the benediction.

In English-language services, the position of one's eyes (open or closed) for either the pastor or the congregation does not seem to be a factor.

Sacramental Practices

Sacrament of Baptism

Most baptisms in Chinese-American churches occur on the high liturgical days of the church year (Easter, Christmas, and Pentecost), although they may also be held, if the parents so choose, on other Sundays in the church year.

Private baptisms are also permitted by some Chinese-American clergy. These may be held in people's homes, in a hospital, or in the church building at a time outside of public worship.

All ages are baptized in Chinese-American churches. Some members in the community choose not to have their child baptized as an infant so that the child can make the decision when he or she is older.

When an infant is being baptized, the pastor meets with the parents at least once in preparation so that they understand the commitment they are making before God. If youth or adults are being baptized, the preparation time lasts from six to thirteen weeks and is sometimes the same preparation as for confirmation.

The liturgy for baptism may come from Methodist prayer books published in Hong Kong or China or the pastor may offer extemporaneous prayers and words about baptism. English-language ministries may use the baptismal liturgy in *The United Methodist Hymnal*. Some pastors include words of blessing over the water, although a blessing of the water is not included in the Chinese Methodist prayer books. Adults who are baptized may share their experience of conversion with the congregation as part of the liturgy.

There are no special requirements or expectations about the dress for baptism. Godparents are not common.

In some Chinese-American churches, the pastor may hold the bowl with the baptismal water while the mother or father holds the infant. The *traditional baptismal formula* is used by most pastors during the baptism. Water is usually sprinkled on the person's head once (some may sprinkle three times for each person of the Trinity). Some pastors also make the sign of the cross on the person's forehead with the baptismal water.

In addition to a baptismal certificate, many churches also present a Bible to the one being baptized. Some congregations also give a rose or flower to the person. Chinese-American churches do not expect the person being baptized to give a gift to the church.

Following baptism, the baptismal party turns to face the congregation and is welcomed by the congregation into the faith-filled community.

Confirmation

Since there are fewer youth who speak only *Cantonese* or *Mandarin/Putonghua*, confirmation is rare in these language ministries. The practice is more common in English language congregations where confirmation serves a dual function. Youths who were baptized as infants make a public proclamation of their faith, and those not previously baptized receive baptism at this time. The usual age for confirmation is between fourteen and sixteen.

Sacrament of Holy Communion

The *Cantonese* translation for *communion* is more akin to "Holy Supper." Communion is celebrated once a month, and in some churches, on special liturgical days as well. The elements are covered until after the sermon when the liturgy of communion begins.

The liturgy surrounding communion is usually a Great Thanksgiving with responses from the congregation. Only ordained clergy are permitted to celebrate communion, although laity assist in distributing the elements. The Chinese hymnal, unlike *The United Methodist Hymnal*, does not include the communion liturgy. However, these are printed in a Chinese Methodist Prayer Book, portions of which are often made available to the congregation. This allows the congregation to participate in the liturgy. It contains thanksgiving over God's acts through Jesus, the *Words of Institution*, and a closing, but does not include words of consecration over the elements. While some pastors choose to consecrate the elements, it is not a common practice in many Chinese-American churches. The bread and cup are elevated during the *Words of Institution* and the bread is broken at this time. It is customary for the clergy and lay servers to partake before serving the congregation.

Traditionally the elements used are wafers and individual cups of grape juice, but today a loaf of bread or unleavened bread and a chalice are also used. In many Chinese-American churches, people kneel at the altar rail to take communion. In some churches the congregation processes to the front to receive communion through *intinction*.

Baptism is usually required before one takes communion. In the *Mandarin/Putonghua* and *Cantonese* communities, baptized children are encouraged to wait until they are confirmed to take communion. However, if parents bring their children forward for communion, they are not turned away. In the English-speaking congregations, it is more acceptable for children who were baptized as infants to receive communion before they are confirmed.

Rituals of Passage

Weddings

As in all cultures, Chinese-American weddings vary according to the wishes of the couple, the involvement of the parents, how "traditional" or how "modern" the couple wants the wedding to be, and whether both the bride and the groom are Chinese-American. In many respects, contemporary Chinese-American weddings have assimilated the customs of the dominant American culture.

The wedding celebration may begin a week or two before the actual ceremony in the Chinese tradition. Close relatives give rings, necklaces, and other jewelry to the bride at a separate occasion or at a special Tea Ceremony. A Tea Ceremony is a time when the bride serves tea to her parents as a symbol of respect and thanksgiving for the life they gave her. If a separate Tea Ceremony is not arranged, the bride may serve her parents tea on the morning of the wedding. Other rituals may include the family of the groom roasting a pig as a gift to the bride's family.

One Chinese custom takes place on the day of the wedding. The bride and her sisters and close female friends gather at her parent's house before the ceremony. The groom and his brothers and close male friends go to the house and knock on the door. The bride and her friends tease the men and make them wait. They ask the groom and his friends for money before they open the door.

48

Premarital counseling sessions are common before the ceremony. The number of counseling sessions varies; some pastors simply meet with the couple once or twice, while others meet with them many times before the wedding. It is permissable to marry persons who are divorced, but this is sometimes frowned upon in the Chinese-American Christian communities.

The wedding ceremony usually takes place in the church but may also be held elsewhere, particularly if the bride and groom are not active church members. The bride usually wears a white gown, and the groom is dressed in a tuxedo. The decoration colors are traditionally red since red is the color of good fortune in Chinese culture. Today in the United States, other colors are also possible.

Bridesmaids, ushers, flower girl, and ring bearer are all possible attendants for the bride and groom. The bride is escorted down the aisle by her father or brother. The music for the procession is usually the "Wedding March" or other Western music. Occasionally Chinese music is used for the procession or sung during the wedding itself.

Scripture is read, the pastor shares words about marriage, vows are made, and rings are exchanged. The couple decides if they will pay respect in some way to their parents during the wedding by bowing to their parents or by presenting a rose or flower to them. After the exchange of rings, it is common in Chinese-American churches to light the Unity Candle. The outer candles are either lit at the beginning of the service by the acolytes or lit by the mothers of the bride and groom. The couple then goes forward to light the center candle with the two outer candles. A blessing is given to the couple and they are pronounced husband and wife.

The couple, along with the wedding party, greet their guests but it varies as to where this "receiving line" takes place. Some couples greet their guests formally at the back of the church immediately following the service, while others choose to greet them at the reception following, and/or at a banquet later that night.

After the wedding, there is usually a reception for everyone in the church hall. Food and drink (no alcohol at the church) are available for the guests. Dancing is not customary, but the bride throws her bouquet over her shoulder to unmarried women and the groom may throw the bride's garter over his shoulder to unmarried men. The couple cuts the wedding cake and feeds one another pieces of it.

After the reception, many couples also have a formal banquet at a restaurant for a limited number of guests. The bride has changed from her wedding dress into other attire (often Chinese garb) for the banquet. Sometimes the bride changes clothes more than once during the festivities. Often red is one of the dress colors symbolizing celebration and good fortune.

Couples who are active church members may expect their pastor to attend the reception and banquet and offer the prayer before the food is served.

At the banquet, the couple moves from table to table greeting their guests. Sometimes the bride is adorned with all the jewelry given to her by her family before the wedding. Several rings and necklaces may be worn at the same time.

Funerals/Memorials

The Chinese term used for the service honoring someone's death translates into English as "memorial" service. For this reason, some Chinese-American pastors refer to this time as the memorial rather than funeral. Other pastors use the term "funeral service." Throughout this section I will use memorial/funeral in reference to this service of worship in the Chinese-American tradition.

When someone dies, the family decides whether to have the memorial/funeral service at the church or at the funeral home. If the person who died or the family of the deceased are active church members, the memorial/funeral service is usually held at the church. Some families also schedule a "viewing" one or two evenings before the service. The pastor is expected to attend on one of these evenings and pray with the family.

The deceased is dressed in clothes chosen by the family (sometimes in special Chinese dress) and a Bible is often placed in the deceased's hand. Occasionally other items of importance are also placed in the casket.

On the day of the memorial/funeral service, it is often the practice in some Chinese-American churches for the pastor to go to the family's home to pray with them and escort them to the place of the memorial/funeral service. At the church or funeral home, the casket is in the front surrounded by flowers and a picture of the deceased. The casket is usually open during the service but can be closed if it is the desire of the family.

As the people enter the church or funeral home for the service (or during the days preceding the memorial/funeral service), it is customary for the friends of the deceased to give *flower money* or *cloth money* (sometimes called *white money*) to the family in a sympathy card. The envelope is given to an usher upon entering the building and the usher keeps a list of names and addresses so the family can send thank-you cards if they wish (although thank-you cards are not required). This money helps the family with the memorial/funeral expenses.

The memorial/funeral service lasts from thirty minutes to over an hour. The liturgy includes prayers, scripture passages, hymns, a sermon and either the pastor or one person from the deceased's family speaks about the one who died. Only those specifically requested to do so by the family may speak at this time.

At the end of the service, the family may stand next to the casket while friends and family process forward and pay their last respects to the deceased. Sometimes this respect is in the form of silent prayer at the casket, pausing for a moment of meditation, or bowing to the deceased (although bowing is associated with Buddhist customs and frowned upon by some Chinese-American Christians). The people then pay their condolences to the family.

As the people leave the church or funeral home, an usher may distribute red packets of dimes or quarters. Each packet contains one coin wrapped in red paper and one wrapped in white paper. This ancient custom signifies that the family's suffering or misfortune is now over and there will be good fortune again.

If the person is being buried, a procession of cars drives from the service to the cemetery. Burial is not necessarily the norm in the Chinese culture. Cremation is equally acceptable. At the cemetery, there is an informal procession from the hearse to the grave site. The pastor leads the procession, followed by the pallbearers carrying the casket, then the family and guests.

The grave site service is short with the reading of scripture (often Psalm 23), prayers for the family, and the Lord's Prayer. At the close of the committal service, the funeral directors distribute a flower to each person present. Family and friends place the flower on the casket just before leaving the cemetery.

After the committal service, there is usually a reception at a restaurant, although sometimes it is held at the church or the family's home.

White is the color for honoring the dead among non-Christians in Hong Kong. Since white is associated with ancestor worship, black is

51

the traditional color for memorial/funeral services for Christians. Black symbolizes mourning.

There are no anniversaries to mark the death, nor are memorial services held for family who have died in China or Hong Kong. If the deceased was an active member of the Chinese-American community at large, Chinese-American clergy from other denominations are invited to participate in the memorial/funeral service.

In every culture, the death of a child brings tremendous suffering to the family. In the Chinese tradition, if a person dies after the age of seventy, the community rejoices that the person lived a long, good life. But if a child dies it is considered tremendous misfortune in Chinese lore. Today, especially in the United States, family and friends mourn the death of a child and honor his or her life during the memorial/funeral service. However, it is possible that some parents who still hold on to old customs may not attend the memorial/funeral service of their child. The belief is that participation in this ritual act may bring more misfortune to the family.

EURO-AMERICAN WORSHIP PRACTICES

with Rev. Dr. Ronald Dunk

The Service of the Word

The Language of the Liturgy

English is the language used in worship in Euro-American congregations.

The Liturgical Space

In most congregations, the American flag and the Christian flag are visible in the sanctuary space. Banners with English writing and Euro-American images may also be present.

Liturgical Time

Worship services usually last between fifty minutes and one and a quarter hours.

Liturgical Garb

Pastors vary in what they wear during worship. Some wear a black pulpit robe, others a white alb, and still others wear no unique clothing that sets them apart from the laity.

Liturgical Seasons and Days

Most congregations celebrate all the seasons of the church year although Epiphany and Pentecost may not receive as much attention as the other seasons. All Saints Day (celebrated on the Sunday closest to November 1) honors those members of the congregation who died in the past year. The Thanksgiving holiday is often celebrated by joining with other churches for Thanksgiving Eve services. Cultural holidays such as Mother's Day (second Sunday in May), Father's Day (third Sunday in June), Labor Day (first Monday in September), Memorial Day (last Monday in May), Valentine's Day (February 14), and Independence Day (July 4) are often recognized during worship. On New

Year's Eve, many churches have a worship service welcoming in the new year. Some use Wesley's Covenant Service to observe this occasion. Most churches also celebrate certain Sundays recognized by the United Methodist Calendar: Laity Sunday, Youth Sunday, Scouting (or 4-H) Sunday, Native American Awareness Sunday, Disability Awareness Sunday, One Great Hour of Sharing, etc.

Beginning Our Praise to God

The opening of worship varies from congregation to congregation. Some churches have chosen to do their announcements before the formal start of worship. Others begin worship with an opening hymn as the choir processes into the sanctuary. Still others begin with a call to worship that is often printed in the bulletin and read responsively between the worship leader and the congregation. The call to worship may or may not be based on a scripture text. Those congregations offering *contemporary worship* services (and those trying to combine traditional worship with contemporary worship) often begin with several praise songs.

Prayer Forms

Prayer forms include: the Lord's Prayer (in various versions), extemporaneous prayers by the pastor, corporate prayers printed in the bulletin, a pastoral prayer, and a corporate prayer of confession followed by words of absolution. In addition, smaller churches may also include prayers of the people (sometimes called "Joys and Concerns") that are offered individually from members of the congregation. Occasionally, extemporaneous prayers are given by a layperson. Most prayer is offered in a sitting posture.

Creeds

The inclusion of a creed in worship varies from congregation to congregation. Many do not recite a creed anymore. Those who continue to include a creed use a variety of options available today: the creed from the United Church of Canada and the creeds available in *The United Methodist Hymnal.* Some churches only recite a creed on Holy Communion Sundays.

Music and Other Art Forms

Every Sunday most Euro-American congregations sing three to four hymns out of *The United Methodist Hymnal* accompanied by a piano or organ. Those churches that offer *contemporary worship* services may also use songbooks that include a variety of praise songs. In place of the songbooks, the lyrics may be copied onto a transparency and projected onto a wall or a screen in the sanctuary by an overhead projector. These praise songs are often accompanied by a variety of additional instruments: guitars, drums, keyboard, tambourines, saxophones, flutes, trumpets, etc. On special occasions, instruments other than the piano and organ may also be used in traditional worship services.

In addition to the music, congregations may also include drama, liturgical dance, clowning, puppetry, and various forms of visual art (fabric art, paintings, sculptures) in their worship.

While there are still many congregations who prefer a quiet, respectful response by parishioners in worship, more and more congregations accept clapping as an appropriate affirmation of the musical and artistic offerings of individuals and choirs. Members of the congregation may also respond by saying "Amen."

Scripture Readings

In a few congregations, only one text is read during worship. However, in most congregations at least two scripture passages are read each week, with many churches reading all three of the lectionary passages for each Sunday. The Psalm text may also be read responsively from the Psalter, which is printed in the hymnal.

While most congregations have the pastor or lay liturgist read the scripture passages, some congregations present a dramatic reading of the text using several voices or actually act out the text in a scripture drama. Others may retell the text in their own words, or become one of the characters in the text in a dramatic monologue. Occasionally the text is found in music form and sung by the choir or a soloist.

Since there are so many translations of the Bible available in English, it is difficult for people to read texts silently in their personal Bible while the pastor or liturgist reads from the pulpit or lectern. In order to rectify this problem, many churches provide Bibles (the same version used by the scripture reader) in the pew racks for the congregation's use.

Preaching

Sermons in Euro-American congregations usually last between ten and thirty minutes. Whether the sermon is located in the middle of the worship service or at the end, most laity still see the sermon as the most important part of the liturgy.

While there are some who preach topically and some who preach *lectuo continuo* (preaching through a book of the Bible verse by verse, chapter by chapter), many pastors use the lectionary texts for each Sunday as the basis for their sermon each week.

There are still some congregations that expect a three-point deductive sermon that has a tight conclusion; however, many congregations appreciate more inductive and alternative styles of preaching.

The expectations laity have regarding the use of notes by the preacher varies. Some believe that using a manuscript is a sign of being prepared while others believe that preaching without any notes is a sign of being prepared. For the most part, however, congregations leave that decision to the pastor.

While still a small percentage, more and more pastors are leaving the pulpit and moving down among the congregation to preach. Many believe this facilitates better conversational communication during preaching and breaks down the barrier between clergy and laity.

Participatory forms of preaching are not traditional in Euro-American worship. However, in small churches, some pastors may ask a question during the sermon and expect people in the congregation to provide the answer, or the pastor may provide visual aids or write the main points/ideas on newsprint or an overhead projector to facilitate communication. In other congregations pastors create study groups prior to the Sunday service in order to get input from various members before writing the sermon, or they establish sermon "talk-back" times after the service where people can offer their own comments and feelings about the text and/or topic of the sermon. Occasionally, pastors preach a shorter sermon and then invite people to add their own testimony to what has been said.

Passing of the Peace

In most congregations, the ritual of Passing the Peace is acceptable. Sometimes it is referred to as the "Ritual of Friendship" or by some other name.

Benediction

In most churches, the pastor pronounces the benediction from the front of the sanctuary (one or both hands raised in a gesture of blessing) while the congregation stands, eyes open to receive the blessing. Some smaller churches form a circle around the sanctuary and hold hands during the benediction.

Sacramental Practices

Sacrament of Baptism

While some persons are baptized during their youth or as an adult, most persons are baptized as infants in the Euro-American culture. Baptisms are usually scheduled at the parents' request. In some large congregations, however, all baptisms during a particular month take place on one Sunday (e.g. second Sunday of the month). Parents who request baptism for their infant meet with the pastor at least once in preparation for the sacrament.

In most congregations it is the decision of the parents whether to ask certain persons to be godparents for the infant. While many congregations prefer that godparents be Christian, that decision also is left to the parents.

Although most baptisms take place during Sunday morning worship, in some congregations, baptisms may take place wherever the faith community is gathered. In the rare case of baptism by immersion, the community gathers at a pool, river, lake or ocean.

When baptisms take place in the church, the water is either poured into a baptismal font before the service begins or during the baptismal liturgy itself. In a few churches, a bowl is used instead of a baptismal font and a lay person holds the bowl for the baptism.

Most congregations use one of the baptismal liturgies from the 1989 *United Methodist Hymnal* or the 1964 *Book of Hymns*. In a few churches, words about baptism and prayers are offered extemporaneously while the questions for the candidate/parents are taken from the hymnal.

The place in the worship service where the baptism occurs varies greatly from congregation to congregation. Some believe that infants should be baptized toward the beginning of worship as a sign that the child is claimed by God before he or she is aware of their faith through the reading of scripture and proclamation of the word. Others include the baptism after the sermon in the response section of the liturgy. Still others view baptism as a means of proclaiming the continuing presence of God among us and schedule the baptism during the Proclamation section of the service before the sermon.

Most baptisms are effected through sprinkling or pouring while the pastor recites some version of the baptismal formula. While the *traditional baptismal formula* is still used in many congregations, alternative baptismal formulas include: "In the name of God, our Creator; Jesus Christ, our Redeemer/Savior; and the Holy Spirit, our Comforter" or "In the name of the Father, Son, and Holy Spirit; One God, Mother of us all."

There is no norm as to the number of times the water is placed on the person's head. Some sprinkle or pour only once while others consider three times more appropriate—one for each person of the Trinity.

The use of other symbols during baptism varies. The tradition has been for infants to wear white clothing although that is slowly changing. Some clergy also anoint the forehead of the infant with oil or with the baptismal water in the sign of the cross. In other churches, the one being baptized is presented with a rose of remembrance, a banner made by children in the Sunday school, or a candle that can be lit every year on the anniversary of one's baptism.

Confirmation

In most Euro-American congregations, there is a period of preparation for those age twelve and older that is followed by a service of confirmation. The preparation period varies from six weeks to a year. While some churches confirm on any Sunday during the year, many churches have confirmation on the day of Pentecost. This is a time for those who were baptized as infants to publicly profess their faith.

Sacrament of Holy Communion

"Holy Communion," "Communion," and "Lord's Supper" are the terms commonly used to name this sacrament which is celebrated once a month after the sermon in most Euro-American churches. Congregations may also celebrate communion on Christmas Eve, Ash Wednesday, Maundy Thursday, Easter Sunday, and the day of Pentecost.

The communion liturgy is often taken from one of the options in *The United Methodist Hymnal*. A few pastors celebrate communion with their own informal narrative on communion themes and offer prayer extemporaneously. Whichever form is used, most clergy include the *Words of Institution* and a consecration of the elements. The one who consecrates the elements is almost always an ordained or licensed minister.

While some pastors break the bread during the *Words of Institution*, others wait until after the Great Thanksgiving Prayer to elevate the cup and break the bread.

When the congregation communes while kneeling at the altar, the most common elements used are small cubes of bread and individual cups of grape juice. These elements may be present on the altar as well during the Great Thanksgiving or a loaf of bread and a chalice may be used by the celebrant. Those congregations that commune through the method of *intinction* also use a chalice and loaf of bread. In a few congregations, unleavened bread or wafers are used.

On Worldwide Communion Sunday, some churches use the staple food of various cultures in place of bread: tortillas, rice cakes, Native American fry bread, etc.

In addition to kneeling at the altar, walking forward, and communing through *intinction*, other methods of distribution include passing the elements to the people in the pews, and passing the elements to one another while standing in a circle around the altar.

The elements are understood to be symbols of the real presence of Christ within and among us. They may or may not be covered during the worship service depending on the tradition of the congregation and the theology of the pastor.

While a few churches prefer that persons be confirmed before they take communion, in most Euro-American congregations, it is acceptable for children baptized as infants and the unbaptized to commune.

Rituals of Passage

Weddings

Prewedding customs and practices have changed greatly over the years in the Euro-American culture. The tradition has been for the man to get down on one knee and ask the woman to marry him and if she says yes, to place a diamond engagement ring on the ring finger of her left hand. Couples may choose to have a party to celebrate their engagement but the pastor is not usually invited and no religious elements are involved. The female family members and friends of the bride may give her a bridal shower weeks before the wedding. Gifts are given to the bride as she begins her new life as a married woman. The male family members and friends of the groom may throw him a bachelor party the week before the wedding. None of these customs are religious in nature and the pastor is usually not invited.

Most clergy do require several premarital counseling sessions before the wedding takes place.

While many weddings are performed in the church, in the Euro-American culture, it is common for weddings to be held almost anywhere.

Some couples still adhere to a traditional belief/superstition that it is bad luck for the groom to see the bride the day of the wedding before she walks down the aisle. Another custom still practiced derives from an old, anonymous English rhyme: "something old, something new, something borrowed, something blue, and a silver sixpence for each of her shoes." Today female family members and friends often present the bride with the first four gifts mentioned: something old, something new, something borrowed, and something blue.

On the day of the wedding, the bride is usually dressed in a white wedding gown and the groom in a tuxedo. The couple is often attended by bridesmaids, ushers, flower girl and ring bearer. Traditionally, the bride is escorted down the aisle by her father. Today however, the bride may choose to have both parents accompany her, or she may choose her best friend. The couple may also decide to walk down the aisle together escorting each other. In some weddings, the groom processes down the aisle with his parents as well. While the "Wedding March" was the most popular music to accompany the procession in years past, today, one finds classical music, rock, jazz, drums, and bagpipes among many other possibilities.

Clergy use a variety of resources for the wedding ceremony: The United Methodist Hymnal and various books on greetings, prayers, and vows from various denominations. Some clergy write their own wedding liturgies that are general in nature or designed specifically for a particular couple.

The wedding service itself may be a simple ceremony of gathering, exchanging vows and rings, and pronouncing the couple husband and wife. The Unity Candle may be lit as a symbolic gesture of the two uniting as one. In weddings where the bride and groom are committed Christians, scripture readings, a sermon/meditation, hymns, and prayers are also included.

In many weddings, there is a time for the couple to pay their respect to their parents by presenting their mothers with a rose, or by greeting them with a kiss of thanksgiving. The wedding ceremony in *The United Methodist Hymnal* also includes a time for the parents and other family and friends to offer their blessing and support for the couple. When either the bride or groom has been married before and children are involved, many clergy include the children in the ceremony offering the children a chance to affirm the union, and offering the soon-to-be stepparent an opportunity to welcome the child/children into their new family.

In some weddings, the sacrament of Holy Communion is included. While the pastor consecrates the elements, the couple distributes the elements to the congregation as their first act as husband and wife.

After the wedding, the couple usually greet their guests in a receiving line either at the back of the church or at the reception following. The reception usually includes various foods, music, dancing, *toasting* (words of hope for the couple), and cutting the wedding cake. The bride may also throw her bouquet over her shoulder to unmarried women and the groom may throw the bride's garter over his shoulder to unmarried men. The superstition is that whoever catches the bouquet and garter will become the next to be married (although not necessarily to one another). As the couple leaves, friends and family may throw rice or birdseed at them. Traditionally this was a ritual gesture of hope that the couple would bear many children. Today the ritual act may be done without the attending symbolism of fertility.

If the pastor is invited to the reception, she or he may be asked to offer a prayer before the food is served.

Funerals

When someone dies in the Euro-American culture, family and close friends immediately visit the bereaved, share stories of the one who died, and help make arrangements for the funeral (if the body is to be buried) or the memorial service (if the body is to be cremated). Both burial and cremation are acceptable in the Euro-American culture today. Often members of the church bring food to the family to relieve some of the burden of daily maintenance. The funeral service usually takes place three to five days after one's death. A memorial service, however, may take place days or even weeks after death.

Between the day of death and the day of the funeral service and burial, there is often one or more evenings set aside for the viewing of the body at the funeral home. During the *viewing* friends and extended family pay their respect to the deceased and offer their condolences to the immediate family. If the pastor attends the *Viewing*, often she or he prays with the family. While there are usually no formal acts of worship during the *viewing*, some churches set aside a time for a prayer service on one of the nights before the funeral.

While funeral services may take place at the church or a funeral home, memorial services are usually held at the church. If it is a funeral, another viewing of the body may take place an hour or so preceding the funeral service. Immediately before the funeral begins, the pastor may pray with the family.

If the service is at the church, the casket is usually closed. When services are held at the funeral home, it may be open. The casket is either placed in the front of the sanctuary parallel to the altar before the funeral starts, or moved into position by a procession led by the pastor, followed by the pallbearers carrying the casket, and then the family. The casket is surrounded by many flowers, an American flag if the person was in the military, and sometimes a picture of the deceased and/or items of importance to him or her.

The pastor designs the funeral/memorial service with input from the family and or information left by the deceased. It usually includes scripture readings and hymns that were important to the deceased, prayers, a sermon, a time of *naming* and a time of *witness*. During the *naming* section, the pastor or a member of the family gives an overview of the person's life. The *witness* section offers various individuals an opportunity to share their memories about the deceased. There may also be special music, reading of poetry, or reading of a letter written by the deceased to the survivors. Today, there may even be a message from the deceased on audiotape or videotape, or a video montage of scenes from the person's life.

If it is a funeral service, there is a car procession from the place of the funeral to the cemetery. Once there, the pastor often leads a procession from the hearse to the grave site followed by the pallbearers carrying the casket, then family, then friends.

The committal service consists mainly of scripture reading, prayer, and committing the deceased to God. At the end of the service, the pastor may throw dirt on the casket, mark a cross on the casket with the dirt, lay a flower on the casket, or give a flower from one of the floral arrangements to each person present to take home with them.

In the northern parts of the United States, the ground may be too frozen in the winter months for graves to be dug. The body is then kept at the funeral home until the ground thaws in the spring. The committal service in these instances usually includes a time of remembering the life of the deceased as well as a short sermon/meditation in addition to the scripture readings and prayers.

Within the Euro-American culture, increasing numbers of persons are being cremated rather than buried. When the body is cremated, the rituals surrounding death may be eliminated or greatly reduced. There is often no viewing and there may or may not be a memorial service. Pastors may be asked to preside over a ritual of spreading the ashes. In some states where spreading the ashes is illegal, this request may pose ethical problems as well as pastoral care concerns.

After the funeral/memorial service, there is often a reception at the church or the family's home. The food for the reception is often supplied by church members and friends.

Friends and relatives may make a monetary contribution to the church or some other charitable organization chosen by the family in honor of the deceased. In many churches, family members contribute flowers for the church's altar on the Sunday closest to the anniversary of the death of their loved one. A poinsettia at Christmas and/or a lily at Easter may be given to the church in honor of loved ones who have died. These flowers are used to decorate the sanctuary on these high celebratory days in the life of the church.

FIJIAN-AMERICAN WORSHIP PRACTICES

with Saimone L. Kete

The Service of the Word

The Language of the Liturgy

The language used in worship is Fijian.

The Liturgical Space

Since Fijian-American churches share the worship space of other congregations, there are usually no cultural images or symbols to identify the space as Fijian.

Liturgical Time

Worship usually lasts between an hour and an hour and a half.

Liturgical Garb

No special liturgical garb is worn by Fijian-American pastors.

Liturgical Seasons and Days

Christmas, Easter, and Pentecost are the liturgical days honored in Fijian-American congregations. On Palm Sunday the children lead the worship service, which begins with a procession outside the church. Everyone waves palms as they enter the sanctuary. Good Friday services are also held. In addition, Fijian-American churches also celebrate Mother's Day, Father's Day, Youth Day, and New Year's Eve. The new year is welcomed in with the beating of the *lali* drums, and the singing of hymns and traditional songs. Worship services are held every evening for the first week of the new year. Fiji Day, October 10, is recognized as the day Fiji was liberated from Great Britain.

Beginning Our Praise to God

Worship begins with an introit sung by the congregation, followed by a Call to Worship which is scripturally based and read responsively between the worship leader and the congregation.

Prayer Forms

Prayer forms in Fijian-American congregations include: the Lord's Prayer, which is recited every week, extemporaneous prayers by the pastor and several lay members of the congregation, a prayer of confession, and a prayer of thanksgiving. Throughout various prayers, people often respond with Fijian words meaning "please Jesus," "thank you, Jesus," etc. The posture of prayer is sitting.

Creeds

The Apostles' Creed is recited once a month on Communion Sunday.

Music

Music in the Fijian culture is similar to that in the Tongan tradition. No musical instruments are used to accompany the hymns, choir anthems, or any other musical offering. The choir director starts to sing the various musical elements (e.g. introit, hymn, or threefold "Amen") and everyone joins in. Three to four hymns are sung every week from the Fijian Methodist hymnal *Vola Ni Sere*. As a sign of appreciation, the congregation may clap following a choir anthem or solo.

Scripture Readings

Two scripture texts are read each week: one from the Old Testament and one from the New Testament. The Old Testament is usually read by a lay liturgist or someone chosen by the preacher. The gospel lesson is often read in unision by the congregation.

Preaching

Preaching usually lasts about twenty minutes in the Fijian-American tradition. Placed at the end of the worship service, the sermon is seen as the most important part of the liturgy. The lectionary is often consulted as the pastor chooses which text to preach on from week to week. Once the text is chosen, one verse from that text is highlighted for the topic of the sermon. Preachers often use stories and illustrations from Fiji in their sermons. Humor is becoming more acceptable in Fijian-American preaching. It is expected that sermons will end with a tight conclusion rather than being open ended.

Sometimes pastors include the congregation in their sermon by asking them to turn in their Bibles to a particular text and read it aloud during the sermon, or by asking them a question that elicits a response from various members.

Passing of the Peace

The Passing of the Peace is not widely acceptable in Fijian-American churches. The sanctuary is seen as a holy place for people to sit quietly and pray. Whenever in the presence of chiefs or anything sacred, respectful behavior requires one to enter, take one's place, be seated, and remain in place throughout the event. Walking around and greeting people during worship is seen as irreverent. Greeting one another is more appropriate before or after the service.

Benediction

When ordained clergy are not available, it is acceptable for lay leaders/pastors to offer the benediction. Usually the pastor and the congregation stand with eyes closed during the benediction. The pastor raises both arms as a gesture of blessing.

Sacramental Practices

Sacrament of Baptism

When a child is born in Fiji, a *Roqoroqo* is held to honor the newborn. Baby-size fine mats and *tapa* cloths along with various foods are presented to the child. The older grandmothers in the community perform traditional dances and sing chants to welcome the child into the world. This tradition is fading away in many Fijian-American communities.

Shortly after birth, the pastor meets with the parents two or three times in preparation for the child's baptism. Except for special situations where the congregation gathers at someone's home for the baptism, most baptisms take place in the church during Sunday worship. The infant being baptized wears white clothing as a sign of purity.

On the day of the baptism, the family presents the pastor with several fine mats and brown *tapa* cloths. These mats are piled on top of one another and placed on the floor of the chancel area. During the baptism, the pastor stands on these mats. This practice is known as *Butubutu*, which literally means "to step on." After the baptism, the mats are given to the pastor as a gift from the parents in thanksgiving for baptizing their child.

The baptismal liturgy is taken from the Fijian Methodist Hymnal and includes words of introduction to the sacrament of baptism, questions for the parents and the congregation, and a prayer of blessing for the infant.

During the baptism itself, a lay leader holds a bowl for the pastor who sprinkles the water on the infant's head three times for each person of the trinity. The baby is baptized with the *traditional baptismal formula*. The pastor then makes the sign of the cross on the infant's forehead with the baptismal water. A baptismal certificate is given to the parents for the child. The congregation takes up a collection to give as a donation to the pastor for performing the baptism. Following the worship service is a feast in honor of the newborn child.

Confirmation

Confirmation is becoming a common practice in Fijian-American churches.

Sacrament of Holy Communion

The most common phrase used to refer to this sacrament is *Na I Vakayakavi ni Turaga*, which translates best as "the Lord's Supper." The Lord's Supper is celebrated once a month after the sermon. A typical Fijian cloth often covers the altar on communion Sundays. The elements used are a loaf of bread which is baked especially for the occasion, and either one chalice or individual cups of grape juice. The elements are covered until the appropriate time in the liturgy. They are understood by the congregation to be symbols of Christ's presence and grace.

The liturgy of the Lord's Supper is taken from the Fijian Methodist Hymnal, which includes an introduction to the sacrament, a prayer of Thanksgiving, the consecration of the elements, and the *Words of*

Institution. The bread is broken at the end of the liturgy before the distribution of the elements.

After the pastor and lay servers commune, the congregation comes forward and kneels at the altar for the Lord's Supper. The elements are distributed with the words "This is the body and blood of our Lord Jesus Christ given for you." A short prayer is offered before each table is dismissed.

People who are not baptized are allowed to take communion. Children commune as early as is physically possible.

Rituals of Passage

Weddings

Before a couple is engaged in the Fijian culture, the prospective groom must first present a Fijian whale's tooth to the bride's parents. If the parents accept the gift, then the groom buys the engagement ring and the date is set for the wedding.

Twenty-one days prior to the wedding, a feast is held in honor of the couple. It is a small gathering of members of both families to confirm that the marriage will take place as planned. If there are any objections or concerns, they are raised at this time. Both families give beds, furniture, food, and other items necessary for a new home. Mats will be set up at the place where the new couple will live.

Most premarital counseling is done by the mother of the bride. After she has talked with the couple several times, the pastor may also meet with the couple in preparation for the wedding. Pastors may perform weddings for those divorced but it is frowned upon.

On the day of the wedding, fine mats and *tapa* cloths are piled on top of one another and placed in the chancel area of the sanctuary. During the wedding, the pastor stands on the mats. After the wedding, the mats are given to the pastor in thanksgiving for performing the ceremony.

The marriage usually takes place in the church, although that is beginning to change in the United States. The bride and groom wear traditional Fijian dress for the occasion. The bridesmaids, ushers, parents, and other assistants, along with the bride and groom, wear leis. The bride is escorted down the aisle by her father while the congregation sings Fijian hymns.

The wedding consists of hymns, prayers, scripture readings, a sermon, the exchange of vows and rings, and the pronouncement that the couple is now husband and wife. In addition, there is a time in the service where the bride and groom thank their parents and their new in-laws. At the end of the wedding, the father of the bride thanks the people for coming and invites them to the reception. As the people exit the church, they formally greet the bridal party at the back of the church.

Following the wedding is a *Magiti* or "wedding feast." It usually takes place in a hall, restaurant, or large shed that was prepared for the occasion. Often the bride changes into a Western-style white dress for the reception. In addition to the feast, the *Magiti* includes music, some modern dancing, words of blessing for the couple, and a ritual of cutting the wedding cake. There are no money dances, traditional dances, or alcohol present at the *Magiti*. At a particular point in the feast, special food is presented to the mother of the bride as a token of love for her role in giving birth and nurturing her daughter through her childhood. *Tambu kaisi* (the best quality mats) are given as gifts to the chief of the tribe and other high-ranked officials. The pastor is expected to offer the prayer before the meal is served.

Funerals

When a person dies in the Fijian-American community, the casket is brought to the funeral home for the *bikabika*, which means "mourners." The *bikabika* is an all-night worship service that includes singing, prayers, and the reading of scripture. Food and *kava* (the national drink of Fiji) is served to the mourners who have gathered. During the *Bikabika*, the casket is closed. Clergy from various churches and denominations may be invited to participate in the *bikabika* and the funeral. The following morning, before the funeral service, the casket is opened for a viewing of the body.

The body is dressed in special clothes and a Bible and high-quality fine mats and *tapa* cloths are placed in the coffin with the deceased. The casket is surrounded by flowers.

The funeral service lasts about an hour and includes hymn singing, scripture reading, the "concluding" sermon, a reading about the facts of the one who died, and someone chosen by the family who offers testimony about the life of the deceased. During the funeral service, the pastor stands on a pile of fine mats and *tapa* cloths. After the funeral, these mats are given to the pastor in thanksgiving for performing the funeral rite.

After the funeral service there is a car procession to the cemetery. Upon arrival, the pastor leads a procession from the hearse to the grave site followed by the pallbearers carrying the casket, then the family and other guests. The grave site service includes scripture reading, prayers, and the "concluding" hymn. Everyone present throws dirt on the casket three times. After the committal service, the people stay until the casket has been lowered and the grave is completely filled in.

Following the grave site service there is a reception for close family members at the family's home. During the reception, the family decides who should wear black clothes, who should wear a black armband, and who should wear a black pin as a sign of mourning. The length of time these items are worn is up to the family. The family stays in mourning until the predetermined date for the "lifting of mourning."

The Sunday after the day of burial is known as "Thanksgiving Sunday." During worship, the deceased is honored with prayers and testimony offered by anyone who wishes to speak.

Memorial services may be held in America for family members who died in Fiji.

FILIPINO-AMERICAN WORSHIP PRACTICES

with Rev. Dr. David H. Marcelo

The Service of the Word

The Language of the Liturgy

The Philippines comprise thousands of islands and around seventy native languages and dialects. The official languages of the Philippines are Pilipino and English. Pilipino is based on *Tagalog* (pronounced Ta-*ga*-log) which is considered to be the richest of all the Filipino languages with the most extensive written literature. It is the language of the largest island, Luzon, which includes the capital city, Manila, and has great influence in the Philippines.[1] Since Methodist missionaries were sent to the island of Ilocos, the *Ilocano* language is also common among Filipino-American United Methodists. *Pampango* is another dialect that can be found in America. Since *Tagalog* is the national language, those who speak *Ilocano* or *Pampango* can understand *Tagalog* but those who speak *Tagalog* often cannot understand the other regional languages.

While some Sunday school classes and Bible study groups may communicate in *Ilocano* or *Pampango*, for the most part, worship services are held in *Tagalog*. There are also Filipino-American churches who use English during worship. Unlike other cultures, English language services are not primarily for second- and third- generation Filipino-Americans. First generation Filipino-Americans may choose to have their services in English since English is also an official language of the Philippines and they are currently living in the United States.

The Liturgical Space

Since many Filipino-American congregations share the church building with another congregation, there is often little in the environment that would identify the space as a place specifically used by Filipino-Americans in worship.

71

Liturgical Time

Worship within the Filipino-American tradition usually lasts between one and one and a half hours. Since it is common for people to arrive late for church, people may enter the congregation at various points during the service.

Liturgical Garb

To lead worship, the pastor may wear a robe or alb or (if male) a Filipino *barong* which is considered special dress or ceremonial garb in the Filipino culture. Stoles may be made of Filipino cloth.

Liturgical Seasons and Days

Advent, Christmas, Epiphany, Lent, Easter, and Pentecost are all celebrated within Filipino-American congregations. Worship services are also held on Christmas Day and on Thanksgiving Day or the night before. Those within the community who died throughout the year are remembered at a special service. This remembrance often takes place on All Saints Day or Memorial Day but may also happen at other times during the year. In addition, the Philippines' Independence Day is celebrated on the Sunday closest to June 12.

Beginning Our Praise to God

The service opens with some form of Call to Worship that is often scripturally based and read responsively between the worship leader and the congregation.

Prayer Forms

Filipino-American congregations have a wide range of prayer forms: the Lord's Prayer, prayers of confession, extemporaneous prayers by the pastor and lay worship leaders, the pastoral prayer, and corporate prayers printed in the bulletin. The posture for prayer is usually sitting.

In addition, in many Filipino-American congregations, individual prayer needs are brought to the pastor before or after the pastoral prayer. During a hymn, the pastor often comes down from the pulpit to the altar rail. As the congregation sings the hymn, various members come and stand at the altar rail. The people whisper their prayer requests in the pastor's ear as he or she walks from one end of the rail to the other. When all the requests are privately received, the pastor returns to the pulpit and offers the pastoral prayer including the general concerns of the people but not including any specifics. The pastor may also pray for concerns of the community and the world. In some congregations these prayer requests may be made aloud rather than in private.

Prayers are also offered for healing of body, mind, and soul. These prayers are accompanied by the anointing of oil in the sign of the cross. While not done every Sunday, prayers for healing are common in Filipino-American churches. Rather than holding separate healing services, the anointing takes place during Sunday worship. People come forward to the altar rail and pray as the pastor anoints each one with oil, offering prayers for healing.

Creeds

While the recitation of a creed is not common in Filipino-American worship, a creed may be said on special liturgical days.

Music

The *Tagalog* hymnal, *Ang Imnaryong Christiany,* used by many Filipino-American churches, is published in the Philippines and used by other denominations in the United States as well.

The piano is the most common instrument in Filipino-American worship although organs may also be used. Increasingly, guitars, drums, synthesizers, and other instruments are incorporated into the worship service as well. A traditional Filipino instrument called the *Banduria* (like a mandolin) may be played on special occasions. In addition, taped music is often used to accompany soloists and some of the choir anthems. The congregation often claps or says "Amen" in affirmation of musical offerings.

Scripture Readings

Two to three scriptures passages are read each week by a lay liturgist as the people read along in their own Bibles. The scriptures may also be read responsively verse by verse between the worship leader and the congregation.

Preaching

Preaching within the Filipino-American tradition usually lasts between twenty and thirty minutes. The sermon is seen by the congregation as the most important aspect of worship but the sermon is often placed in the middle rather than at the end of the service. Humor is acceptable and storytelling is often expected. Illustrations often come from the Filipino context: historical figures, folktales, and contemporary struggles.

Filipino-American pastors often employ a range of participatory styles of preaching. Many clergy intentionally ask questions in the middle of their sermon which require a short, but audible response from persons in the congregation. A pastor may also ask the congregation to find a particular text in the Bible and read it aloud. Some pastors invite laypersons to come forward after the sermon to share their thoughts about the topic and/or text of the sermon. Others give their sermon "notes" to the Sunday school teachers so that the various classes can discuss the sermon after the service in Sunday school.

There are many laypersons in the Filipino-American church who believe that the pastor should preach without any notes at all as a sign that the preacher is truly being led by the Holy Spirit and is convicted by what he or she says. Sermons are often judged by how they touch one's emotions, not one's intellect.

Blessings

Blessings are a very important aspect of Filipino-American Christian tradition. Since all of life is in the realm of the sacred and used in service to God, a pastor is often asked to bless objects as well as people. It is common for a pastor to be called upon to bless a house or a car or even a pet. Some of these blessings may take place in Sunday worship while many take place in people's homes or elsewhere. Every aspect of daily life is ritualized, made holy, and blessed. Worship is not kept for a specific time and place but is brought into the home and the workplace —wherever the people carry out their various ministries in the world.

Passing of the Peace

It is common in many Filipino-American churches to include the Passing of the Peace in the weekly liturgy. In the United States, the members of the congregation share God's love with one another with handshakes, hugs, and kisses.

Benediction

It is traditional in Filipino-American churches for ordained clergy to pronounce the benediction with both hands raised in a gesture of blessing. Local pastors who offer the benediction may or may not use the gesture of blessing.

Sacramental Practices

Sacrament of Baptism

Most persons baptized within Filipino-American churches are baptized as infants. Usually the pastor has at least one counseling session with the parents before the baptism takes place.

The baptismal liturgy used for the sacrament varies from pastor to pastor. Some pastors use a formal liturgy with preprinted prayers and questions for the parents (or adult being baptized), while others ask the formulated questions but pray extemporaneously. Still others prefer to do the questions and prayers extemporaneously.

During the baptism itself, water that has been placed in the baptismal font prior to the service is sprinkled (sometimes poured) on the baby's head three times, once for each person of the Trinity. Some pastors also anoint the infant's head with oil in the sign of the cross. Although somewhat rare, adults who are baptized may be baptized by immersion in a river, lake, pool, or ocean. The adult being baptized often shares her or his faith journey and conversion experience with the congregation. The person being baptized is given a certificate and perhaps some small gift (e.g. a cross). In some Filipino-American congregations it is expected that the person (or family) being baptized will give a monetary gift to the church.

The *traditional baptismal formula* is used. "Holy Spirit" is always used since the word *ghost* as in "Holy Ghost" implies (as in one English definitions) a spirit from the dead in the *Tagalog* language.

Because of the strong Roman Catholic influence in Filipino culture, it is common for members of the congregation to follow Catholic customs of requesting (and expecting) private baptisms in their homes rather than during Sunday worship. The home setting often impacts the liturgy that surrounds the baptism. Home rituals tend to be more informal with extemporaneous prayers and questions rather than a formal liturgy, and a bowl is used instead of a font. While Sunday worship is encouraged as the setting for baptisms, private baptisms are such a part of the Filipino culture that they are sometimes hard to avoid. These baptisms in the home are not devoid of the community of the faithful since members of the church are often invited to these private baptisms.

Baptisms are also a big social occasion within the Filipino-American community. The celebration and festivities are supported by the broader community as the parents ask various individuals to be *kumpadres* and *kumadres* (literally godfathers and godmothers)—spiritual guides—for the child as well as to provide support for various aspects of the celebration. For example, someone might be asked to be godmother for the clothes the child wears at the baptism, which would mean she would buy the baptismal gown. Someone else might be godfather of the cake served at the party after the baptism. In this way, the extended family and broader community contribute to the celebration of the child's incorporation into the family of God.

Confirmation

Many Filipino-American United Methodist churches have confirmation for those in their early teen years. The preparation time varies but could last up to one year. The service of confirmation may take place on any Sunday of the year.

Sacrament of Holy Communion

"Holy Communion" and "Lord's Supper" are the most common terms used in the Filipino-American church to describe this sacrament. It takes place once a month and is open to the baptized and unbaptized alike. The elements used for Holy Communion vary: wafers, small cubes of bread, one loaf, and either one chalice or individual cups. A form of rice is sometimes used in place of bread to honor the staple food of the Philippines. The altar is sometimes covered with a white embroidered cloth from the Philippines called a *tapete*. The elements are usually covered throughout the service until the time for Holy Communion.

The distribution of the elements varies: kneeling at the altar rail, processing forward and communing by *intinction*, or having the elements passed to the congregation sitting in the pews. The words that accompany the distribution of the elements is a dilemma for some Filipino-American United Methodist clergy. Because the Philippines is 85 percent Roman Catholic, it is common for the people to have a belief in *transubstantiation* or *consubstantiation*. While some pastors still distribute the elements with the words "This is the body and blood of our Lord Jesus Christ given for you," some clergy use alternative language ("Receive these elements and be thankful") so as not to reinforce doctrines of *transubstantiation* and *consubstantiation* among their parishioners. Efforts are made to teach doctrines of real presence and the understanding that the elements are symbols of Christ's life-giving, hope-filled presence and grace.

The liturgy surrounding Holy Communion also varies from pastor to pastor within the Filipino-American context. While some use stylized Great Prayers of Thanksgiving with the *Words of Institution*, the consecration of the elements, and responses by the congregation, many clergy offer words about communion and pray extemporaneously consecrating the elements before reciting the *Words of Institution*, while others simply pray extemporaneously without repeating the *Words of Institution* or specifically consecrating the elements. Some pastors break the bread during the *Words of Institution* and others break after the Great Prayer of Thanksgiving before the invitation to the table and distribution of the elements.

Rituals of Passage

Weddings

Filipino-American weddings are diverse and varied in the traditional elements included in the engagement, wedding, and reception rituals. There are many factors that contribute to this diversity: the number of years the person has lived in the United States, how involved the parents are, whether the future spouse is also Filipino-American or not, and personal likes and dislikes. The descriptions that follow are all possible practices one might experience, and requests one might receive if serving as the officiating clergy at a Filipino-American wedding.

Preparation for a wedding in the Filipino-American culture may begin with the *Pamanhikan*. In Filipino tradition, the parents of the (hopeful) groom go to the house of the family of the bride-to-be and ask permission for the two to be married. This *Pamanhikan* establishes the engagement of the couple.

Once the date for the wedding has been set, the bride is measured for her white wedding gown, but she is not allowed to try it on because it is considered a sign of bad luck. The groom wears either a tuxedo or a Filipino *barong*, which is traditional ceremonial garb for men.

It is preferable that weddings be held in the church but it is acceptable for a wedding to take place in a garden or at someone's home. Usually two to four premarital counseling sessions are required before persons are married in the Filipino-American church.

Bridesmaids, ushers, flower girl(s), and ring bearer(s) are all possible attendants for the bride and groom. The bride processes down the aisle escorted by her father.

The wedding ceremony consists of a rite, of the father "giving the bride to the groom," the reading of scripture, prayers, sermon or meditation, solos (often including a *Tagalog* love song), exchange of vows, and the giving and receiving of rings. In addition, several elements are unique to Filipino-American weddings.

After the vows and the giving of rings, the couple may pay respect to their parents with the ritual of "kissing of the hands." The couple leaves the chancel area and go first to the bride's parents, then the groom's. The "kissing of the hand" does not involve actual kissing, but rather the bride takes her mother's right hand and touches the back of her mother's hand to the bride's forehead, bowing into it simultaneously. The bride repeats this ritual with her father. Then the groom likewise "kisses the hand" of his new in-laws. The couple then go to the groom's parents to repeat this ceremony of respect.

After the "kissing of the hands" is completed, the couple returns to the chancel area and kneels for the ceremony of the cord and veil. One end of a prelooped cord is placed around the neck of the groom and the other end around the neck of the bride. This yoke is symbolic of binding the two together in love. It also signifies strength as well as elasticity. "When two work together the burdens of life become easier to carry."[2] Then a veil is placed over the heads of the couple. The veil symbolizes the canopy of God's love that encompasses them as well as the notion of a home that should be hospitable to all.

After the ceremony of the cord and veil, some couples choose to have the gift of coins bestowed upon them. The couple chooses someone to be the "coin bearer" for the wedding (the "coin bearer" may also process in with the other attendants). This "coin bearer" hands the minister a bundle of several gold novelty coins wrapped in netting to present to the couple. These coins not only symbolize God's rich blessings but also God's call to be good stewards of the resources entrusted to us.

A Bible (white or black) with the couple's name engraved on the front (Mr. and Mrs.——) may also be presented to the couple at this time. A prayer is offered for the couple, then the veil and cord removed.

The Unity Candle is becoming more and more common in Filipino-American weddings. If the Unity Candle is lit, it takes place at this time. The outer candles are lit along with the candelabra or altar candles before the procession by the "candle sponsors" (usually one of the bridesmaids and one of the ushers). During the lighting of the Unity Candle, the bride and groom go forward, remove the outer candles and with them light the center candle. The outer candles are blown out as a sign of the two becoming one. Following this, the officiating minister pronounces the couple as husband and wife.

The couple greet their guests either after the wedding at the back of the church or at the place of the reception. The bride stays in her wedding gown for the reception, which usually includes a sit-down dinner, dancing, *toasting* with words of blessing, health, and happiness, and a ritual of cutting the wedding cake and feeding each other. The bride often throws her bouquet to unmarried women. In addition, it is customary at many Filipino-American wedding receptions to have a time when doves are released. Two doves are kept inside a paper decoration in the shape of a bell. At the appropriate time in the reception, the couple pulls an attached cord that opens the bell and releases the two doves. The guests then try to catch the two doves. Once caught, the two doves are made to kiss which is a sign for the couple to kiss. Once the doves are caught, they are returned to their custodian to be kept until the next wedding in the community.

Another tradition at Filipino-American wedding receptions is the money dance. After the release of the doves, the guests line up and receive pins. The men form a line in front of the bride while the women wait their turn to dance with the groom. The guests who want to dance with the bride and groom pin bills (often $20 bills and above) on the clothing of the bride and groom. Their dance only lasts a short time, then it is the next one's turn. After the reception, some couples join a family gathering at someone's house before going on their honeymoon.

As is the custom at baptisms, there are also godparents or "sponsors" of various aspects of the wedding. These *kumadres* and *kumpadres* are usually older friends of the family or couple. The primary role of the godparents is to provide spiritual guidance for the couple. Today, however, it is also expected that they will give financial gifts to the couple or be a sponsor for the various elements necessary for the celebration: the wedding gown, the flowers, cake, etc. The larger community contributes in this way to the cost of the ceremony and festivities.

Funerals

After someone dies within the Filipino-American community, a prayer service is immediately organized while plans for the funeral service and burial are being made. This prayer service may take place at the funeral home, the church, or the family's home and can last from thirty minutes to a few hours. It is a time when the community gathers more informally for prayer, scripture reading, and singing. During the prayer service the casket is open and people have a chance to pay their last respects to the deceased. Depending on the wishes of the family, there may be similar prayer services on various evenings between the day of death and the day of burial. If the deceased was involved in more than one faith community, the family may ask representatives from each of these groups to lead the prayer service on various nights or to participate in the funeral service.

Both black and white are appropriate colors for the prayer service and the funeral service. Black represents mourning and white symbolizes eternity, goodness, and resurrection.

Immediately prior to the funeral service, some parishioners expect the pastor to come to their home, pray with them, and accompany the family of the deceased to the funeral.

During the funeral service, the casket is in place at the front surrounded by flowers, candles, a flag if the person was in the military, and a picture of the one who has died. Often the casket is closed, but sometimes it is open upon request of the family. The deceased may be dressed in special clothes, and a Bible or other items of importance in the person's life may be placed in the casket as well.

The funeral service includes prayers, singing, scripture reading, preaching, and testimony about the person who died. While some families select a few persons in advance to share their memories of the

80

deceased, often everyone is given this opportunity. After the funeral service, there is often a car procession from the funeral to the cemetery. Cremation is still rare within the Filipino tradition. Once at the cemetery, there is a procession from the hearse to the gravesite. The pastor leads the procession, followed by the pallbearers carrying the casket, honorary pallbearers (if chosen), family, and friends. A brief service is held with prayers and the reading of scripture. Sometimes dirt is thrown on the casket by the minister (occasionally by all). It is more common, however, for the family and friends to place a flower on the casket as they leave. After the committal service, there is a reception at the family's home or at the church.

If a family member dies in the Philippines, it is common to have a memorial service for that person here in the United States. There are worship services that mark the anniversary of someone's death. These services take place on the fortieth day after death, on the first year anniversary, and every year thereafter. Occasionally the ninth day after death is also ritually honored. These services take place at the family's home and include prayers, preaching, and the sharing of memories of their ancestor.

Notes

1. Robert McHenry, general editor. *The New Encyclopaedia Britannica*, vol. 25, 15th Edition, Chicago: 1992, p. 540.
2. *Pacasiana*—Filipino—p. 1, written by Rev. Dr. Anatalio Ubalde, Rev. Juan Ancheta, Rev. Leonard Autajay.

FORMOSAN-AMERICAN WORSHIP PRACTICES

with Rev. Frank Yang

The Service of the Word

The Language of the Liturgy

Fukienese is the language used in Formosan-American Worship. People who speak *Fukienese* are called Formosans. They come from three basic areas: the island of Taiwan, the area of China previously known as Fukien, now Fujian, and those *Fukienese* speaking persons who immigrated to the Philippines. All three groups are represented in Formosan-American churches.

English may also be used in worship to accommodate those Formosan-Americans born in the United States. While some services may be entirely bilingual (*Fukienese* and English), often only the scripture reading and the sermon are translated into English. Separate English services may be offered for the second and third generations.

Though *Fukienese* is the primary spoken language of the liturgy, the written language of the bulletin is in Chinese. The Chinese characters are read aloud in the Fukienese dialect.

The Liturgical Space

Since most Formosan-American churches borrow the sanctuary space from other congregations, the worship setting is often devoid of any cultural symbols that would identify the space as Formosan.

Liturgical Time

Worship in the Formosan-American tradition lasts about one hour.

Liturgical Garb

Regular street clothes (suit for men) with a clerical collar or a pulpit robe are worn by clergy for Sunday worship services.

Liturgical Seasons and Days

In some congregations, all the seasons of the liturgical year are celebrated. In other congregations, Advent, Christmas, Holy Week, Easter, and Pentecost are celebrated, but Epiphany and the season of Lent receive little or no attention.

Mother's Day, Thanksgiving, and New Year's Day (January 1) are also celebrated liturgically. In addition, most churches celebrate the Chinese New Year (usually in February or March), which is determined by the lunar calendar.

Beginning Our Praise to God

Worship begins with a Call to Worship that is often based on a Psalm text.

Prayer Forms

Prayer forms in the Formosan-American tradition include: the Lord's Prayer, a pastoral prayer, and extemporaneous prayers by the pastor and lay liturgist. In some congregations corporate prayers of confession are also offered. Individual prayer needs of the people may be offered during weekday prayer meetings. The posture of prayer is sitting.

Creeds

The recitation of a creed may be weekly or only sporadically throughout the year.

Music

Two to four hymns are sung during the worship service. The hymns are taken from hymnals published in Taiwan by the Holiness Church of Taiwan and the Presbyterian Church of Taiwan. In addition, a hymnbook entitled *Pak-Bi Seng-Si* is often used. This hymnal is published by the Taiwanese Christian Church Council of North America. The hymnal used most often in Formosan-American churches depends on which denomination the pastor belonged to in Taiwan and what affiliations have been made in North America. English-speaking services use *The United Methodist Hymnal.*

The prelude, postlude, and hymns are played on a piano or organ. The congregation sings the hymns in unison. In addition, short, repetitive praise songs may also be offered. Overt expressions of appreciation for soloists or choir anthems depend on the congregation. Some congregations remain silent while other congregations may clap.

Scripture Readings

One to two scripture passages are read each Sunday. Sometimes it is only one verse. It is read by the pastor or lay liturgist. In addition, a Psalm text may be read responsively between the lay liturgist and the congregation.

Preaching

Sermons usually last between twenty and thirty minutes. The sermon is seen as the most important part of the liturgy whether it is placed in the middle of the service or toward the end. Topical sermons are most common, utilizing humor and illustrations from Taiwan. The use of notes in the pulpit is acceptable and is sometimes viewed as a sign of preparation.

Participatory forms of preaching are not usually practiced in Formosan-American congregations. Occasionally, a preacher may ask the people to turn in their Bibles to a particular text and read it aloud.

Passing of the Peace

The ritual of Passing God's Peace to one another is not common in Formosan-American congregations.

Benediction

Only clergy are permitted to pronounce the benediction. The pastor stands in the pulpit with eyes closed and one or two hands raised in a gesture of blessing. The congregation stands to receive the benediction with eyes closed and heads bowed. Following the benediction, the congregation may sit for the postlude. For the first few minutes of the postlude, members of the congregation may close their eyes and bow their heads in silent prayer. Before the postlude ends, however, the people may stand and leave the sanctuary space.

Sacramental Practices

Sacrament of Baptism

The appropriate age of baptism in Formosan-American congregations varies. Theological preference for adult baptism or infant baptism is often influenced by the denomination of the pastor before moving to the United States and becoming involved in The United Methodist Church, and by the number of years the pastor has lived in North America.

For those churches that prefer adult baptism, infants are often presented at a dedication service in which the parents promise to raise the child in the Christian faith. A candle is given to the child in hopes that the candle will be lit every year on the anniversary of the dedication service until the child is baptized.

The traditional age of baptism in these congregations is fourteen years of age and older. A few classes of education and preparation are usually required before one can be baptized. Since adult baptism is the practice of the Holiness Church of Taiwan, the liturgy of baptism is usually taken from a resource by this denomination that includes questions and prayers for the person being baptized, and a thanksgiving over the water. The candidate for baptism may share their faith journey or conversion experience with the congregation as part of the liturgy. The pastor scoops water from a baptismal font with the palm of the hand and pours the water over the person's head with the words of the *traditional baptismal formula*. A Bible and baptismal certificate are given to the one being baptized. The person (or their family) often gives a large monetary gift of appreciation to the church.

In those churches that practice infant baptism, the parents attend one or two sessions in preparation for the sacrament. The liturgy from the United Methodist *Book of Worship* may be used or the pastor may ask questions and offer prayers extemporaneously. The water is either in a baptismal font or in a bowl that is held by a lay leader from the congregation. The water is sprinkled one time on the infant's head while the pastor recites the traditional baptismal formula. A certificate is often given to the parents.

Confirmation

Those churches that practice adult baptism have no need for confirmation. Those that baptize infants often confirm their youth after

85

several classes of preparation. Some churches confirm the youth between the ages of thirteen and fifteen while others prefer to wait until they are eighteen years of age before they receive confirmation.

Sacrament of Holy Communion

"Holy Communion," "Communion," and "Lord's Supper" are the most common terms to refer to this sacrament. It is celebrated once every two or three months as well as on some special liturgical days. While the sacrament usually takes place after the sermon, it may occur before the sermon.

The elements are understood by the congregation to be symbols of Christ's presence and grace among us. Individual cups of grape juice and either wafers or small cubes of bread are covered until the appropriate time in the liturgy.

While an abbreviated version of the communion liturgy from the United Methodist Book of Worship is sometimes adapted for use in the Formosan-American context, the use of any formal liturgy often depends upon the denomination of the pastor while living in Taiwan. If the pastor was from the Holiness Church, the communion liturgy is taken from their worship resource. It includes a prayer of confession, a prayer of thanksgiving, responses by the laity, a blessing of the elements, and the *Words of Institution*. The bread is broken during the Institution.

If the pastor was Presbyterian, Congregational, or from some other denomination in Taiwan, often no formal liturgy is used to celebrate communion. Prayers and words about communion are offered extemporaneously. The *Words of Institution* are offered followed by a blessing of the elements. The bread is broken during the Institution.

The elements are usually distributed to the people while they are sitting in the pew with the words "This is the body/blood of our Lord Jesus Christ given for you." When the people are served in the pew, the pastor and lay servers commune simultaneously with the congregation. In some small congregations, the people may stand in a circle around the altar to receive communion. In this case, the pastor and lay servers commune after the congregation.

Those churches that believe in adult baptism require baptism before a person can take communion. Those churches that practice infant baptism usually leave it up to the parents to decide at what age their child is ready to commune.

Rituals of Passage

Weddings

Once a couple decides to be married, there is usually some form of an engagement ritual and party. The couple and their families decide which traditional Formosan elements will be included. Often the relatives of the bride present her with gifts of various kinds of jewelry. Between the engagement ritual and the wedding, the couple attends two to five premarital counseling sessions with the pastor.

Some pastors believe that Christians should only be married in the church. Others believe that it is acceptable for weddings to take place outside the church as well—in a garden or at someone's home. The groom is usually dressed in a tuxedo and the bride in a white wedding gown. The traditional color for weddings, however, is red, a symbol of happiness and good fortune. Decoration colors often reflect this custom.

Bridesmaids, ushers, flower girl, and ring bearer serve as attendants to the bride and groom. Before the procession begins, the mothers of the bride and groom (or other representatives from each family) light the candles on the altar. The bride is escorted down the aisle by her father to the accompaniment of the "Wedding March" or other Western-style music.

The wedding consists of prayers for the couple, hymns, scripture reading, sometimes a sermon, the exchange of vows and rings, and the pronouncement that the couple is husband and wife. The lighting of the Unity Candle is becoming more and more popular in Formosan-American churches. Usually the bride and groom or the mothers of the bride and groom light the outer candles. At some point in the service there may be a time for the couple to pay respect to their parents by bowing to them or presenting them with a rose.

The couple formally greet their guests at the back of the church after the wedding or at the banquet following. Both a wedding reception at the church or a hall *and* a formal banquet at a restaurant are accepted occasions following the wedding. Some choose one over the other, while others can afford to have both.

The reception is open to everyone and includes "finger food" and music. If there is to be no banquet later, the couple also cuts the wedding cake, throws the bride's bouquet to unmarried women and the bride's garter to unmarried men during the reception. The formal banquet would be by invitation only. During the banquet, the bride often changes into traditional Chinese dress for the occasion. A traditional dress for the occasion is a red dress with symbols of a dragon or rose on it. The bride often wears all the jewelry that was presented to her by her relatives before the wedding. At the banquet, the wedding cake is cut and the bride's bouquet and garter are also thrown to unmarried guests (if there was no reception where this took place earlier). Pastors are often asked to attend the reception and/or banquet and pray before the meal is served.

Memorials/Funerals

Traditionally, the term most commonly used for the final service honoring a person's life in the Formosan community is "memorial" rather than "funeral." In America, the term "funeral" is gradually replacing "memorial" for this occasion. The body is often present. Memorial/funeral services without the body may also be held for family who have died in Taiwan.

In Taiwan, the family often waits at least one month before burying or cremating the deceased. Waiting is a sign of being a good son or daughter. In the United States, customs have changed. Some families still set the funeral date for a week to ten days after death. When this is the case, invitations may be printed and sent to family and friends announcing the day and time for the memorial/funeral service. Others have adapted to Western customs, scheduling the funeral within a week of the time of death.

Between the day of death and the memorial/funeral service, family and friends gather at the funeral home to view the body and offer their condolences to the family. The family may decide to offer prayers and sing hymns at this time, or they may ask the pastor to facilitate this short devotional time.

The tradition of giving "flower money" or "cloth money" to the family before the day of the memorial/funeral service may still be practiced by some. This is given by close family members and friends to help with expenses.

The memorial/funeral service may take place at the funeral home or the church. If the deceased was associated with other churches, it is customary to invite the other pastor(s) to participate in the memorial/funeral service. On the morning of the memorial/funeral, some families expect the pastor to come to their home and accompany them to the place of the service.

The casket may be open or closed depending on the preference of the pastor or the wishes of the family. Flowers, candles, and a picture of the deceased often surround the casket. The service consists of hymns, prayers, scripture reading, a sermon, and one person chosen by the family to testify about the life of the deceased. The service may last from one to two hours. At the end of the service, the family often stands next to the casket as the guests come forward and pay their last respects to the deceased and offer words of condolences to the family.

If a child dies before his or her parents, it is possible that the parents will not attend the memorial/funeral service. The death of a child is considered to be a bad omen in Chinese and Taiwanese lore. Some believe that participation in the memorial/funeral service may bring more misfortune upon the family.

Burial and cremation are acceptable within the culture. If the body is being buried, there may be a car procession from the place of the memorial/funeral service to the cemetery. The grave site service consists of scripture reading, prayers, and a committal of the body to God. Everyone places a flower on the casket after the service. The family may also choose to throw dirt on the casket. During the service, family members may wear a cloth or ribbon tied around their upper arm as a sign of mourning.

After the grave site service, there is usually a reception at a restaurant, the church, or the family's home.

At the family's request, the pastor may lead a worship service in the family's home on the yearly anniversary of someone's death.

GHANAIAN-AMERICAN WORSHIP PRACTICES

with Rev. Samuel Acquaah Arhin

The Service of the Word

The Language of the Liturgy

Ghana has several language systems stemming from regional and tribal localities. The two most commonly used systems in United Methodist Churches are *Akan* and *Ga*. *Ga* is its own language. *Akan* however, is an umbrella term for four linguistic subgroups: *Twi*, *Fanti*, *Asanti*, and *Akwapim*. Of these four subgroups, *Twi* and *Fanti* are currently used in Ghanaian-American churches. Because of British colonialism in Ghana and the tremendous diversity of regional languages, English is also taught in Ghana as a language intended to unify the diverse population. Since Ghanaians in America come from various regions of Ghana, most worship services include a combination of at least two of the above languages, as well as English.

In those churches where *Twi* and *Fanti* dominate, hymns tend to be sung in *Fanti* (or English) since Methodist missionaries first settled among the *Fanti*-speaking people of Ghana and published the first hymnal in *Fanti*. A Methodist hymnal in English based on the British hymnal (lyrics only, no musical notation) may also be used. It is common for some to be singing in *Fanti* while others are singing the same hymn in English.

The Liturgical Space

Both Christian symbols and cultural symbols are present in the sanctuary of a Ghanaian-American congregation. African *kente* cloth may be used as an altar cloth, made into the pastor's stole, or fashioned into the clothing of many members of the congregation. Ghanaian drums and other musical instruments are visible as well as a wooden tithing box and a wooden offering bowl. In some churches, the flag of Ghana may also be present.

90

Liturgical Time

Worship in Ghanaian-American churches usually lasts about two hours.

Liturgical Garb

Liturgical garb may be African dress, a pulpit robe with *kente* cloth stole, or a suit (for men) with a clerical collar.

Liturgical Seasons and Days

Some churches celebrate all the seasons of the church year while others focus on Christmas, Lent, Easter, and the day of Pentecost. In some churches, New Year's Eve, Mother's Day, and Thanksgiving are also honored liturgically. In addition, March 6 may be remembered as Ghana's Independence Day.

In Ghana, there are several festivals commemorating certain events or honoring the gifts of the earth: a Full Moon Festival, a Harvest Festival, a Fishing Festival (among others). While these festivals are not practiced in America, churches may offer prayers at these times for those in Ghana.

Beginning Our Praise to God

Worship is opened with music and a Call to Worship that is scripturally based. This may be proclaimed by a lay liturgist or read responsively between the liturgist and the congregation. Throughout the service, whenever the pastor or lay liturgist says "Praise the Lord," the congregation responds with "Alleluia!"

Prayer Forms

Prayer forms in the Ghanaian-American tradition include the Lord's Prayer recited weekly, extemporaneous prayers offered by the pastor and various laypersons, and a pastoral prayer that includes prayers of petition. Often one of the prayers offered by a layperson includes a confession.

The laypersons who offer prayer during a worship service are not necessarily the person designated as the lay liturgist for that Sunday. It is common for persons to begin praying extemporaneously from where they are standing or sitting. Before the person prays, he or she may first begin singing a song. The entire congregation joins in the singing.

91

During the prayer, various members of the congregation respond with "Amen" or "Yes" or a few short claps in affirmation.

Another unique prayer form in the Ghanaian-American tradition is the "silent" prayer time. During this "silent" prayer, many people quietly voice their individual prayers aloud simultaneously (similar to the Tong Song Kido Prayer of the Korean Church).

All-night prayer vigils are held on a regular basis (often monthly). These vigils include prayer, singing, and testimony.

The posture of prayer may be sitting, standing, or kneeling. When seated, many members lean forward with their eyes closed and their heads lowered.

Creeds

The Apostles' Creed is recited weekly in worship. Other creeds may be used on special occasions.

Music

Music is a predominant feature in Ghanaian-American worship. Four to six hymns are sung each week accompanied by some form of a keyboard instrument. The hymnals (in *Fanti*, *Ga*, and English) come from the Methodist Church in Ghana. Occasionally Ghanaian instruments are also used.

In addition to the hymns, several songs are sung. While the choir may choose some of these songs in advance, many are begun spontaneously by anyone in the congregation. These songs are accompanied by traditional Ghanaian instruments: the *conga drums* (two large wooden drums on a stand), the *dondo drum* (hit with a curved wooden stick), the *fritwa* (two metal cones hit with a wooden stick), the *akasaa* (a gourd wrapped in beads strung together in a pattern that, when shaken, sounds like a maraca from the Latino cultures), and the *frutweaa* (two metal objects—one that fits on the thumb and one on the first finger—that when hit together produces a high pitched sound). Tambourines may also be used.

In Ghana, when the chief has a message for the people, the *fritwa* is sounded as a way to call the village together. It may also be used at the beginning of worship as a way to call the people to worship because God has a message for the people.

During these praise songs, the choir moves out and dances in a line to the front of the sanctuary (on level with the congregation) and dances around in a circle. As they dance back to their seats, one side of the congregation moves out row by row and dances in the same fashion up to the front, around in a circle, and back to their seats. They are followed by the other side of the congregation. As they return to their seats, the pastor(s) and lay liturgist(s) dance down from the chancel area and complete the dance. All the while, the people are singing songs accompanied by the various instruments while the congregation claps to the beat.

This *Dance of Life* is repeated several times during the worship service. It occurs during the songs of praise, during the offertory as people bring their offering forward, and to welcome the newly baptized as members of the household of God. The dance may also occur at the end of the service as the choir and congregation dance forward to greet the pastor(s) and any visitors in attendance. Whenever the *Dance of Life* occurs, it is accompanied by the various instruments and congregational singing. This form of dancing during worship is an important element in Ghanaian-American worship. They believe that all life is worship and that worship is life. As such, worship is a time of celebrating that "circle of life."

Offering

In preparation for the offering, a large, carved wooden bowl is brought out and placed on a wooden stand in the front of the sanctuary. In addition to this wooden offering bowl, there is a wooden tithing box placed on or near the altar rail. While the congregation sings and the musicians play the various instruments, the people dance forward and place their tithe (a true one-tenth) in the tithing box or their offering (less than one-tenth) in the offering bowl. Some contribute to both the tithing box and the offering bowl. After the congregation has returned to their seats, the choir dances their offering forward followed by the pastor(s) and liturgists.

On the first Sunday of the month, people may bring their offerings forward according to the day of the week on which they were born. As someone calls out each day of the week, those born on that day dance their offerings forward.

Scripture Readings

Three scripture passages are read each week: an Old Testament lesson, an Epistle lesson, and a Gospel lesson. Each passage may be read in a different language. The texts may be read by the pastor or lay liturgist while the congregation reads along in their own Bibles, or the text may be read responsively verse by verse between the worship leader and the congregation.

Preaching

Sermons usually last thirty to forty-five minutes in Ghanaian-American churches. The sermon is not seen as the most important part of worship, however. The music and *dance of life* are equally important if not more important for many in the congregation.

There are certain expectations, however, regarding preaching in the Ghanaian-American context. The congregation prefers that the pastor preach without any notes as a sign of being inspired by the Holy Spirit. The preacher also tends to receive a greater response from the congregation if he or she leaves the pulpit and preaches down among the people. Humor is greatly appreciated, as are stories and illustrations from Ghana.

Several forms of participatory preaching are practiced in Ghanaian-American churches. The "call and response" form is the most common. During the sermon, members of the congregation respond with "amen!" or "Yes!" as they offer their agreement to something the preacher has said. Often the pastor asks the congregation to turn in their Bibles to a particular text and read it aloud or the preacher begins a Bible verse and various persons complete the remainder of the verse. Sometimes the pastor asks a question during the sermon and someone calls out the answer.

In Ghanaian-American preaching, it is acceptable for anyone who feels touched by the sermon to stand in their place and begin singing spontaneously. The congregation joins in the song. The pastor is expected to suspend the sermon until the song is over.

Passing of the Peace

The Passing of the Peace may not be a formal liturgical element in the Ghanaian-American church but it takes place at several parts in the worship service: as the people gather, as they dance forward during the songs of praise, as they dance forward for the offertory, and at the end as they greet visitors and one another.

94

Benediction

Only ordained clergy are permitted to give the benediction in the Ghanaian-American tradition. The benediction is pronounced standing in front of the congregation with eyes closed and one or two hands raised in a gesture of blessing. The congregation receives the benediction standing with their eyes closed as well.

Sacramental Practices

Sacrament of Baptism

Seven days after the birth of a child, the pastor, family, and friends gather at the family's home before sunrise. At dawn, they go outside and raise the infant up and down three times. The pastor asks what name is given the child. The father announces the infant's name (always named after an ancestor). Then the pastor addresses the infant as if he or she can understand.

The pastor puts water or some other form of drink into the baby's mouth with an admonition similar to: "When you say water, let it be water, when you say soda, let it be soda. Be sincere in your thoughts. Let your 'yes' be yes and your 'no' be no." Then money is put in the infant's hand with words that encourage the child to save it and help his or her family with what he or she will earn. Sometimes, a pen is also given the child with words of encouragement to become educated. An offering is taken and kept as a "savings bond" for the child. The naming ceremony is followed by a feast for the family and friends. A date is then set for the festival that celebrates the birth of the child. The festival often last throughout the night until sunrise.

Baptism often takes place as soon after the naming ceremony as possible. Occasionally parents wait until the child is twelve years of age or older and able to make his or her own decision to be baptized. For the baptism of infants, parents go through a preparation period of five to eight sessions. For youth who are being baptized, the preparation period of catechesis lasts for one year.

Baptisms only take place in the church during Sunday worship. A bowl filled with water is held by a layperson for the baptism. The baptismal liturgy may be a formal liturgy from a Ghanaian resource or the questions and prayers may be offered extemporaneously by the pastor. If youth or adults are being baptized, they may share their faith

95

journey with the congregation or share their story with the pastor who then conveys it to the congregation during worship. Water is sprinkled three times on the person's head as the pastor recites the *traditional baptismal formula*. The sign of the cross is then made on the person's forehead with oil or with the baptismal water.

After the baptism, each person is given a baptismal certificate and often a Bible. The newly baptized are then greeted by the congregation. The church elders come forward first and welcome them with a hug. Then the entire congregation begins singing and dances forward in line to greet each one.

Confirmation

Persons who were baptized as infants may go through a six-month period of preparation after the age of fourteen. Confirmation often takes place on Easter Sunday.

Sacrament of Holy Communion

"Holy Communion" is the most common term used to name this sacrament. It is celebrated once a month and takes place after the sermon. The communion elements are covered until the appropriate time in the liturgy. The elements are viewed by some as the literal body and blood of Jesus while others understand them to be signs of Christ's presence among us.

The communion liturgy consists of words about communion and prayers led extemporaneously by the pastor as well as the *Words of Institution* and a consecration of the elements.

Wafers and individual cups of grape juice are the most common elements used although a loaf of bread may be used on occasion. Compared to the exuberant *dance of life* that is prevalent in Ghanaian-American worship, there is a quiet, solemn procession as the people come forward and kneel at the altar rail for the sacrament of Holy Communion. The elements are served to them with the words "This is the body and blood of our Lord Jesus Christ given for you" or "The body and blood of Jesus Christ destroyed on Calvary so that we might live." A blessing is given to the people before they return to their seats.

The sacrament of Holy Communion is reserved for those who are baptized. If children are baptized as infants, they wait until after confirmation before they take communion.

Rituals of Passage

Weddings

Before a couple is married, they have an engagement ceremony. This ceremony lasts three to four hours and is presided over by the minister. This ceremony honors not only the future joining of the man and woman but also the joining of the two families. While the tradition has been for the bride's family to bring out three or four women (the bride-to-be presented last) and ask the groom if this is the one he wants to marry, this practice may or may not take place in the United States.

During this engagement ceremony, the pastor facilitates the exchange of gifts from the groom's family to the bride. Traditional gifts include a ring, money, powder, and cloth. If the woman is educated, she receives an additional bag of gifts deemed essential for her future. The groom's family also gives gifts to the bride's mother and father, grandparents, aunts, and uncles.

In return, the bride's family cooks a feast for the groom and his family. When the bride's family accepts the gifts, it is a sign that they support the engagement. When the groom's family eats the food that has been prepared for them, it is a sign that they accept the upcoming marriage.

If the parents of both the bride and groom support the marriage, the pastor does not hold premarital counseling sessions with the couple. If there is disagreement, then the pastor may counsel the couple prior to the wedding.

Weddings usually take place at the church or at home but it may also occur during regular Sunday worship. The bride and groom may be dressed in a white gown and tuxedo respectively or they may be dressed in African garb for the occasion. They are often attended by bridesmaids and ushers, a flower girl and ring bearer. The father of the bride (or some father-figure) is the only appropriate person to walk the bride down the aisle. The processional music may be the "Wedding March," but most often it is Ghanaian music or some form of African drumming.

The wedding ceremony consists of singing, the reading of scripture, words about marriage, the exchange of vows and rings, a prayer of blessing for the couple, and the pronouncement that the couple is now husband and wife. In the United States, the couple may also light the Unity Candle. After the pronouncement, the pastor lays a broomstick

97

on the floor and the couple joins hands and jumps over it. This is an ancient ritual from Africa that seals the vows made between the couple and affirms their being husband and wife.

After the wedding, there is a reception with food, music and dancing. Clergy are expected to attend the reception and pray before the meal is served. Speeches are made by the father of the bride and others wishing the couple long life and prosperity. The couple cuts the wedding cake and may or may not participate in the Western ritual of throwing the bride's bouquet and garter.

The first Sunday the couple attends church after the wedding, they address the congregation. They thank their parents for nurturing them to this point in their lives, thank the congregation and the pastor for their support, and sing a song of thanksgiving. Then, arm in arm, the couple dance in a circle (the *dance of life*) in the front of the sanctuary as the congregation sings.

Funerals

In the Ghanaian-American tradition, the funeral service takes place a month or more after the day of death. A quick burial is associated with the burial of animals, not humans. If burial takes place before a month has passed, it is considered a disgrace. Consequently, after someone has died, the family takes their time in consulting with friends and relatives to make sure that everyone can be present for the funeral service, the funeral festival, and the committal service. In the United States, the family pays the funeral home to keep the body until the set date.

When the day of the funeral finally arrives, some people expect the pastor to come to the family's home, pray with them, and accompany them to the place of the funeral. The funeral usually takes place at the funeral home in the evening. The casket is placed in the front and is surrounded by flowers and possibly a picture of the deceased. The casket is open and the deceased is dressed in special clothing depending on the specific Ghanaian organization to which the person belonged.

The service includes singing, praying, scripture reading, preaching, and testimony about the life of the deceased. In addition, the spouse of the deceased (or closest family member) rips a black and white (or sometimes blue and white) cloth into strips and gives a strip to everyone present. The people wrap the strips around their wrist, neck, or forehead. One strip is placed in the casket with the deceased. The strip of cloth is worn throughout the funeral service, the funeral festival, and the committal service. It is also worn during the Memorial Thanksgiving that is held during Sunday worship at a later date.

After the funeral service, the gathered community (often upwards of one thousand people) go to a hall that has been rented for the night. From nine in the evening until five in the morning the large crowd joins in the Funeral Festival, which celebrates the life of the deceased. The pastor may open the occasion with prayer, which is followed by singing, dancing, eating and drinking. People may share stories of their memories of the one who died.

At daybreak, the people travel in a car procession to the cemetery for the burial and committal service. The pall bearers carry the casket from the hearse to the grave as the family follows. The committal service includes singing, reading of scripture, a short sermon, prayers for the family, and a committal of the deceased to God. The pastor throws dirt on the grave and in some funerals, everyone lays a flower on the casket. A reception follows at the family's home. At this time, a date is set for the Memorial Thanksgiving, which takes place during Sunday worship.

During the Memorial Thanksgiving, the family of the deceased comes forward and reads an account of their loved one's life. The congregation prays for the deceased and the surviving family members. A moment of silence is kept before the pastor offers a final prayer.

Special worship services are held on the fortieth day after death and again on the first-year anniversary.

Memorial services may be held for family members who died in Ghana.

It is common courtesy to invite Ghanaian-American clergy from other churches and denominations to participate in the funeral activities.

99

HAITIAN-AMERICAN WORSHIP PRACTICES

with Rev. Sony Augustin[1]

The Service of the Word

The Language of the Liturgy

The native language of Haiti is *Creole*. However, French is the language of the educated and elite classes in the country.

While the large, historic Methodist Church in the capital city of Port au Prince conducts worship services solely in French, churches in the suburbs and provinces use *Creole* as well. The Bible may be read in French or *Creole* and hymns may be sung in either language. The sermon, however, is almost always in *Creole*. In America, English is also used to communicate with children and youth who were born in the United States.

The Liturgical Space

There may be banners with Haitian images or words of praise in French or Creole that are visual reminders of the community that worships in that space.

Haitian-American worship space is devoid of any candles because candles are associated with Roman Catholic and Voodoo ritual practices and are not acceptable for Haitian Christian worship.

Liturgical Time

Worship in the Haitian-American tradition usually lasts between one and a half to two hours.

Liturgical Garb

For male clergy, a suit with a clerical collar or a black pulpit robe is the most common liturgical garb worn during worship. On special occasions, however, traditional Haitian clothing may be worn.

Liturgical Seasons and Days

In some Haitian-American churches, all of the seasons of the church year (although Epiphany is often omitted) are celebrated. In others, however, only Christmas, Holy Week/Easter, and Pentecost receive liturgical attention.

In addition, Thanksgiving, Mother's Day, and New Year's Eve are celebrated during worship. Haitian Independence Day is recognized on the Sunday closest to January 1.

Beginning Our Praise to God

Worship begins with a Call to Worship that is based on a scripture text and either read by a worship leader or read responsively between the liturgist and the congregation.

Prayer Forms

Prayer forms include: the Lord's Prayer, extemporaneous prayers by the pastor and lay worship leaders, corporate prayers printed in the bulletin, prayers of the people offered individually from the congregation, and a corporate prayer of confession. When a prayer of confession is included, the words of forgiveness are often offered in a sung response.

The posture of prayer in Haitian-American congregations may be sitting, standing, or kneeling.

Creeds

Haitian-American congregations tend to recite some form of creed at least once a month.

Music

The hymnbook most commonly used in Haitian-American churches is *Chants D'Esperancy,* which is an ecumenical resource with hymns in both French and Creole. The hymnal is British in style with only the words printed; no musical notations are included.

Five to six hymns are sung every week. In addition, some churches have special musicians for contemporary songs of praise. Most hymns are sung in unison. The organ is the most common instrument to accompany the hymns. Guitars, modern drums, and tambourines may be used to accompany the contemporary songs of praise. Clapping and saying "Amen" are acceptable responses to musical offerings.

In addition to music, drama and liturgical dance may also be used on certain occasions.

Scripture Readings

Usually two scripture passages are read during Haitian-American worship: one from the Old Testament and one from the New Testament. The texts are read by the pastor or lay liturgist, or read responsively verse by verse between the pastor/liturgist and congregation.

Preaching

Sermons usually lasts twenty-five to forty-five minutes in Haitian-American churches. Placed at the end of the service, preaching is seen by the congregation as the most important aspect of worship.

Sermons tend to be topical in nature, utilizing stories from Haitian resources. Humor is both appropriate and expected in preaching. While most in the congregation have no expectations regarding the preacher's use of notes during the delivery, some feel that the preacher should preach without notes as a sign of being inspired by the Holy Spirit.

Participatory forms of preaching vary within Haitian-American congregations. Some people say "Amen" to affirm something the preacher has said. At other times, the preacher asks the congregation a question during the sermon and people call out the answer. The pastor may also ask the congregation to turn in their Bibles to a particular text and read it aloud collectively. Other churches have a sermon "talk-back" time after the service.

Passing of the Peace

The Passing of the Peace is not common during worship in Haitian-American churches.

Benediction

The benediction, pronounced by either clergy or laity, is often offered with one or both hands raised in a gesture of blessing. The congregation and the person giving the benediction stand with their eyes closed.

Sacramental Practices

Sacrament of Baptism

There is division within the Haitian community in America over the issue of infant baptism. In Haiti, the Roman Catholic Church is the largest Christian influence. Because they have developed relationships with those from the Voodoo religion, Protestants in Haiti often design their practices in opposition to the Roman Catholics (e.g. eliminating candles from the worship space —see "Liturgical Space" above). Since Roman Catholics practice infant baptism and because Baptists are a very strong Protestant presence in Haiti, adult baptism is popular among many denominations.

In The United Methodist Church, however, infant baptism is the norm. Therefore, there are some Haitian-American churches who practice infant baptism and some who practice adult baptism only. The choice depends on many factors: the denomination of the pastor before joining The United Methodist Church, the number of years the pastor and members of the congregation have been in the United States, and the denomination of the members when they were in Haiti.

When an infant is baptized, the pastor usually meets with the parents a couple of times in preparation for the sacrament. It is common for the parents to choose godparents for their child but it is strongly recommended that the godparents be Christian. The infant often wears white clothing as a symbol of innocence and purity.

A bowl of water is held by a layperson during the baptism, which takes place after the sermon in the "response" section of the worship service. The baptismal liturgy is taken from a liturgical resource from Haiti that includes questions for the parents and prayers for the child. The infant is baptized with the *traditional baptismal formula*as the pastor sprinkles water on the baby's head three times. The parents are given a baptismal certificate and the infant is introduced to the congregation.

For those Haitian-American churches that prefer adult baptism, the parents usually bring their newborn infant to the church for a dedication service. Once the child has reached the age of twelve, preparation classes are held for a couple of months before the baptism.

The worship service takes place in the church, then the congregation goes to a designated body of water (ocean, river, lake, pool) for the baptism. The baptismal candidates (dressed in white gowns) are asked questions, prayers are offered, and the candidates share their faith journey with the congregation. The candidates are then immersed once while the pastor baptizes him or her with the *traditional baptismal formula*. During the baptism itself, the congregation sings hymns. A baptismal certificate is presented to each candidate and they are introduced to the congregation. Adult baptisms often take place immediately following revival meetings or other special occasions in the life of the church.

Confirmation

Those congregations that practice infant baptism confirm persons twelve years of age and older after several months of preparation. Confirmation usually takes place on Easter Sunday.

Sacrament of Holy Communion

"Holy Communion" is the most common term used to describe this sacrament although "Lord's Supper" and "Eucharist" are also used on occasion. It is celebrated once a month after the sermon in the "response" section of the liturgy. Since the altar is usually against the front wall, a special table is brought out on communion Sundays so the pastor can stand behind it to celebrate the sacrament.

The elements most commonly used—small cubes of bread and individual cups of grape juice—are covered until the appropriate time in the communion liturgy. The elements are understood to be signs or symbols of Christ's presence and grace.

The communion liturgy consists of a Great Thanksgiving with responses by the laity,which are printed in one of the liturgical resources from Haiti. This usually includes a consecration of the elements and the *Words of Institution*. Many Haitian-American clergy break the bread during the *Words of Institution* although some opt to break it after the Great Prayer of Thanksgiving. For the most part only ordained clergy participate in the celebration of Holy Communion; however, in many churches laity assist in the distribution of the elements.

The congregation kneels at the altar to commune. Traditionally, the pastor communes before the congregation. In America, however, the pastor may choose to commune after the congregation. The elements are distributed with the words "This is the body and blood of our Lord Jesus Christ given for you."

The sacrament of Holy Communion is reserved for the baptized only. Children who have been baptized as infants wait until they have been confirmed or until they are twelve years of age or older before taking communion.

Rituals of Passage

Weddings

Before a couple is married in the Haitian tradition, an engagement ceremony takes place at the bride's home. The two families are brought together for a time of affirmation and celebration. Usually, this occasion is limited to the two families. However, if the pastor is invited, he or she is expected to offer a prayer of blessing for the couple.

Between the engagement ceremony and the wedding, the pastor meets with the couple four to six times in preparation for their upcoming marriage.

It is customary for Christians to be married in the church. However, in America, it is becoming more acceptable for weddings to take place elsewhere.

The bride wears a white wedding gown and the groom a tuxedo. They are attended by bridesmaids, ushers, flower girl and ring bearer. The bride's father or some "father-figure" is the most appropriate escort for the bride as she processes down the aisle to the "Wedding March" or other Western-style music. Haitian songs may be sung as solos during the wedding ceremony.

The wedding ritual includes the reading of scripture, words about marriage, prayers for the couple, and the exchange of vows and rings. Since candles are not acceptable in Haitian-American worship, there are no candelabras, candles on the altar, or lighting of the Unity Candle.

At the end of the ceremony, the couple greet their guests informally at the back of the church. Following the wedding service is a reception. Clergy are expected to attend the reception and offer a prayer before the meal is served.

The reception usually includes a catered meal, music, and speeches (always one by the best man) of blessing and hope for the couple. In some receptions, dancing and a ceremonial cutting of the wedding cake are also part of the festivities. The American custom of throwing the bride's bouquet to unmarried women and the bride's garter to unmarried men may also be practiced.

Funerals

Between the death of a person and the day of the funeral and burial, there is an evening where the community gathers at the funeral home for a *wake* or "prayer service" and a time of viewing the body. The casket is open and a Bible is placed in the deceased's hand. The coffin is surrounded by flowers and often a picture of the deceased.

This *wake* or "prayer service" always includes the reading of scripture, the singing of hymns, and prayers offered for those who are grieving. The pastor may also be expected to preach a sermon and people present may be given an opportunity to witness to the life of the deceased. This service may last from one to four hours.

On the day of the funeral and grave site service, the pastor is expected to go to the family's home and accompany the family to the church for the funeral service.

The casket may already be in place in the front of the sanctuary or it may be moved into place with a procession led by the pastor followed by the pallbearers carrying the casket, and then the family. The service includes singing, scripture reading, a sermon, many prayers, and testimony about the life of the deceased. This service may last a couple of hours. If testimony was not a part of the prayer service/viewing before the funeral, usually everyone is given an opportunity to share during the funeral service. If testimony was included in the prayer service/viewing, then often the family selects a few people to offer a time of witness.

After the funeral service, there is a car procession from the church to the cemetery. The grave site service includes scripture reading and prayer (no sermon). Toward the end of the service, everyone places a flower on the casket. The last act of the committal service is for the pastor (and sometimes the family as well) to throw dirt on the casket with the words "Ashes to ashes, dust to dust."

After the grave site service, friends and relatives gather at the family's home for a reception.

Notes

1. Special thanks also to Rev. Jocelyn Jean-Baptiste Adhemar for his invaluable information on Haitian worship practices.

HISPANIC-AMERICAN WORSHIP PRACTICES

with Rev. Myriam Escorcia

The Service of the Word

The Language of the Liturgy

While some congregations are predominantly Puerto-Rican or Cuban, most Hispanic churches throughout the country are composed of people who trace their ancestry to Mexico, and other Central and South American countries. Spanish is the language that unifies the people from various Latino cultures, but various cultural heritages contribute to a diversity of worship practice.

The Liturgical Space

Banners with words in Spanish, flags from the various nations represented by the members in the congregation, or colorful woven cloth from one of the many Latino countries may be found in the worship space of Hispanic-American churches.

Liturgical Garb

There is no consistent liturgical garb for leading worship in the Hispanic traditions. Some clergy wear regular street clothes, while others prefer a black pulpit robe, a white alb, or a poncho or chasuble. Stoles made in Guatemala are popular not only in Hispanic-American churches but among Euro-American clergy as well.

Liturgical Seasons and Days

In many Hispanic-American churches, all the seasons of the church year are honored although Epiphany may receive less attention. Protestants may choose to downplay this particular season in the church year because of its strong association with Catholicism's large celebrations on the Day of Epiphany, January 6, known as *El Dia de los Reyes* or the "day of the kings."

Palm Sunday, Holy Thursday, and Good Friday services mark Holy Week. Services may also be held to celebrate Thanksgiving and New Year's Day. During Sunday worship, Mother's Day and Father's Day often honor members of the congregation.

During Advent, some protestant churches may have a service of *Las Posadas* in preparation for, and anticipation of, the birth of Jesus. *Las Posadas* began in 1587 and is a reenactment of the journey Mary and Joseph made to Bethlehem, seeking shelter for the night. Traditionally, eight church members offer their homes for the eight nights prior to Christmas Eve. Each night, the people gather and process on foot (or by car if the distance is too great) to someone's home. Often children are dressed as shepherds, magi, Mary, and Joseph. People carry candles as they walk and sing songs appropriate to the occasion. They may stop at several houses on the way seeking shelter, but each time they are turned away. When they have reached the house of the church member, there is a ritual that takes place between the people seeking shelter and those inside the home. (For a sample of this ritual, see *Las Posadas*, the Service of Shelter for the Holy Family found on page 266–68 of the United Methodist *Book of Worship*.) When the family finally decides to let the people take shelter in their home, food and drink are provided, as well as a piñata for the children.

> The piñata represents the devil, who cannot be recognized, and therefore the child is blindfolded. The child is fighting against evil with the rod of virtue, symbolized in the stick provided to break the piñata. When the child perseveres to the end, the glory of God will come down on everyone, as shown by the candy hidden within the piñata.[1]

This ritual occurs every night at a different home for eight nights. On Christmas Eve, a similar ritual takes place at the church. People representing Joseph and Mary, along with the youth and children, knock on the sanctuary door. When the door is open, they ask for shelter and again, a conversation ensues between those inside and those outside. (For a sample of this ritual, see p. 281–84 of the United Methodist *Book of Worship*.) Once the people are admitted inside, a worship service ensues. After the service, food is served and the piñata is broken.

Quinceañeras are also celebrated liturgically in many Hispanic-American churches. When a girl turns fifteen years of age, the community honors this moment in her life with a worship service and a fiesta.

108

The birthday girl chooses fourteen girls and fourteen boys who are fourteen years of age or older to serve as her attendants. When the community is smaller, seven of each may be chosen. The girls carry bouquets of flowers, the boys carry Bibles. The birthday girl wears a pink or white dress with roses on it. The service takes place in the church outside of Sunday worship.

The attendants process into the sanctuary and line up down the aisle with the girls on one side and the boys on the other. The attendants then raise their arms toward one another to form an arch under which the birthday girl processes to the front of the sanctuary. Everyone is seated for the worship service, which includes scripture reading, prayers, special poems, a sermon, and much singing. Toward the end of the service, the birthday girl kneels for her vows. She promises to consecrate herself to God, to make scripture the main source of her guidance, and to respect and honor her parents. She places her hand on the Bible for the blessing prayer. At the end of the service, the birthday girl speaks to the congregation and thanks her parents. She is presented to the congregation and everyone stands and claps. She then leads the recession as the attendants follow.

After the worship service, there is a banquet at a hall with music and dancing. In some Central American cultures, the music is played on the marimba. In the Mexican-American culture, usually mariachi bands play at the fiesta. The birthday girl, along with her attendants, perform a special dance at the party. (For a sample blessing, see p. 531 in the United Methodist *Book of Worship*.)

Beginning Our Praise to God

Most Hispanic-American churches begin their worship with verses from Scripture. Sometimes the scripture-based Call to Worship is read responsively between the worship leader and the congregation.

Prayer Forms

Prayer forms in the Hispanic-American traditions may include: extemporaneous prayers by the pastor or lay liturgists, prayers of joy and concern offered aloud from various members, a pastoral prayer, and the Lord's Prayer (recited weekly or, in many churches, on Communion Sundays only). A few congregations include corporate prayers that are printed in the bulletin.

109

After certain musical selections by the choir, one of the musicians may offer a prayer. Members of the congregation sometimes join in offering their own prayers in a soft voice simultaneously. In some Hispanic-American congregations, people come an hour or so before the Sunday activities begin in order to pray at the altar rail.

The posture of prayer may be sitting, standing (possibly with arms raised), or kneeling at the altar rail.

Creeds

The reciting of a creed varies in Hispanic-American worship. Some churches do not include a creed at all. Other congregations recite a creed on certain occasions. When a creed is used, it may be the Apostles' Creed or the Hispanic Creed written by Justo L. González.

Music

Three to four hymns are sung every week during worship. The hymnbooks used vary, although many use *Mil Voces*, which is the United Methodist Spanish hymnal. The hymns are often accompanied by the piano or organ.

In addition, many congregations also sing *coritos*, which are short songs repeated several times. The music and lyrics to the *coritos* are often written by persons from the various Latino cultures. In most churches, the people have memorized these songs and therefore have no need of songbooks. *Coritos* are usually accompanied by guitars, modern drums, and maracas. Traditional drums of the various cultures, tambourines, harmonicas, and the fish and clave (a grooved, wooden object in the shape of a fish that is hit or scraped with a wooden stick) may also be used.

Clapping and calling out words of affirmation ("Amen" or "*Gloria a Dios*"—"Thanks be to God") are common responses to soloists, choir anthems, and musical offerings of the *coritos*. There are a few congregations, however, who prefer silence over these more overt expressions of affirmation.

Scripture Reading

Two to three scripture passages are read each week in worship. Sometimes the entire text is read by the pastor or lay liturgist. At other times, the text may be read responsively, verse by verse, between the liturgist and the congregation. The lectionary is consulted (although not always used) by many Hispanic-American clergy as they choose which texts to read each week.

Preaching

Preaching in Hispanic-American churches varies greatly. Some clergy preach twenty minutes while other sermons last more than an hour. In some churches, the sermon is seen as the most important part of the liturgy, but music is increasingly becoming equally important to the sermon.

Stories and illustrations often come from the histories, folktales, and issues found in the various Latino cultures. The use of humor in Hispanic-American preaching is both appropriate and appreciated. In many congregations, the people prefer sermons to have a tight conclusion.

In some congregations, preaching without any notes is a sign of being inspired by the Holy Spirit. In other congregations, however, preaching with notes is a sign of preparation on the part of the preacher.

Participatory styles of preaching are not very common in Hispanic-American preaching. However, occasionally the preacher may intentionally ask the congregation a question during the sermon that requires a short, verbal response; or, various members of the congregation may say "Amen" as an affirmative response to something the preacher said; or, the pastor may pass out scripture passages in advance and ask them to read the text during the sermon; or, immediately following the sermon, pastors may invite laypeople to respond to the sermon or add their own testimony about the topic or text. A few pastors may write the main points of the sermon on newsprint or an overhead projector during the sermon.

Passing of the Peace

The passing of the peace is becoming more acceptable in Hispanic-American worship. In some protestant congregations, it is seen as "too Catholic" and therefore avoided. However, it is included in many congregations in the United States today.

Benediction

While clergy usually offer the benediction, lay leaders are also permitted this privilege in some Hispanic-American congregations. Most clergy who pronounce the benediction raise both hands in a gesture of blessing. In some contexts, it is not acceptable for lay leaders to use any gesture of blessing. It is traditional for both the person pronouncing the benediction and the congregation to be standing. Whether one's eyes are closed or open in giving or receiving the benediction is not a crucial factor.

Vigilias

Vigilias or vigils are held once every month or so. They usually begin about seven o'clock on a Friday evening and continue until six o'clock Saturday morning. Other churches, choirs, and music groups may be invited to participate in the vigil. It is a time of spiritual renewal and fellowship. There is much singing and praying along with a sermon. The most important aspect of the vigil is the testimonies given by the laity. Often each person shares their journey of faith or some time in their life when they have felt touched by God. People bring food from their various cultures, which is served at midnight. There are breaks throughout the night for more eating and socializing.

Sacramental Practices

Sacrament of Baptism

Before baptisms take place, most clergy meet with the persons involved one to four times. Baptisms take place whenever the need arises. While most infant baptisms occur in the church during Sunday worship, adults are often baptized by immersion at some other location. Baptisms may also take place in the hospital in emergency situations.

When infants are baptized, sprinkling is the form most commonly used. A few pastors may pour water over the infant's head rather than sprinkling. If a bowl is used, a layperson holds it for the pastor during the baptism.

The liturgy varies according to the pastor and the congregation. Some pastors use a formal baptismal liturgy with prayers, a thanksgiving over the water, and questions for the parents or adult being baptized. Others use a standard set of questions, but do the rest of the liturgy extemporaneously, while still others use no formal liturgy at all. Adults being baptized may share their faith journey during the liturgy.

Those being baptized usually wear white clothing as a sign of purity. Most Hispanic-American pastors baptize with the *traditional baptismal*

112

formula. A few, however use words similar to "I baptize you in the name of God, our Creator; Jesus Christ, our Savior; and the Holy Spirit, our Comforter." Whether the water is sprinkled or poured once or three times is up to the pastor. After the baptism, the one being baptized is given a baptismal certificate, and sometimes a Bible and/or rose.

Occasionally persons who have experienced a conversion as an adult request rebaptism. Pastors are then faced with the dilemma of whether to rebaptize an adult who was baptized as an infant.

Godparents are an important part of many Hispanic-American baptisms. Known as *padrino* and *madrina*, they function solely as spiritual guides for the child in those families who come from Nicaragua and other Central American countries. In the Mexican-American culture, however, there are several *padrinos* and *madrinas*. Each one also contributes financially to the activities surrounding the baptism. There may be a *madrina* of the baptismal gown, or a *padrino* of the cake for the party afterwards, or a *madrina* of the mariachi band to entertain the guests. Adults being baptized also have sponsors for their baptism, likewise called *padrino* and *madrina*. If a bowl is used instead of a baptismal font, often one of the *madrinas* holds the bowl during the baptism.

Following the baptism is usually a *fiesta* or party with music, food, and piñatas for the children.

Confirmation

The practice of confirmation varies from congregation to congregation. Some churches do not practice confirmation at all, while others offer confirmation classes for youth between the ages of twelve and fourteen.

Sacrament of Holy Communion

In the Spanish language, the most common terms used for this sacrament are *Santa Cena* (Holy Supper) and *Santa Communion* (Holy Communion). When speaking of the sacrament in English, "Lord's Supper," "Communion," and "Eucharist" are also possible terms, although "Eucharist" often carries Catholic connotations.

The Holy Supper is usually celebrated once a month after the sermon. Some churches also include communion on special liturgical days. While the celebration of communion is usually reserved for clergy only, in some Hispanic-American churches, lay leaders may assist in the celebration as well as the distribution of the elements. The liturgy surrounding the Holy Supper varies. Some pastors use a formal Great Thanksgiving with responses by the laity or some shortened version of the Great Thanksgiving. Other pastors offer extemporaneous prayers and words about communion, then consecrate the elements and recite the *Words of Institution*. Most Hispanic-American clergy break the bread during the Institution. While many clergy partake of communion before the congregation in order to purify themselves in preparation for feeding others, there are some who believe the pastor should be the servant of the people, serving the congregation first and partaking last.

The elements most commonly used are small cubes of bread and individual cups of grape juice. Sometimes one loaf and one cup are used. Wafers tend to be avoided because of their association with Catholicism. Those who come from Roman Catholic backgrounds may still understand the elements to be the body and blood of Jesus. Those who are influenced by protestant theology believe the elements are symbols of Christ's presence and grace. The elements are usually covered until the appropriate time in the liturgy. Occasionally, the cloth on the altar is from one of the Latino cultures represented in the congregation.

In most churches, the elements are distributed to the congregation as they kneel at the altar rail. In a few small congregations, the people may commune standing in a circle around the altar. When one cup is used, the people commune through *intinction*. Various words accompany the distribution of the elements: "This is the body and blood of our Lord Jesus Christ," "This is the Bread of the Covenant and the Cup of Salvation," or "Take this in remembrance of Him."

The communion table is open for all who wish to come regardless of one's baptism. Parents decide at what age they feel their children are ready to partake.

Rituals of Passage

Weddings

The law in Mexico and many Central and South American countries is that persons must first be married by the state before they can be married in the church. Many Hispanic couples continue this practice in the United States, and pay to be married by a Justice of the Peace before the church wedding. It is important for Hispanic couples to understand that the civil ceremony is not necessary in America, since clergy are legal representatives of the state and are licensed to perform weddings.

Approximately one month before the wedding, some couples have an engagement celebration at the bride's family's home. On the morning of the wedding, the bride may kneel before her parents to receive their blessing.

Three to six premarital counseling sessions are common in preparation for marriage. Marrying divorced persons is acceptable and carries no overtly negative connotation.

Padrinos and *madrinas* (godfathers and godmothers) are very common in Hispanic-American weddings. In families from Nicaragua and other Central American cultures, they provide advice and guidance to the young couple. In these cultures it is the responsibility of the groom to pay for all the wedding expenses. In the Mexican-American culture, the family of the bride and groom asks various friends and family members to be *padrinos* and *madrinas* for necessary elements of the wedding festivities. There may be a *madrina* of the wedding dress, or a *padrino* of the mariachi band. *Padrinos* and *madrinas* contribute to the expenses of the wedding. They may give the wedding cake, the honeymoon trip, or a set of bedroom furniture. In this way, the broader community shares resources with the couple as they begin their new journey together.

The bride usually wears a white gown and the groom wears a tuxedo. Bridesmaids, ushers, flower girl, and ring bearer serve as attendants to the bride and groom. In addition, the *padrino/madrina* of the *lazo* and the *padrino/madrina* of the *arras* (gold-colored novelty coins) also serve as attendants. The altar candles are lit just prior to the ceremony by acolytes or a representative from each family. If the Unity Candle is used, the two outer candles may be lit by the mothers of the bride, other family members, the bride and groom, or acolytes. The ushers enter from the side at the front of the sanctuary. The groom, however, is often not visible when the procession begins.

The procession begins with the bridesmaids walking down the aisle followed by the flower girl, ring bearer, and the bride with her escort(s). While the father of the bride is the most common escort, occasionally both parents of the bride, the bride's best friend, her widowed mother, a brother, or uncle are the escort. In some traditions, the flower girl

115

processes first and places a white Bible on the altar. The Bible has the couple's name engraved on the front (i.e. Mr. and Mrs.——) and is a gift for the couple. The procession is usually accompanied by Western-style music although latino music or hymns may also be used.

At the beginning of the wedding ceremony, the pastor asks, "Who gives this woman away?" or "Who presents this woman for marriage?" The escort responds, "I do" and sits down. The pastor then asks, "Who will receive this woman?" At this point, the groom enters from the side and says, "I do."

The ceremony continues with prayers, the reading of scripture, a sermon, music, exchange of vows and rings. Some couples may choose to sit for the scripture reading and sermon. There may be a time in the wedding for the couple to pay their respect to the parents. Sometimes, however, this takes place in the form of a *toast* at the reception, or at the home before the couple leaves on their honeymoon.

In many Hispanic cultures, after the couple is pronounced "husband and wife" the couple kneel and the pastor or *madrina* wraps a *lazo* (lasso) around the couple symbolizing the two becoming one. Then the *padrino/madrina* of the *arras* presents the couple with a bag of many gold colored novelty coins. The coins symbolize the wishes of the community for wealth, health, and happiness.

After the ceremony, the father of the bride or groom may stand and thank the people for coming. In many Hispanic-American weddings, the bridal party remains standing at the front of the church as the congregation files by offering their congratulations. If the receiving line does not take place at the church, there is often one at the reception.

Mariachi bands often wait outside the church and/or reception place entertaining the guests as they come and go. The reception may be informal with finger food, or a more formal setting with a catered meal. Clergy are often expected to attend the reception and pray before the meal is served. Reception practices include much music and dancing (although in the Puerto Rican context, dancing is sometimes forbidden). The bride throws her bouquet over her shoulder to unmarried women, and the groom throws the bride's garter over his shoulder to unmarried men. Various people offer words of hope and blessing for the couple in the form of toasts. The couple cut the wedding cake and feed each other.

It is customary in many Hispanic-American weddings for the first dance to be led by the bride and her father, and the groom and his mother. After that, the bride and groom dance together. Occasionally, a "money dance" may take place at the reception. During the "money dance," the friends of the bride place bills or checks into the bride's clothes and the friends of the groom stick money into the groom's clothes.

Funerals

The pastor is often expected to help the family make the various funeral arrangements. If the person is well known in the Hispanic community, clergy from other churches may be invited to participate in the funeral.

White and black are both common colors for funerals. White is associated with purity and being one with God. White is also associated with *luto*, sharing in another's pain. Black means sadness or mourning and is worn as a sign of respect.

The night before the funeral, a worship service is held at the funeral home. The casket is open, the deceased is often dressed in special clothes, and items of importance to the deceased may be placed in the casket. Often this includes a Bible, a cross ,or other religious object. The casket is surrounded by flowers, candles, picture(s) of the deceased, and possibly banners, or objects of importance to the deceased. The service at the funeral home includes scripture reading, singing, a sermon, prayers, and testimony by family and friends about the life of the one who died. Food is often brought by various guests and served to the people after the service.

The morning of the funeral, many families expect the pastor to pray with them at their home and accompany them to the place of the funeral. While most Hispanic-American funerals take place at the church, some choose to hold the final service in the funeral home.

In many Hispanic-American funerals, the casket is open throughout the service. The open casket may already be in place before the service begins, or the closed casket may be brought to the front of the sanctuary/chapel in a procession, then opened when in place. During the funeral, prayers are offered, scripture is read, a sermon is preached, and music is sung. In some Hispanic cultures, it is appropriate for the pastor alone to speak about the deceased. In other cultures, the family selects a few persons in advance to speak. In still other cultures, the pastor offers a general invitation to the congregation to share a brief memory about the one who died.

117

In some traditions, cars follow each other to the cemetery. Some families expect the pastor to ride with them to the cemetery. While burial of the body is still preferred, cremation is slowly becoming more acceptable in Hispanic-American communities.

At the cemetery, there may be a procession from the hearse to the grave site. If so, the pastor leads the procession followed by the pallbearers carrying the casket, then the family and guests. The committal service includes prayers, singing, and scripture reading. Often the Lord's Prayer and Psalm 23 are recited, and sometimes a short sermon is preached. In some traditions, everyone throws dirt on the grave at the point in the service where the pastor reads "ashes to ashes, dust to dust." Flowers may also be placed on the casket after the service by the pastor only or by everyone present.

After the committal service, there is often a reception at the family's home. If numbers are too large for the home, the reception may be held at the church.

In some traditions, memorial services are held in America for family members who died in the native country. There are no special worship services marking the anniversary of a person's death. Family may give flowers for the church altar on the Sunday closest to the anniversary. If the family has the financial means, they may give a larger gift to the church at this time.

Notes

1. *United Methodist Book of Worship* (Nashville: The United Methodist Publishing House, 1992), p. 266.

HMONG-AMERICAN WORSHIP PRACTICES

with Rev. Kham Dy Yang

The Service of the Word

The Language of the Liturgy

Hmong people come from the high mountain area of Laos. They identify themselves as Hmong, not Laotian, because their culture and dialects are different from the other people of Laos. Two dialects of the Hmong language are spoken by Hmong people: *Hmoob Ntsaub* (meaning Blue Hmong) and *Hmoob Dawb* (meaning White Hmong). While these two dialects are slightly different in their written and spoken forms, those who speak *Hmoob Ntsaub* can understand those who speak *Hmoob Dawb* and vice versa.

Worship services in Hmong-American churches in the United States may be in *Hmoob Ntsaub*, *Hmoob Dawb*, or both. When both dialects are used, there is no need for translation to take place. Worship leaders communicate in whichever dialect is most comfortable for them. As recent immigrants to America, most Hmong persons prefer to conduct services in the native dialects. A few, however, are beginning to provide ministries in English for the children who were born in the United States.

The Liturgical Space

A traditional Hmong *paudau* (colorful embroidered cloth) is often found hanging in the worship space. The embroidery on a *paudau* usually depicts scenes in the life of Jesus. Banners with Hmong writing or images may also be hanging in the worship space.

Liturgical Time

Regular Sunday worship services usually last one to one and a half hours.

119

Liturgical Garb

Clergy in the Hmong-American tradition wear robes, albs, or regular street clothes in the pulpit. Some wear clothing made from the *paudau*.

Liturgical Seasons and Days

While Christmas and Easter are the liturgical days that are celebrated by all Hmong-American churches, a few also celebrate Advent, Lent, Epiphany, and Pentecost. Holy Week is often not celebrated liturgically, but Easter is an important celebration.

New Year's Day (January 1) is a significant day in the life of the community. It is a time for confession, letting go, and blessing. Mother's Day, Father's Day, and American Thanksgiving are also honored liturgically.

Beginning Our Praise to God

Worship services often begin with a welcome, a hymn, and an opening prayer. There is no official call to worship.

Prayer Forms

Prayer forms in the Hmong-American tradition include: the Lord's Prayer, extemporaneous prayers by the pastor and lay liturgist, a pastoral prayer, prayer of confession, and a prayer before and after the sermon. At times corporate prayers printed in the bulletin and prayers of the community offered aloud by individual members of the congregation are also included.

The usual posture of prayer is standing. This reflects the influence of the Christian Missionary Alliance denomination, which was the first protestant denomination in Laos and Vietnam, and which remains strong in the region.

Creeds

The use of a creed in weekly Sunday worship varies. Some congregations recite the Apostles' Creed and others choose to use a creed only on specific occasions.

120

Music

The hymnbook most commonly used is called the *Cov Ntseeg Yesxus Phoo Nkauj*, which was developed by a United Methodist Hmong-American congregation in St. Paul, Minnesota. Three to five hymns are sung every week. The organ or piano is used to accompany the hymns. Some churches also sing "praise" songs, which may be accompanied by guitars and drums. On special occasions, some churches use a traditional flute.

Clapping is the most common response to soloists and choir anthems although some feel that silence is more appropriate for the worship setting.

Scripture Readings

Two scripture passages are usually read. These two passages can come from anyplace in the Bible. It is not always the case that one is from the Old Testament and one from the New Testament. The scripture texts are read by lay liturgists. People in the congregation often read along in their own Bibles. The translation of the Bible used is *Vaajtswv Txujlug Cog Tseg Kws Cawm Taubneeg Txujsy,* which means "God's Word Promised for the Salvation of Humankind."

Preaching

The length of sermons in the Hmong-American tradition varies greatly. Some preach ten to twenty minutes while others preach forty-five to sixty minutes. The sermon is often placed in the middle of the service and is seen by the congregation as the most important part of the worship experience.

The structure of the sermon and tone of delivery also vary from preacher to preacher. Many sermons are topical in nature, although expository sermons are also common.

Many sermon illustrations come from the life experiences of the Hmong living in the United States, Hmong stories from Laos, Hmong history, and folktales. Humor is sometimes used in sermons.

Some Hmong-American congregations prefer their pastor to preach without any notes as a sign of being inspired by the Holy Spirit. Other congregations voice no preference as to whether the pastor uses notes in the pulpit.

Many Hmong-American preachers try to involve the congregation as much as possible in the sermon by employing some participatory

121

preaching techniques. Preachers may intentionally ask a question in the sermon which requires a short, verbal response from the congregation. Others ask the congregation to turn in their Bibles to a particular text and read it aloud. One church has a sermon "talk-back" time after the worship service so the laity can discuss the preacher's sermon and add their own thoughts about the sermon's text and/or topic.

Passing of the Peace

This ritual is acceptable but not very common in the Hmong-American tradition.

Benediction

Although benedictions are usually pronounced by ordained clergy only, some congregations permit laypersons to offer the benediction. It is not, however, appropriate for a layperson to use any gesture of blessing. Ordained clergy often stand in the front of the congregation with two hands raised in blessing. Whether one's eyes are open or closed to give or receive the benediction does not seem to be of great importance in the Hmong-American tradition.

Sacramental Practices

Sacrament of Baptism

While United Methodists baptize infants, the Hmong-American community tends not to bring their children for baptism, preferring that they be baptized as adolescents. This, too, is a result of the Christian Missionary Alliance influence in Hmong Christian culture. Thus, most persons baptized within the Hmong tradition are usually age thirteen or older. Those families who have been in the United States for some time are more apt to present infants for baptism. Before a person is baptized, Hmong pastors may meet with the person or family at least once.

Immersion is the most common method of baptism among Hmong United Methodists. Because United Methodist churches do not have baptisteries, the Hmong-American community often gathers at a river once a year for baptism by immersion. A full worship service is conducted at the river's edge with singing, praying, and preaching. After the sermon, and prior to baptism, the persons being baptized often testify to their faith. When an infant is baptized, the water from a baptismal font is poured from a baptismal font over the baby's head. No special baptismal apparel is expected of either the youth or infants being baptized although some choose to wear white.

The baptismal liturgy within Hmong-American churches varies. Some use a preprinted baptismal liturgy while others use only the preprinted questions. Still others conduct the entire liturgy extemporaneously. The *traditional baptismal formula* is said as the person is baptized. Some pastors then make the sign of the cross on the person's forehead with the baptismal water. Occasionally, a baptismal candle is lit in honor of the newly baptized.

A baptismal certificate is given to each person baptized and some churches give a Bible or a cross as well. It is not expected that the persons being baptized will give a gift to the church.

Confirmation

Since infant baptism is not very common, most Hmong-American churches do not have confirmation. As more and more Hmong-American children become baptized as infants, confirmation may become incorporated into the life of the church.

Sacrament of Holy Communion

In Hmong-American churches, this sacrament is usually referred to as the "Lord's Supper" or "Communion." Some may refer to it as the "Eucharist." The sacrament is held once a month and sometimes on special liturgical days as well. The communion table may be covered with a *paudau*.

The celebration of the Lord's Supper takes place after the sermon. A variety of elements are common: wafers, small cubes of bread, one loaf of bread, and grape juice in individual cups or one chalice. The elements are covered to respect the sacred mystery contained within them. Some Hmong-Americans believe in the doctrine of *transubstantiation* or at least in the doctrine of *consubstantiation*. Others within the community see the elements as symbols of Jesus' body and blood representing Christ's grace and presence in our lives.

The liturgy surrounding the celebration of the Lord's Supper contains extemporaneous prayers and "words" about communion. In some Hmong-American churches, these "words" about the sacrament are actually a second sermon preached on communion Sundays. This additional sermon which takes place at the beginning of the Eucharistic liturgy deals with themes of communion, thanksgiving to God, and confession of sins. All Hmong-American churches use some version of the *Words of Institution*. Some congregations also include words of consecration over the elements. The bread is elevated and broken during the *Words of Institution*.

The elements are often passed to the people in the pews and the pastor and lay servers commune simultaneously with the congregation. Some congregations commune by processing forward to the altar rail and receiving the elements standing through the method of *intinction*. Occasionally, the congregation kneels at the altar rail. When these latter methods are practiced, the pastor and lay servers partake before the congregation communes. The elements are distributed with the words "This is the body and blood of our Lord Jesus Christ given for you."

The sacrament of Holy Communion is reserved for the baptized in Hmong-American churches. Since parents tend not to bring their infants for baptism, it is unusual for children to take communion. However, as more infants born in America are baptized, more children will begin to take communion in Hmong-American churches. While the tradition prefers baptized persons taking communion, the hospitality of the table is such that if unbaptized children are brought forward for the sacrament, they are not turned away.

Rituals of Passage

Weddings

In traditional Hmong weddings, the pastor may have no role in the wedding itself, but plays a major role in the feast after the wedding. It is traditionally at the feast, not the wedding, where scripture is read, hymns are sung, the word is preached, and the pastor blesses the couple. Some couples choose to have a Western-style church wedding in addition to the traditional wedding. While a few of the cultural wedding practices vary among different Hmong clans, what follows is a general description of a traditional Hmong wedding.

Weddings in the Hmong culture begin with the elder of the bride and the elder of the groom making arrangements between the two clans for the marriage. Premarital counseling is not common since the elders take responsibility for arranging the marriage. The wedding itself takes place at the bride's house and is presided over by an elder from the bride's clan and an elder from the groom's clan in the Blue Hmong tradition, *Hmoob Ntsaub* (two elders from each clan in the White Hmong tradition, *Hmoob Dawb*). A table is set up as the center for the ceremony, but the table is devoid of any religious or cultural symbols.

The groom goes to the bride's house the morning of the wedding. He brings with him his family's "umbrella." It is a large, black umbrella tied with a woman's hair ribbon. The groom's elder gives the umbrella to the bride's elder. The groom has two attendants with him when he goes to the bride's house: a "best man" type of person and the "carrier" of a blanket. The blanket is plain in color and wrapped in a cloth tie. Once at the bride's house, the bride's family sends the groom to pick up the bride's elder and bring him to the wedding.

The bride is dressed in a red and black traditional dress while the groom is dressed in a suit and tie. The bride is assisted by a female cousin or sister of the groom. There is no procession or escort for the bride.

Once both elders are present at the bride's home, the elders discuss among themselves the commitment between the couple, the commitment between the two families, and the commitment between the two clans. During this time, the groom is present and listening to the conversation. In some clans, the bride is also present. In others, the bride and the groom must be separated. The bride, then, is usually in the kitchen or some other part of the house.

The elders eventually call the bride into their presence (if separated from the group) and ask her if she is willing to marry the groom. If she says "yes," the wedding continues. If she says "no," the ceremony ends. When this part of the wedding draws to a close, all the family and friends present gather around the couple, bless them, and share with them advice about married life. The couple make vows to one another and exchange symbols if any are used. At various points throughout the wedding, there is Hmong chanting. The groom and "best man" bow to the bride's family, bow to her ancestors, and bow to the elders who participated. According to Hmong tradition, they are now married.

Some Hmong-American couples choose also to have a Western-style wedding in the church. In the church wedding, the bride is escorted down the aisle by her father and rings are exchanged. Most also choose to have the Unity Candle. Either the bride and groom or their respective mothers light the outer candles. There is also a time in many weddings where the couple pay respect to their parents by presenting them with a rose or other flower. The parents may also give their blessing to the couple.

When a traditional wedding is held in the bride's home, the feast after the wedding is held there as well. If the couple also has a church wedding, the feast is held at the church after the church wedding.

At the feast, both tribes are present and the minister is expected to attend. After traditional Hmong weddings, it is here at the feast where Christian prayers are offered for the couple, hymns are sung, a sermon is preached, and a blessing is given to the couple. The minister signs the marriage license to make the wedding legal in the United States.

After a traditional Hmong wedding and feast at the bride's family's house, there is another feast at the groom's family's home. The bride's elder gives the umbrella (brought to the bride's house by the groom) to the groom's elder. The groom's elder takes it to the groom's house, blesses the umbrella, and gives it to the groom's father. The bride's family also gives the blanket back to the carrier who then takes it to the groom's house and gives it to the groom's elder. The groom's elder blesses the blanket and gives it to the groom's father. During the feast, the father gives the umbrella and blanket to the groom with words of blessing. The blanket is a symbol of fertility, blessing the couple with many children. The groom, along with his brothers, bow in thanksgiving for these words of blessing, they bow in respect to God, the groom's ancestors, elders, parents, aunts, and uncles.

Three days after the wedding, the grandmother of the groom opens the umbrella, unties the blanket, and blesses the couple.

Funerals

When someone who is Hmong dies, the entire Hmong-American community gathers regardless of one's denomination. On the day of death, the body is washed, perfumed, and dressed in elaborate Hmong burial clothes. The feet are wrapped in white gauze, and black cloth shoes are placed on the feet. Many *paudau* are placed in the casket with the deceased.

For seven days the body is usually at the funeral home, although some still prefer the family's home. It is expected that there will be three services each day (morning, afternoon, and evening) for the six days between the death and the burial seven days later. Each service lasts one to two hours.

The pastor of the deceased is responsible for the structure and content of the services, but if there are clergy from other Hmong-American churches in the area, they come to assist in leading the services. These clergy may be accompanied by the choir or other laity from their congregations. The minister of the deceased decides which ministers will conduct each service.

The casket may be open or closed for these services. It is surrounded by flowers and a picture of the deceased. Red and black are the traditional colors for funerals in the Hmong tradition.

Every service includes singing, reading scripture, praying, preaching, and testimony about the person who died. On the seventh day, the body is moved from the funeral home to the church, where the final service is held.

For the seven days people also gather at the family's home and stay all night keeping watch. The deceased's son's wife is expected to keep watch over the body at the funeral home all day, every day. The minister may also stay at the family's home keeping watch all night.

Once the final service at the church has ended, there is a car procession from the church to the cemetery. At the cemetery, there is a procession from the hearse to the grave site. The sons are the pallbearers (when appropriate), with the oldest son holding the casket at the head and leading the procession. The family and friends make their own way to the grave site. The committal service includes prayers, scripture reading, and a short sermon. At the end of the service, it is common for the family to place a flower on the casket. In some cases, everyone who has gathered does the same.

Family and friends stay after the service while the casket is lowered into the grave. The oldest son first shovels dirt on the grave, then everyone else takes turn until the casket is well covered. After this, a cemetery representative completes the filling of the grave with dirt brought for that purpose on a truck. Once the grave is completely covered, the people usually go to the family's home for a meal.

Since it is not common for services to be held in the United States for family who have died in Laos, and cremation is not an acceptable form of disposing the body, there are no memorial services in the Hmong tradition. The body must always be present.

There are no special worship services marking the anniversary of a person's death.[1]

Notes

1. For "Hmong for Life" resources, including a video depicting a Hmong funeral, contact Rev. Kham Dy Yang through the Moore Multicultural Resource Center at the School of Theology at Claremont, 1325 N. College Ave., Claremont, CA 91711.

INDIAN-AMERICAN WORSHIP PRACTICES

with Rev. Dr. Winson Josiah[1]

The Service of the Word

The Language of the Liturgy

There are literally hundreds of languages and dialects in India, with fifteen regional languages recognized by the government. In the United States, the most common languages used in worship are *Gujarati, Hindi, Malayalam, Tamil, Telugu, Urdu,* and English.

While a church's worship service may be in one language, Bible study and Sunday school classes may be offered in one of the other languages. English may be used as a common language when tremendous language diversity exists within a congregation or as a way to include the children of the congregation who do not speak the native languages.

Because many who speak *Hindi* do not read the *Hindi* alphabet, printed bulletins and songs may often be transcribed into the English alphabet. The letters of the English language are used phonetically to portray the pronunciation of *Hindi* words.

While *Hindi* and *Urdu* are similar languages and are often understood by speakers of each language, there are some differences in terms and in pronunciation.

The Liturgical Space

Cultural images are absent from most worship spaces. On special occasions the flag of India may be present. Women often wear a *sari* to church that evokes a particular cultural identification.

Liturgical Time

Most worship services last about one hour.

129

Liturgical Garb

A pulpit robe or a suit with a clerical collar (for men) is the most common clothing worn by clergy to lead worship.

Liturgical Seasons and Days

Some churches celebrate all of the seasons of the church year. However, Christmas, Holy Week, and Easter receive the most attention. Thanksgiving, New Year's Day, and Mother's Day are also honored liturgically. In addition, August 15 is celebrated as India's Independence Day.

Beginning Our Praise to God

Worship often begins with a Call to Worship which is based on scripture and offered by one person or read responsively between the worship leader and the congregation.

Prayer Forms

Prayer forms in Indian-American churches include: the Lord's Prayer, extemporaneous prayers by the pastor, a pastoral prayer, a corporate prayer of confession, other corporate prayers printed in the bulletin, and prayers offered individually from the congregation. The posture of most prayer is sitting.

Creeds

A creed (usually the Apostles' Creed) is recited at least every other week.

Music

Three to four hymns are usually sung each week during Sunday worship. The hymns are taken from hymnals from the Church of India in the Gujarati language and the Hindi language. *The United Methodist Hymnal* is also used. Several songs written by persons from India in one of the native languages are also sung. The piano or organ is used to accompany the hymns. A keyboard, tambourines, traditional Indian drums, and a harmonium may be used to accompany the traditional songs. Drama and liturgical dance are other art forms that may be utilized to proclaim God's Word. Cultural dance forms may be performed on special occasions.

Clapping and saying "Amen" are acceptable responses to choirs, soloists, and other artistic offerings.

Scripture Readings

The number of scripture passages read each week varies. It may be one, two, or three. The text(s) are usually read by the pastor or lay liturgist while the people read along in the Bible. Psalm texts are often read responsively verse by verse between the worship leader and the congregation.

Preaching

Sharing worship space with another congregation often places forced time limits on the length of worship and therefore the length of the sermon. In India, sermons usually last thirty to forty minutes. In the United States, sermons usually last between fifteen and thirty minutes.

Whether the sermon is in the middle of the service or towards the end, it is seen as the most important part of worship. The lectionary is usually consulted but not necessarily followed as texts are chosen each week.

In some congregations humor is acceptable in preaching. The history and folktales of India as well as the issues facing Indians in America are often used as sermon illustrations.

It is acceptable to leave the sermon open ended or bring it to a tight conclusion with a call to discipleship. While the congregation has no expectations regarding a pastor's use of notes in the delivery of the sermon, good eye contact is required when notes or manuscript are used.

For the most part, there is little outward participation by the congregation during the sermon. However, individuals may say "Amen" to affirm something the preacher said or the preacher may ask the congregation to turn in their Bibles to a particular text and read it aloud. Occasionally the pastor may intentionally ask a question and members of the congregation are expected to call out the answer.

Passing of the Peace

While it is not common, the Passing of the Peace is acceptable in some congregations.

131

Benediction

Usually only ordained clergy are permitted to give the benediction. On special occasions, a lay person may be given this honor. The congregation and the pastor stand with their eyes closed. One or both hands raised in a gesture of blessing often accompanies the benediction.

Sacramental Practices

Sacrament of Baptism

Persons of all ages are baptized in Indian-American churches in America. Baptisms take place whenever the need arises and on special days in the life of the church such as Christmas and Easter. Infants are baptized in the church before the sermon during Sunday morning worship. The method of baptism is sprinkling.

Godparents are not traditional, but if the family chooses godparents for their infant, the preference is for godparents to be Christian. Some churches encourage parents to choose members of the congregation. The pastor may meet with the parents in preparation for the baptism.

When adults are baptized, classes in preparation for the sacrament are required. Adults may be baptized in the church or at the ocean, lake or river when immersion is requested. They often share their experience of conversion at some point during the service.

When baptisms take place in the church, the water may already be in the baptismal font before the service begins, or it may be poured into the font during the Thanksgiving over the water section in the liturgy. Many Indian-American pastors use the baptismal liturgy from the United Methodist Hymnal. Some, however, use a set of questions for the parents of the infant or the adult being baptized, but the rest of the liturgy is given extemporaneously.

During the actual baptism, water is taken from a baptismal font and sprinkled three times on the person's head with some version of the baptismal formula. The *traditional baptismal formula* is often used but alternative formulas may also be used ("I baptize you in the name of God, our Creator; Jesus Christ, our Redeemer/Savior; and the Holy Spirit, our Comforter"). Persons who are baptized are given a baptismal certificate and sometimes a small gift (for infants) or a Bible (for adults).

132

Confirmation

Confirmation is common within the Indian tradition. Those age twelve and above attend confirmation classes that usually last nine to twelve months. At the end of the classes, the youth publicly affirm the vows their parents made for them at their baptism.

Sacrament of Holy Communion

The most common term used to name this sacrament is "Holy Communion." It is celebrated once a month after the sermon. A loaf of bread and one chalice or small cubes of bread and individual cups of grape juice are the most common elements used.

While some believe in the doctrine of *transubstantiation* and others believe in the doctrine of *consubstantiation*, most believe that the elements are symbols of Christ's presence and grace. The elements are covered until the appropriate time in the liturgy.

The liturgy may come from one of the United Methodist resources or the pastor may lead the communion service extemporaneously including the *Words of Institution* and a consecration of the elements. Usually the bread is broken during the *Words of Institution*. In India, only clergy are permitted to say the words of the communion liturgy and distribute the elements. In America, laity are permitted to assist in the distribution of the elements.

The elements are distributed to the congregation as they kneel at the altar. When one loaf and one cup are used, the congregation partakes through *intinction*. The elements are distributed with the words "This is the body and blood of our Lord Jesus Christ given for you." The clergy and lay servers may take communion before the congregation or after they have been served.

While it is traditional for persons to wait until after they have been confirmed or baptized to take communion, those who are not baptized are not discouraged from coming to the table.

Rituals of Passage

Weddings

Before the wedding day, there is a special gathering of the two families and their friends. This party usually takes place at the bride's family's house or a hall rented for the occasion. This celebration includes lots of food, Indian dances and a ceremony of giving gifts to

133

the couple. The groom's family often gives a ring and traditional Indian dress to the bride. The bride gives a ring and maybe a suit to the groom. The pastor is expected to attend for at least a short portion of this event and offer a prayer for the couple.

Premarital counseling is not traditional but many pastors in America meet with the couple before the wedding, with the number of sessions varying. Divorce is frowned upon in the Indian Christian community, so divorced persons who request to be remarried pose theological and pastoral care issues for some pastors.

One or two nights before the wedding, the women relatives and friends may gather with the bride and groom to participate in a ceremony involving the spice turmeric. The turmeric is mixed with water until it is in a liquid form. The women rub the turmeric on the face, arms, and legs of the bride and on the chest, back, face, arms, and legs of the groom. This ritual is an act of beautification as the turmeric mixture makes the skin soft and shiny for the wedding day.

As the groom's family and friends arrive for the wedding festivities, the bride's family often welcomes them with garlands of flowers. Members of the bride's family place a garland around the neck of the groom and each of those accompanying him. This is known as *Barat*.

Immediately before the wedding begins, the groom's sisters and female relatives bring gifts of rings, necklaces, bracelets, and other jewelry to the bride's house along with a special *sari*. The women dress the bride for the wedding, adorn her with jewelry, and put on her makeup. The bride's family gives household gifts to the couple: pots, pans, furniture, appliances, etc.

The church is the only acceptable place for a wedding to take place. The bride wears either a white gown or a traditional Indian *sari*. The groom wears a dark-colored suit or tuxedo.

Bridesmaids, ushers, flower girl, ring bearer, friends, and relatives are all possible attendants in the wedding. The bride is escorted down the aisle by both of her parents or by her father only. The music accompanying the procession is either the "Wedding March" or traditional Indian music.

During the wedding, hymns are sung, scripture is read, prayers are offered, and a sermon is preached. The couple exchange vows and rings before they are pronounced husband and wife. The Unity Candle is seldom used but when a couple chooses to include it, the outer candles are lit by the families of the bride and groom. There is often a time in the wedding for the couple to pay respect to their parents. The form this takes varies. Some bow to their parents while others give them a rose or a kiss.

Immediately following the service, the couple greet their guests in a formal receiving line. Sometimes the bridal party remains up front for this and sometimes they process to the back of the church and greet their guests there.

As the couple leaves the church to go to the reception, someone often gives the groom a garland to place around the neck of the bride. Then in like fashion, the bride places a garland on the groom. These garlands are made out of a shiny, thin metallic material (similar to a Christmas tree garland) with a large decorated heart at the bottom.

The reception may take place at a hall or restaurant. If the bride wore a white Western gown at the wedding, she usually changes into traditional Indian dress for the reception. The pastor is expected to say the prayer before the food is served. Included in the reception are music, modern dancing, many Indian dances performed by various people present, words of hope and blessing for the couple, and cutting the wedding cake. Sometimes the bride throws her bouquet over her shoulder to unmarried women.

Traditionally, the bride goes back to her parents' home and the groom goes back with his family and friends for the wedding night. The following day is the ceremony of *vidai* (sometimes pronounced "bidai"). The bride's family cooks breakfast for the *barat* (groom and his family and friends) before they take the bride with them to the groom's family's home. It is a time of weeping as good-byes are said. Here in America, the ritual of *vidai* may be omitted as the couple leaves immediately after the wedding for the honeymoon.

Funerals

Between the death of someone and the day of burial, there is usually one or two services in addition to the funeral itself. These worship services or prayer meetings may take place at the church, the funeral home, or the family's home. If the pastor speaks the native language of the congregation, the pastor is expected to design and lead these services. If the pastor is not fluent in the native language, often friends and family take over this responsibility. If the family was involved in other faith communities, the family may request that pastors from other churches be invited to participate in the prayer services or the funeral. These gatherings may also be more informal with spontaneous singing and prayers.

135

The prayer meetings include viewing of the body, singing, scripture reading, praying, preaching, and sharing memories about the life of the deceased. Each service may last a couple of hours. The body may be dressed in traditional Indian attire or Western clothing depending on the wishes of the family. The casket is surrounded by flowers and possibly candles or a picture of the deceased.

On the day of burial, some traditions require the pastor to pray with the family at their home and accompany them to the church or funeral home for the funeral. The funeral service is often shorter than the prayer meeting(s) on the previous nights. The casket is usually closed during the funeral but may be open upon request of the family. The funeral includes scripture reading, singing hymns, praying, a short meditation about God's gift of eternal life, and sometimes preaching and testimony about the deceased.

After the funeral service, there is a car procession to the cemetery. The pallbearers carry the casket to the grave site but there is usually no formal procession. The grave site service is short with the reading of scripture and offering of prayers for the family. Dirt is thrown on the casket by either the pastor or everyone present. Often the family places a flower on the casket before they leave. In some communities, people stay until the casket is lowered and the grave is completely filled in. The pastor then offers a final prayer.

While cremation is not practiced by Christians in India, on rare occasions a person in America is cremated so that the deceased's ashes can be taken back to India.

A reception usually follows the grave site service at the family's home, the church, or a restaurant.

Memorial services may be held in America for persons who died in India.

There are no special worship services that mark the anniversary of someone's death but often the family places flowers on the church altar on the Sunday nearest the yearly anniversary, and the pastor offers a prayer of remembrance during the service.

Notes

1. Special thanks to Lamuel J. Jacob who provides pastoral leadership for the Hindi/Urdu Worship Services of the Sepulveda United Methodist Church.

JAPANESE-AMERICAN WORSHIP PRACTICES

with Rev. Dr. Yasuhiko Richard Kuyama
and Rev. Keith P. Inouye

The Service of the Word

The Language of the Liturgy

Japanese is the language used in the worship services of many Japanese congregations. Japanese language congregations are referred to as *Nichigo* or *Nihongo*. However, because people of Japanese ancestry have been in the United States for several generations, there are also many English language congregations served by Japanese-American pastors. Especially in this century, Japanese-Americans tried hard to learn English and assimilate to American values and customs so they would not be singled out as foreigners or as the enemy (e.g, when Japanese-Americans were put in concentration camps during World War II).

The result of both assimilation and the high rate of "out-marrying" among Japanese-Americans (marrying persons who are not of Japanese ancestry) is that the English language ministries associated with Japanese ministries are often comprised of the second and third generations of various Asian cultures. Rather than being oriented solely to the Japanese community, these English language ministries are becoming pan-Asian communities. Occasionally in these services Japanese words are used, but the diversity of the congregation requires that the words be explained in English.

The Liturgical Space

Flowers are always present in the worship space and are an important part of Japanese churches. In addition to flowers, Japanese churches may also have banners with Japanese writing or images on them and a Japanese screen that functions not as a divider, but as art. Japanese cloth may be used on the altar or in other places in the sanctuary.

Liturgical Time

Worship services in both the Japanese and English language ministries usually last one hour.

Liturgical Garb

A black robe, white alb, or street clothes are acceptable clerical attire. Some clergy may wear stoles made from Japanese textiles.

Liturgical Seasons and Days

All the seasons of the church year are celebrated although Epiphany receives the least attention. Holy Week is marked by a Good Friday service. American Thanksgiving and New Year's Day are also honored liturgically.

In addition, several cultural days are celebrated. In *Nichigo* (Japanese language) congregations, March 3 is "Girl's Day" or "Doll's Day." Dolls and handmade crafts are displayed and songs are sung. The dolls represent health and happiness for families. Originally paper dolls were put on paper ships and sent afloat on the river or the sea to take away bad elements. Today, dolls are given to girls by their parents. Some of these dolls may be new but many are passed down from generation to generation.

May 5, Children's Day, also honors children. It, too, is celebrated with crafts and singing. Symbols of this celebration include armor and flying carp. The armor represents the strong growth of children and the flying carp symbolizes the strength of swimming upstream against all odds.

Memorial Day is celebrated the last Monday in May in some Japanese *Nichigo* communities. The broader ecumenical and interfaith Japanese community may gather at a cemetery and have a service that includes scripture reading, hymns, and often two short sermons, one in Japanese and one in English. The names of those in the community who died the past year are read and a Floral Tribute is given (see section on "Funerals" for a description of the Floral Tribute). In communities with a large Japanese population, there is often one cemetery with a Japanese Memorial Tower where these services take place. In English language ministries, services may be held at the church on Memorial Day or during worship the Sunday before. The lives of those who died the year before are remembered at this time.

Some churches also honor the Day of Remembrance (February 19, 1942) when Roosevelt signed an order that sent Japanese-Americans to the concentration camps during World War II.

Beginning our Praise to God

Services often begin with a Call to Worship that is scripturally based (often from the Psalms) and read responsively between the worship leader and the congregation. Some services also include an Introit, an invocation, or a greeting.

Prayer Forms

Prayer forms in Japanese language ministries include the Lord's Prayer, extemporaneous prayers by the lay liturgist, and a pastoral prayer. Individual prayers of the community are sometimes included but few in the congregation are willing to raise their hands and speak aloud in a worship setting. The cultural norms encourage people not to stand out. Many tell the pastor their prayer needs before the service, and the pastor is expected to remember those and include them in the pastoral prayer. The pastoral prayer also includes the "Memorial Prayer" and prayers for those who are in the hospital or recovering at home. The Memorial Prayer is unique to the Japanese community. Prayers are offered for every person in the congregation who died during that week in years past.

In some English language ministries, the Lord's Prayer is recited occasionally in worship but not always every week. These services may also include a corporate prayer of confession printed in the bulletin.

The posture of prayer in both Japanese language and English language services is sitting.

Some *Nichigo* congregations have prayer services before worship early on Sunday mornings. These services include prayer, singing, reading scripture and testimonies given by the laity. Some English language ministries do not utilize the early morning prayer services, but they do include lay testimonies during Sunday worship several times a year.

Creeds

Reciting a creed is not a common practice in *Nichigo* congregations. The Apostles' Creed may occasionally be included in English language services.

Music

The hymnal used in most Japanese language services, *Sambiky*, is the hymnal published by the United Churches of Christ of Japan, which is the merger of Japanese Methodist, Presbyterian, Congregationalist, and some Baptist denominations that occurred during WWII. Several other hymnals are available and used by *Nichigo* congregations. English language ministries use the United Methodist Hymnal.

Usually two to three hymns are sung during Sunday worship.

Organ and piano are used to accompany the hymns. Guitars are used more by the young people. English language ministries may also sing "praise" songs or offer contemporary services where guitars, modern drums, saxophone, and other instruments are used. Japanese instruments are not common in either worship context.

In both Japanese and English language services, there are few overt responses to soloists and choir anthems. Clapping is becoming more acceptable in the English language ministries.

Scripture Readings

One to two scripture readings are usually read in Sunday worship by the pastor or lay liturgist. Many in the Japanese language congregations read along in the pew Bibles. These texts often come from the lectionary.

Preaching

Sermons in Nichigo congregations usually last fifteen to twenty minutes. The sermon is usually at the end of the liturgy and is seen by the congregation as the most important part of worship.

Scripture texts are often taken from the lectionary. Some pick a topic from the text and preach topically, while others preach the text exegetically.

Humor is appropriate in Japanese congregations. Storytelling is also common in preaching. While *Nichigo* congregations use illustrations from Japanese stories, folktales, and classic literature as well as from life experience, English language sermons tend to develop the illustrations primarily from everyday life experience.

In sermon delivery, most congregations appreciate passion, but some frown on emotional, revivalistic styles. Many congregations have no expectations regarding the use of manuscript or notes, however good eye contact is crucial. There are a few, however, who feel that extemporaneous preaching is a sign of being inspired by the Holy Spirit.

In *Nichigo* congregations, sermons tend not to be participatory in nature. Throughout the year, lay speakers may preach on certain occasions. In English language services, immediately following the sermon, the pastor may invite members of the congregation to respond by offering their thoughts about the text or sermon topic. Other churches have a sermon "talk-back" time after the service. Some pastors use a more informal style of preaching and invite the congregation to divide into small groups during the sermon to discuss an issue that has been raised. The main points of a sermon may also be written on newsprint during the delivery.

Passing of the Peace

This ritual is practiced in both Japanese language and English language services.

Benediction

Ordained clergy pronounce the benediction with either one or both hands raised in a gesture of blessing. Whether the one giving the benediction or those receiving it have their eyes open or closed does not seem to be of great importance in the Japanese context.

Sacramental Practices

Sacrament of Baptism

Within the Japanese tradition in America (unlike Japan), most persons are baptized as infants in the church during Sunday worship. Occasionally, private baptisms take place in someone's home or in the church outside of Sunday worship. Sprinkling is the only form acceptable in *Nichigo* congregations. Baptisms often occur at the beginning of the Easter and Christmas services. Communion is often celebrated after the sermon on days when someone is baptized.

In English language congregations, baptisms occur whenever the parents or individuals request it. Sprinkling is the most common method. Parents requesting baptism for their child (or adults wanting to be baptized) meet with the pastor at least once before the baptismal vows are made. When adults request baptism, or seek to join the church, at least three classes are required of these persons prior to baptism. Sometimes these classes are called confirmation.

Both congregations often use formal liturgies for the sacrament. Some may choose to include only the questions printed in the liturgy, offering their own extemporaneous words about baptism. In *Nichigo* congregations, if adults are baptized they often share their faith journey with the congregation as part of the liturgy. English language services often include the blessing over the water.

Water is poured into a baptismal font (or bowl if there is no font) before the service begins. The person is baptized with the *traditional baptismal formula*. Sprinkling water on the person's head once or three times is up to the pastor. Some ministers also make the sign of the cross on the person's forehead with the baptismal water.

White clothing is not part of Japanese baptismal tradition. However, in English language ministries, some have adopted the Euro-American cultural practice of dressing infants in white for the baptism. Appointing godparents is not a practice in Japanese-American churches, but in English language ministries it is acceptable.

Before the time of internment in concentration camps in the United States, a Bible and a blanket were given to the person being baptized in Japanese-American churches. Today, however, a certificate and a rose are given. In *Nichigo* congregations, the family of the one being baptized (or the adult being baptized) often gives a special offering to the church. This practice is not expected in most English language ministries.

Confirmation

In Japan, persons are usually baptized as adults so there is little need for confirmation. However, in English-speaking Japanese-American congregations, the practice of infant baptism leads some larger congregations to offer confirmation classes for their youth.

Sacrament of Holy Communion

The sacrament of Holy Communion takes place once a month after the sermon. The elements are understood to be symbols of Christ's presence and grace.

The communion liturgy usually consists of a shortened version of the Great Thanksgiving with no congregational responses. This liturgy includes the *Words of Institution* and a consecration of the elements.

English language ministries often use a full Great Thanksgiving with congregational responses, although the shortened version is also acceptable. Both congregations break the bread during the Institution. Only clergy can celebrate communion, but laypeople assist in the distribution of the elements.

The elements are often covered until the proper time in the service. Traditionally, cubes of bread and individual cups are passed to the people in the pews. Some pastors however, use a loaf of bread and one chalice. The congregation comes forward and receives the elements through *intinction* while standing. The elements are often distributed with the words "This is the body and blood of our Lord Jesus Christ."

On New Year's Day, rice cakes are sometimes used in place of bread. In English language ministries, rice and tea are sometimes substituted for the bread and grape juice on communion Sundays. *Nori* (a flat sheet of seaweed) is used to pick up the rice.

In many Japanese and English language ministries, the ministers and lay servers take communion after the congregation has received. In Japanese culture, it is important to let others go first and to serve oneself last.

While the nonbaptized are not allowed to take communion in Japan, that is not an issue in America. Parents decide at what age they want their children to begin taking communion. In some churches, the children come forward in their Sunday school classes as a group to partake.

Rituals of Passage

Weddings

In Japan, weddings are very elaborate and often business oriented. Now that the man is married, he is viewed as being more reliable and responsible. Often, a boss or some business associate is asked to be the "go-between." The wedding becomes an occasion for the groom to be introduced to the business community. "Go-betweens" are not used in America where weddings are more family oriented.

Japanese-Americans have assimilated many of the wedding customs of the Euro-American culture. Before the wedding, the couple may drink a special tea made from salted cherry blossoms, but other than that, prewedding rituals are not present.

Prior to performing the marriage ceremony, most Japanese pastors require one to four counseling sessions with the couple.

While many pastors encourage the couple to be married in the church, weddings can take place anywhere.

When persons from the *Nichigo* congregation are married, there is often a receptionist at the entrance to the church who collects envelopes containing monetary gifts for the couple. The receptionist keeps a record of the name and address of each person who gives a gift. This is very important since the couple is expected to give a gift back to everyone who gave them money. The cost of these thank-you gifts must be factored into the total cost of the wedding. This practice is known as *hikidemono*.

When it is time for the wedding to begin, the mothers of the bride and groom or other persons chosen by the couple light the candles on the altar and the outer candles of the Unity Candle if used.

The wedding begins with a procession of the bridesmaids, flower girl, and ring bearer, followed by the bride who is often escorted by her father. The groom and his attendants enter from the side at the front of the sanctuary. Today, however, different configurations of the procession involving both men and women are becoming more popular. The bride is dressed in a white wedding gown, the groom wears a tuxedo.

Japanese weddings are often bilingual. In some weddings, the Declaration of Intent is in one language and the Vows in the other. It has never been the tradition in Japanese weddings for the father to "give away" the bride.

In the English language congregations that use the service in the United Methodist *Book of Worship*, the parents give their support and blessing to the couple. In *Nichigo* congregations, there is no place in the service for the parents to give their blessing to the couple or to receive symbols of respect from them. Occasionally, however, a couple may present a rose or Hawaiian lei to the parents.

After the wedding, a reception includes a sit-down meal with music, dancing, and toasting. The bride throws her bouquet over her shoulder to unmarried women, the groom throws the bride's garter over his shoulder to unmarried men, and the couple cuts the wedding cake and feeds each other. A receptionist is also present at the reception to record the gifts given to the couple.

If the couple is strongly connected to the Japanese culture, they often wear traditional Japanese clothing at the reception for a short time. The groom wears black and the bride wears a kimono. While in Japanese dress, the couple may break open a *sake* barrel with a wooden mallet. Later in the reception, the couple changes back into their tuxedo and wedding gown.

The couple moves from table to table greeting their guests. When the dancing begins, some English-speaking couples choose to have a form of "money dance." The women pay an usher (often $5 or $10) to dance with the groom, and the men pay to dance with the bride.

Some couples include a *banzai* toast at the reception. The couple shouts *banzai* and the people raise their glasses and say *banzai* in return. This goes back and forth three times. Because *banzai* was used by kamikazes in preparation for war, if other Asians are present at the reception, the *banzai* toast may be eliminated.

Brides who come from the Japanese-Hawaiian[1] culture may make 1,001 origami cranes, which signify long life. Her friends help her make these cranes, which are often in gold, or sometimes silver and red. In the past, the custom was to hang them on a tree branch and, at the reception, people took a crane home with them. Now they are often preserved by mounting them in the form of an image (i.e. a fan) that can be hung and displayed permanently.

The minister is usually invited to the reception and is often asked to pray before the meal is served.

Funerals

On one or more nights between one's death and the day of the funeral, there is usually a viewing of the body at the funeral home. The pastor is expected to attend and offer prayer with the family.

In Japan, cremation is more common than burial today. However, in the U.S. cremation and burial of the body are practiced. If the body is cremated, the ashes are placed in a box rather than an urn. The box is covered with a *furoshiki*—a square white cloth tied in Japanese style over the box. The box is often taken to the cemetery and sealed in a vault. White is a symbol of Christian resurrection and new life.

Memorial services are held when the body is not present. In place of the casket, pictures of the deceased are positioned in the front.

Though not customary, some families may request the pastor to pray with them at their home the morning of the funeral. More often, the pastor prays with the family at the place of the funeral before they enter the sanctuary or chapel. The funeral can take place at either the

145

church or the funeral home. Occasionally there is a viewing of the body immediately before the funeral begins.

Many in the Japanese community still practice the tradition of *koden*, a practice of mutual support. As the people gather for the funeral, people bring sympathy cards with money inside. The amount of money given is determined by one's relationship to the family. As the guests sign the registry, a designated person receives the cards, makes sure the address is clear, and may even number the card with the number next to the person's name in the registry. It is important to keep track of the gifts so the family can send thank-you cards or gifts.

Traditionally, the family was required to send tea, sugar, or a hankerchief to each family as a thank-you gift for the *koden*, but that is not practiced today. thank-you cards are sufficient. In the Japanese-Hawaiian tradition, families often include a book of stamps in the thank-you card. In many communities, the funeral home prepares the thank-you cards and the money received is often given by the family to the church or some other charitable organization.

If the service is at the funeral home, and if the body is present, the casket is already in place. If the funeral takes place at the church, the pastor often processes in, followed by the pall bearers carrying the casket. Traditionally the casket is closed for the service, although upon request of the family, it may be open.

Surrounding the casket are candles, a picture of the deceased and many flowers. In addition to western floral arrangements, some of the flowers are Japanese *ike bana* in style. Inside the casket, items of importance to the deceased are placed. Sometimes this includes a Bible or other mementos. Sometimes children, grandchildren, and great grandchildren write letters to the deceased expressing their love and grief. These letters are also placed in the casket.

The funeral service includes a sermon, the reading of scripture, music, and prayers. A few people are often chosen by the family to speak about the deceased. The culture does not encourage spontaneous speaking from the congregation. Telegrams or faxes from Japan and letters sent from other parts of the United States are also read in the service.

In addition, funerals within *Nichigo* congregations also have a "Floral Tribute" and/or a "Final Respect Floral Tribute." The Floral Tribute involves representatives from the various organizations to which the deceased belonged. Representative friends and family may also be included. Each representative's name is called and he or she comes forward and places a flower on the casket. Some people may bow before they lay the flower down. The "Floral Tribute" may also be practiced in English-speaking congregations if the deceased had strong ties to organizations.

The Final Respect Floral Tribute takes place at the end of the service. The casket is sometimes opened at this point. Whether open or closed, the congregation processes forward, takes a flower, and places it in or on the casket. The people pay respect to the deceased by bowing to the deceased, praying before the body, or simply walking by in silence. They then give their condolences to the family before they leave. In English language congregations, the "Final Tribute" does not include flowers. The guests come forward at the end of the service and pay respect to the deceased and the family. Flowers are only placed on the casket at the grave site service.

Sometimes cars drive in a procession to the cemetery. Once people have arrived, the family and friends seat themselves by the grave. The pastor leads a procession from the hearse to the cemetery followed by the pallbearers carrying the casket, then the honorary pallbearers. The committal service includes the reading of scripture, prayers, and occasionally a short sermon. At the end of the service, everyone places a flower on the casket.

In the Japanese-Hawaiian tradition, the people remain until the grave is filled in with dirt, or the urn is sealed in the vault.

After the committal service, there is often a reception at the family's home or at a restaurant.

The yearly anniversary of a person's death is remembered in the Memorial Prayer during Sunday worship services.

The expected time of mourning is one year, called *mochuu*. During this time, the person in mourning does not send or receive greeting cards.

Notes

1. Special thanks to Rev. Gail Messner for her information regarding Japanese-Hawaiian traditions.

KOREAN-AMERICAN WORSHIP PRACTICES

with Rev. Dr. Seog Wan Cho

The Service of the Word

The Language of the Liturgy

Korean-American congregations gather to praise and worship God in their native tongue—the Korean language. However, many Korean-American churches also have English language ministries for those within the community who were born in Korea but came to the United States early enough to receive an American education (1.5 generation), and for second and third generation Korean-Americans.

The Liturgical Space

While Korean-American churches may hang banners in the sanctuary with Korean script on them, or have a Korean flag in a stand opposite the American flag, often there is nothing in the worship space to identify the space as Korean.

In Korea, there are several pairs of slippers on the steps leading up to the chancel area. It is customary for clergy to remove one's shoes and wear the slippers before one enters the chancel area. Removing one's shoes is common before entering anyone's home, certain offices, and restaurants. This practice is not as common in Korean-American churches.

Liturgical Time

Sunday services last about an hour and a half.

Liturgical Garb

Most Korean-American clergy wear a black or white pulpit robe. Often the black robe is worn in the winter and the white robe during the summer months. On New Year's Day (solar calendar) or other special occasions, traditional Korean garb may also be worn.

Liturgical Seasons and Days

Christmas and Easter are the two primary liturgical days of the church year that are celebrated in Korean-American churches. Some Korean-American churches also celebrate Advent, Epiphany, Pentecost, and Lent. The English language ministries are more likely to celebrate all the seasons of the liturgical year. Korean-American churches celebrate Thanksgiving on the third Sunday of November.

In addition to the special days in the life of the Christian calendar, other cultural occasions are also honored liturgically. While some celebrate the Lunar New Year (usually in February or March), most Korean-American churches have special services on the solar New Year, January 1. On this day, many in the congregation attend in traditional Korean dress. March 1 (the date that honors the Independence movement's unarmed uprising to protest Japanese occupation) may be recognized on the Sunday closest to that day. Likewise, on the Sunday closest to August 15, Korean-American churches often celebrate Korea's liberation from Japanese rule.

Beginning Our Praise to God

The opening words offered by the pastor to begin the worship service are usually scripturally based.

Prayer Forms

The Lord's Prayer, extemporaneous prayers by the pastor and lay elder, and a pastoral prayer are all common prayers in the Korean-American church. The pastoral prayer often includes themes of confession and forgiveness as well as prayers of petition for needs of individuals and the broader community. In a few Korean-American churches, the people offer their individual prayers aloud in worship. The posture for prayer is sitting.

Tong Song Kido is a unique prayer form in Korean-American churches but it is used more often during weekday evening or early morning worship services than during Sunday morning worship. During *Tong Song Kido* prayer time, everyone in the congregation prays aloud their own individual prayers. The result is a great cacophony of voices merging together in supplication, confession, and praise. It also functions as "bidding prayers" as the pastor bids the congregation to pray for a particular thing, then as the voices subside, the pastor calls them to pray for something else. This bidding can go back and forth

149

between the pastor and the people several times as the people offer their prayers of petition to God. The posture of *Tong Song Kido* praying is either sitting with the upper body leaning forward or kneeling with heads bowed and eyes closed.

Creeds

Reciting a creed is part of the weekly worship service in Korean-American congregations. It may be the Apostles' Creed, the Korean Creed, or the Social Creed. However, in the English language ministries of the Korean-American church, reciting a creed is not as common. In some of these ministries a creed is not included at all.

Music

The hymnal published by the Korean Christian Publishing House is used not only by United Methodist Korean-American congregations but by almost every Korean-American congregation regardless of one's denomination. The English language ministries, however, usually use *The United Methodist Hymnal*. The organ and/or piano are commonly used to accompany hymns. Some Korean-American churches also sing "praise songs" which are usually accompanied by the piano. In the English language ministries of Korean-American churches, these "praise songs" may be accompanied by guitars, drums, tambourines, or a synthesizer. Traditional Korean drums may be used on special occasions.

Responses to soloists and choir anthems vary. Some believe that silence is the most respectful response in the sanctuary while others may clap or say "Amen." Clapping and verbal affirmations are much more common in English language services.

Scripture Readings

Two scripture passages are read each week: one reading from the Old Testament and one from the New Testament. Korean-American Christians are very Word centered. Each person brings his or her own Bible to church to read along with the pastor. Occasionally the scripture text is read responsively (verse by verse) between the pastor and the congregation.

Preaching

Sermons in the Korean-American church are approximately thirty minutes in length. In the English language services, they are much shorter—usually fifteen to twenty minutes long. The sermon is seen as the most important part of the liturgy. The lectionary is often consulted, but not always followed. Three-point deductive sermons are still quite common, but many Korean-American clergy now vary the sermon structure from week to week. Most sermons are topical in nature but some may be expository or exegetical.

Humor is acceptable, although one's use of humor varies greatly. Illustrations often come from the Korean context in America, or from folktales, legends, historical figures, and issues of Korea. It is assumed by many in the congregation that the sermon will have a tight conclusion but it is becoming more acceptable in America to leave the sermon open ended.

Some Korean-American congregations prefer the pastor to preach without any notes or manuscript as a sign of being inspired by the Holy Spirit. In other congregations it does not matter as long as the preacher maintains good eye contact. In the English language ministries, it is more common for the congregation to view the use of notes as a sign of preparation on the part of the preacher.

For the most part, Korean-American preaching is the sole responsibility of the pastor in both preparation and delivery. The congregation participates at their own internal level but no outward participation is involved.

In more informal settings, some Korean-American pastors occasionally use a variety of methods to include the congregation in the sermon. Some preach for a shorter time, then ask laity to offer their thoughts about the text or topic. Other pastors intentionally ask a question in the sermon that requires a short, but verbal response from the congregation. The "call and response" method (most common in the African-American church) is also used in some congregations. Laity may say "Amen" in affirmation of what the preacher is saying during the sermon.

Passing of the Peace

This ritual is not commonly found in first generation Korean-American congregations. The Passing of the Peace is more acceptable in English language services.

Benediction

It is very clear in the Korean-American church that only ordained clergy are allowed to pronounce the benediction. The pastor stands in the front with eyes closed and one or two hands raised in a gesture of blessing. The congregation also stands with their eyes closed to receive the benediction. Having one's eyes closed is important in Korean-American churches because the benediction is often seen as a prayer. Sometimes benedictions in Korean-American churches are long prayers that end with a dismissal or blessing.

The notion that a benediction is a prayer is less prominent in English language ministries and therefore whether one pronounces or receives the benediction with eyes closed is less important.

Sacramental Practices

Sacrament of Baptism

Baptism in Korean-American churches is an important event in the life of the church. Persons are baptized at various ages (although infancy is the most common) on special liturgical days such as Easter and Christmas. For infants, the parents' responsibility and commitment to raise the child in a Christian context is stressed; for youth and adults the focus tends to be more on participation in the death and resurrection of Jesus as well as repentance and cleansing of sin. For everyone, incorporation into the body of Christ is something to celebrate. Unless there is an emergency situation, almost all baptisms take place in the church in the context of worship.

In some Korean-American churches, there is a practice of presenting a flower to the parents on the first Sunday they attend worship after the birth of the baby (before the baptism). Then the pastor meets with the parents at least once in preparation for the sacrament of baptism to make sure they are fully aware of the commitment they are making for the child.

In Korea, youth and adults who want to be baptized must attend the church for six months and undergo a time of study. At the end of the six months, if the person passes a written test and a personal interview, he or she receives the status of *hakseup* membership. After attending for another six months and passing another written test and interview, the baptism takes place. If the person is over the age of eighteen, *ipkyosik* (full membership) is also bestowed upon the person. In the United States, usually there are no written tests nor is a waiting period required, although attendance at church and Bible study for six months to a year is strongly encouraged before baptism.

The baptismal liturgy is usually taken from the Korean Methodist Book of Worship, which includes words about baptism, and prayers and questions to ask the parents or adult being baptized. When youth and adults are baptized, there may also be a time of sharing one's faith journey or conversion experience. English language ministries pastored by 1.5, second, or third generation Korean-Americans may pour the water into the bowl during the service and include a thanksgiving over the water in addition to the prayers and questions.

There are no expectations about special dress for the baptism, nor is it common for godparents to be chosen. In some churches, adults being baptized have a sponsor from the congregation who guides them and keeps in touch with them in the months following the baptism.

Baptismal fonts are not always common in Korean-American churches. Often water is poured into a bowl before the service begins, with the bowl placed on the altar during the service. At the time of baptism, a lay elder or associate pastor holds the bowl for the baptism.

The most common method used in baptism is sprinkling although a few pastors pour the water using their hand as a cup. Water is placed on the person's head just once (although three times is becoming more common among second and third generation Korean-Americans in English language ministries) while repeating the *traditional baptismal formula*. Some Korean-American pastors also make the sign of the cross on the person's forehead with the baptismal water.

A baptismal certificate is given to the person being baptized and in some churches, a Bible is given to adults as well. It is common in most Korean-American churches to expect that the person being baptized (or family of the infant) will give a monetary gift to the church. This is based on the Korean custom of hospitality where it is assumed a person would not go to one's elders or superiors "empty handed." Since God is the ultimate "person of honor," it is expected that the greatest hospitality will be offered to the church.

Confirmation

Confirmation is not a traditional practice in many Korean-American churches. Many churches, however, practice the Korean tradition of *ipkyosik*, which is a unique ceremony taking place when a person reaches the age of eighteen. It is a time for the person to publicly renew her or his baptismal vows and become a full member of the church.

Confirmation is more common in the English language ministries of the Korean-American church. Youth over the age of twelve spend six weeks to six months in preparation.

Sacrament of Holy Communion

The term for this sacrament in the Korean language is best translated into English as "Holy Supper" although Holy Communion is also used. The sacrament of the Holy Supper is celebrated several times a year in Korean-American congregations but it is not a monthly ritual in most churches. Holy Communion may be offered on certain liturgical days, other special days, or during retreats. When Holy Communion is celebrated during Sunday worship, it often takes place before the sermon. In many Korean-American churches, a separate communion table is brought out to celebrate the sacrament.

The liturgy itself may come from the Korean Book of Worship, which includes prayers for communion and a consecration of the elements. The elements are consecrated before the *Words of Institution* are recited. Most Korean-American clergy break the bread during the *Words of Institution*. When the Korean Book of Worship is not used, clergy offer extemporaneous prayers and words about communion in addition to a blessing of the bread and cup, and the *Words of Institution*.

The ordained clergy celebrate the liturgy of Holy Communion and may be assisted by lay elders in this act. Laity also assist in the distribution of the elements. The tradition in Korea is for the pastor and lay assistants to partake before the congregation so that they are worthy to serve the people of God, but this practice is not always followed in Korean-American churches.

The elements usually take the form of wafers and individual cups of grape juice, or a loaf of bread and a chalice. The elements are covered until the appropriate time in the liturgy. The elements are distributed in a variety of ways. In many Korean-American churches, the congregation comes forward and kneels at the altar rail to partake. Those who use a loaf and chalice may have the people process to the altar and receive while standing, using the method of *intinction*. In a few congregations, the elements are passed to the members while they are sitting in the pews. The elements are distributed with the traditional words "This is the body and blood of our Lord Jesus Christ given for you." While some laypersons believe in the doctrine of *consubstantiation*, most members understand the elements to be signs of Christ's real presence and grace among us.

In some Korean-American churches children can take communion only if they were baptized as infants. In other congregations, unbaptized children can also partake.

Rituals of Passage

Weddings

Korean-American weddings are a unique blend of Western and Korean cultural influences. While many couples participate in an Engagement Ceremony (printed in the Korean Methodist Book of Worship), this ceremony is not required before persons can be married.

Prior to the wedding, the groom's friends (sent by the groom's family) take gifts to the bride in a box. The box usually contains things for the bride to wear or use at the wedding. In return, the bride buys presents for the groom's family members. The bride's family usually gives a watch and a suit to the groom.

While premarital counseling is not very common in Korea, pastors in the United States meet at least once with the couple before the wedding. Divorce is strongly discouraged in the Korean-American Christian community. If legal divorce papers are presented, however, many Korean-American pastors will marry persons who are divorced although it is frowned upon by some in the congregation. Weddings can take place anywhere, but use of the church is encouraged.

Decoration colors for the wedding are up to the bride but yellow is not used with white since yellow and white are associated with funerals. Bridesmaids, ushers, flower girl, and ring bearer are all common attendants at Korean-American weddings.

As the guests gather for the wedding, there are two tables set up near the front door—one for the groom and one for the bride. Ushers stand behind the tables and collect "envelopes" from guests (usually filled with money). The money given to the bride's table is given to the bride's family to help with the cost of the wedding. The money given to the groom's table is given to the groom's family. If the bride's family is solely responsible for the wedding expenses, there may only be a bride's table. In weddings of second and third generation Korean-American, gifts for the bride and groom (other than money) are also common.

While ushers escort the people to their seats, the groom escorts the mothers to their seats. Prior to their being seated, the mothers of the bride and groom light the altar candles and the outer candles of the Unity Candle.

The groom is fully visible, greeting guests as they arrive. Only the bride is hidden from view. The groom is in a tuxedo and the bride in a white wedding gown.

The traditional procession (to the "Wedding March" or other Western music) involves the groom and his attendants walking down the side aisle and the bride's attendants walking down the center aisle. The father of the bride is the most appropriate escort in first generation Korean-American weddings. In second or third generation weddings, it is also possible for ushers to escort the bridesmaids down the center aisle. The groom then processes alone, followed by the flower girl and ring bearer together, and finally the bride and her father.

In Korean weddings, the bride stands to the left of the pastor and the groom to the right (opposite Western tradition). Korean-American pastors who are of the second and third generations often use the Western positions for weddings.

The wedding proceeds with a greeting, prayers, scripture readings, a sermon, music (sometimes Korean music), exchange of vows, the giving and receiving of rings, and the pronouncement that the couple is now husband and wife. After the pronouncement, the couple makes a deep bow (once or three times) first to the bride's parents, then to the groom's parents, and finally to the congregation. At the very end of the service the father of the bride or groom or someone influential in the community speaks to the congregation, thanking the people for coming and inviting them to the reception.

Some couples choose to have a formal receiving line with the entire bridal party at the back of the church after the wedding. Others greet their guests more informally at the reception.

Between the wedding and the reception, the bride changes her clothes (often into Korean dress) and the couple goes through another bowing ritual with their parents and other elders.

Following the wedding is a reception at the church, a hall, or a restaurant. At the place of the reception are two receptionist tables and two receptionists (one for the bride, one for the groom). People who did not give their envelopes or gifts at the wedding leave them with the receptionist. The name of the giver is registered with a number that is placed on the envelope or gift. This facilitates the couple sending out thank-you notes and protects the gifts from being lost or stolen.

Clergy are expected to attend the reception and are often asked to offer the prayer before the meal is served. The reception includes a sit-down dinner with music, but usually no dancing. Words of blessing and hope for the couple are given but not in the form of "toasting" since alcoholic beverages are very rare in Christian wedding receptions. The bride throws her bouquet over her shoulder to unmarried women, and the couple cut the wedding cake and feed each other. The couple also goes through the ritual of bowing to various elders and people of importance at the reception. The presider at the reception may ask the couple to sing or do something in fun.

One unique aspect of some Korean-American weddings either takes place before the wedding or at the reception. The groom's friends may "beat up the groom." They hang him upside down and beat the souls of his feet with a stick or taunt him in other ways. To free her husband, the bride performs tricks or does whatever the friends demand in order to release him. While this practice is traditional, it is becoming less frequent in the United States.

Funerals

The term "funeral" is used in the Korean tradition for the final worship service offered on the day of burial. The term "memorial" is used to describe the worship services that honor the anniversary of someone's death. English language ministries of Korean-American churches may use the term "memorial service" in relationship to a funeral service where the body is not present.

Immediately after a death, the pastor is called. He or she is expected to go immediately to the hospital (or home) before the body is removed to the morgue (usually about a four hour time frame). The pastor offers words of comfort, reads scripture and prays with the family while the body is still present. The pastor then assists the family in making the arrangements, often accompanying them to the funeral home.

Since burial of the body is the most common (cremation is frowned upon as a Buddhist practice, and some believe the "resurrection of the body" is not possible if the body is cremated), the body is dressed in special clothes (sometimes Korean dress) and placed in the casket along with a Bible and possibly other items such as rings.

In some Korean-American churches an all night prayer vigil takes place the first night after death at the funeral home with the casket open for viewing. Other churches have a service of *ipkwonsik* the night before the funeral.

In Korea, *ipkwonsik* is the ceremony of laying the body in the coffin. Here, the funeral directors take care of the body but there is still a service that takes place at the funeral home (but not necessarily in the funeral chapel). The service of *ipkwonsik* takes place at the beginning of an evening of viewing the body. The service includes prayers, hymns, reading of scripture, a short sermon, and sharing about the person who died. After the service, family and friends may stay for the duration of the viewing offering comfort and support for the family. The pastor is not expected to remain for the entire evening.

On the day of the funeral, the community gathers at the funeral home (sometimes the church) for the service. As they enter, there is a reception table with a receptionist to receive envelopes with money inside brought by guests to aid the family with the funeral expenses. The envelope is numbered and the number is registered in a book with the person's name and address.

During the funeral service the casket is closed or open depending on the family's wishes. The casket is already in place in the front. It is surrounded by flowers and a picture of the deceased draped in a black ribbon. Scripture is read, prayers are offered, a sermon is usually preached, hymns are sung, and a few people are chosen in advance to share memories of the person who died. The service usually lasts about an hour.

After the funeral, there is often a car procession from the place of the funeral to the cemetery. At the cemetery, there is a procession from the hearse to the grave site. The pastor leads the procession with the oldest son (or someone comparable) carrying the picture of the deceased draped in the black ribbon. Then follows the casket carried by the pallbearers, then the family.

The service includes the reading of scripture, and the offering of prayers (sometimes a short sermon as well). The pastor throws dirt on the casket during the liturgy and the people place a flower on the grave before they leave. After the committal service, there is often a reception at a restaurant.

Upon request of the family, clergy from other denominations may be asked to participate in the funeral service.

Funeral services may be held in America for family who have died in Korea even though there is neither casket nor body present. In addition to funeral services, there are also memorial services held in the family's home on the yearly anniversaries of the death. The pastor is often invited but is not always required to attend.

In Korea, there is a belief among some that a child who dies before a parent is being "undutiful" or is bringing the parents bad luck. The pain and suffering they experience at this time are great. Some parents will not attend the funeral service of their child because of this. This belief and practice is very rare in Korean-American churches in the United States but depending on the family and how recently they moved here, pastors may face this situation.

LAOTIAN-AMERICAN WORSHIP PRACTICES

with Rev. Dr. John C. Kounthapanya

The Service of the Word

The Language of the Liturgy

Lao is the language used in worship. The Lao community are recent immigrants and just beginning to experience the need for English language services.

The Liturgical Space

Since most Laotian-American churches share the sanctuary space with other congregations, the worship space is usually devoid of overt Lao symbols or images.

Liturgical Time

Worship lasts approximately one hour.

Liturgical Garb

Nothing is worn by the pastor during worship that identifies him (there are no women Lao-American clergy to date) as a member of the clergy; no robes, stoles, or clerical collar are worn.

Liturgical Seasons and Days

Christmas and Easter are the main liturgical days celebrated by Laotian-American congregations. Holy Week services are uncommon. Thanksgiving and the Lao New Year (April 13 or 14 depending on whether it is a leap year) are also celebrated liturgically.

Beginning Our Praise to God

Worship begins with a greeting, hymn, opening prayer, and scripture verses that are taken from the Psalms.

Prayer Forms

Prayer forms include the Lord's Prayer, extemporaneous prayers by the worship leader(s), a pastoral prayer, and prayers of the people offered up by individuals within the congregation. The posture of prayer is either sitting or standing.

Creeds

The Apostles' Creed is recited every week during worship.

Music

Three hymns are sung each week from the hymnal of the Lao Evangelical Church which is published in Laos. Included in this hymnal are both western hymns that are translated into Lao and hymns utilizing Lao tunes and lyrics.

The piano and organ are the most common instruments used to accompany the hymns. On certain occasions (Christmas, Thanksgiving, Lao New Year), modern guitars and drums may also be used for special music. It is common for the congregation to clap as a sign of their appreciation for soloists and choir anthems.

Scripture Readings

Two scripture passages are read each Sunday by a lay liturgist: one from the Old Testament and one from the New Testament. In addition, a Psalm text, which is taken from the Psalter printed in the Lao hymnal, is read responsively between the worship leader and the congregation.

Preaching

The sermon is usually placed in the middle of the worship service and lasts between twenty and thirty minutes. It is seen by the congregation as the most important part of the liturgy. Sermons tend to be topical. The pastor chooses the topic first and then identifies a scripture passage that speaks to the topic.

The use of humor is appropriate in preaching but one of the most important ingredients are stories and illustrations from Laos. Good eye contact is also crucial, but it is acceptable to use an outline or notes to guide one through the delivery of the sermon. The congregation does expect that the sermon will have a tight conclusion. It is not appropriate to leave a sermon open-ended.

Participatory forms of preaching are not very common in Laotian-American churches. Occasionally the pastor asks a question during the sermon with the expectation that people will verbally answer it, or the pastor asks the congregation to turn in their Bibles to a particular text and read it aloud.

Passing of the Peace
This ritual is common in Laotian-American congregations.

Benediction
Usually ordained clergy pronounce the benediction (unless no one ordained is present). The pastor stands in the front of the congregation with eyes closed and hands positioned in a posture of prayer. The congregation receives the benediction standing with their eyes closed as well.

Sacramental Practices

Sacrament of Baptism
The most common age of baptism in Laotian-American churches is adolescence (influenced by the Christian Missionary Alliance church, which was the primary protestant denomination in Laos until 1960 when the independent Lao Evangelical church was formed), although membership in The United Methodist Church does not preclude infant baptism. It is still rare, however, for parents to present their child for infant baptism. Usually when an infant is born, there is a service of dedication where the parents present the infant to God and promise to raise the child in a Christian home until the child decides to become baptized. Once a child has reached the age of twelve, he or she may request baptism.

After four weeks of preparation, the community gathers at a river or lake for baptism by immersion which is the most common form of baptism. Occasionally the congregation borrows the facilities of a church that has a baptistery. When the people gather by a river or lake, the service includes singing, scripture reading, a sermon, and prayers for the candidate. There is no formal liturgy that is followed. The pastor asks several questions of the ones being baptized as they proclaim their faith. The person is immersed once while the pastor recites the *tradi-*

tional baptismal formula. Occasionally, persons are also anointed with oil on their forehead in the sign of the cross. After the baptism, the person is presented with a baptismal certificate.

Confirmation

Since the majority of Lao are not baptized until they are twelve years of age or older, there is no need for confirmation.

Sacrament of Holy Communion

"Holy Communion" is the most common term used to identify this sacrament. It is celebrated once a month after the sermon. The elements, understood by the congregation to be symbols of Christ's grace and redemption, are a loaf of bread and individual cups of grape juice or sometimes one cup is used. They are covered until the appropriate time in the liturgy.

There is no formal liturgy that is used to celebrate Holy Communion. The pastor offers words about communion and prays extemporaneously. The bread is broken as the *Words of Institution* are given, then the elements are blessed.

The most common form of distribution is to pass the elements to the people sitting in the pew (another influence of the Christian Missionary Alliance denomination). When this is done, the pastor partakes simultaneously with the congregation. Occasionally, the congregation gathers in a circle around the altar for communion. The pastor then partakes after the congregation has communed. The elements are distributed with the words "This is the body and blood of our Lord Jesus Christ given for you."

Communion is reserved for the baptized only which means that since infants are not usually baptized, only those twelve years of age and older take communion.

Rituals of Passage

Weddings

In America today, "arranged marriages" are still practiced in some families. The parents choose a spouse for their son or daughter, ask for his or her consent, make the arrangements with the other family, and set the day and time for the wedding. In other families, the son or daughter takes the initiative to choose his or her future spouse and asks the parents for their approval. If the parents give their permission, the parents then take responsibility for making the arrangements with the other family and negotiating the day and time of the wedding. The "arrangement" is usually made three months to a year before the wedding is to take place. While arranged marriages may still be practiced, there is usually no dowry involved in weddings in the United States. Both families share the costs of the wedding and reception.

Once all the agreements have been made, there is an engagement ritual that makes the formal announcement to the community. During the engagement ritual, the pastor presides and offers prayers for the couple and their families, reads scripture, preaches a sermon, exacts vows from the bride and groom, and facilitates the gift giving that is an integral part of the ritual. The bride and groom vow to keep themselves chaste until the wedding night and to eventually be bound together in marriage. The groom gives the engagement ring to the bride and gifts are given to the bride's parents. After the ritual, food is served and a party ensues.

Between the engagement ritual and the wedding, the pastor meets with the bride and groom a couple of times in preparation for the ceremony. The wedding almost always takes place at the church.

On the day of the wedding, the bride and groom are dressed in a white wedding gown and tuxedo respectively or traditional Lao dress. Bridesmaids, ushers, flower girl, and ring bearer are all possible attendants for the bride and groom. The groom and his attendants enter from the side at the front of the church and take their places. The bride's attendants process down the aisle followed by the bride who is escorted by her father. The music "The Wedding March" usually accompanies the procession.

The wedding includes hymns, scripture reading, sometimes a sermon, prayers for the couple, the exchange of vows and rings and the pronouncement that the bride and groom are now husband and wife. Special Lao music may be sung during the ceremony. In addition, lighting the Unity Candle is becoming more and more popular in Lao-American weddings. The acolyte usually lights the outer candles before the service begins. At the end of the ceremony, the father of the bride thanks the people for coming and invites them to the reception.

The bridal party formally greet their guests at a receiving line at the reception which usually takes place at the church or in a larger hall. The minister is expected to attend the reception and offer the prayer before the food is served. The reception includes food, music, occasionally dancing, words of blessing and hope for the couple, and cutting the wedding cake. The bride throws her bouquet over her shoulder to unmarried women and the groom throws the bride's garter over his shoulder to unmarried men.

After the reception, the couple and their families go back to either the groom's parents' home or the bride's parents' home for the "forgiveness ceremony." This is a ritual performed by the bride and groom before their elders according to rank. The bride and groom present a flower to each of their elders as a symbol of respect and thanksgiving for his or her influence on each of their lives. The couple asks their forgiveness for whatever wrongs they have committed against them. Kneeling on the floor with hands near their face in a "praying hands" position, the bride and groom bow to the floor before each elder. After the "forgiveness ceremony," the couple leaves for their honeymoon.

Funerals

Once the pastor has been informed that someone from the community has died, the pastor goes immediately to the family's home to pray with them. Friends and family also gather at the home and a prayer service is conducted. The service includes singing, praying, reading scripture, and preaching. The guests bring flowers and gifts to the family.

The pastor then helps the family make the funeral arrangements. If the family was associated with other churches (even other denominations), it is common to invite the pastors to participate in the funeral service.

A viewing of the body takes place at the church or the funeral home one or two nights before the funeral. The casket is surrounded by flowers, candles, and a picture(s) of the deceased. During the time of viewing, the pastor is expected to be present and offer prayer for the family and the community gathered.

The funeral service takes place at the church or the funeral home. If the funeral is in the church, the casket is moved to the front of the sanctuary with a procession led by the pastor followed by the pallbearers carrying the casket, then the family. Once in place, the casket is opened for a final viewing of the body. When it is time to begin the funeral service, the casket is closed.

The funeral includes singing, scripture reading, prayers, and a sermon. The family chooses at least one person to speak about the life of the deceased. After the service, there is a car procession to the cemetery and another procession from the hearse to the grave site. Burial is the common practice in the Lao Christian community since cremation is commonly associated with Buddhist practice. However, pastors may go along with the wishes of the family if they strongly advocate for cremation.

The grave site service is mostly comprised of scripture reading and prayers. Occasionally a short sermon and singing are also included. At the time in the liturgy where the text "ashes to ashes, dust to dust" is quoted, dirt is thrown on the casket by the pastor first, then the family, then by everyone. Sometimes people also put a flower on the casket after the service has ended. The people stay at the grave site until the groundskeepers at the cemetery have lowered the casket and filled in the grave. After the grave site service, there is a reception at the family's home or at the church.

It is very common for the family to ask the pastor to preside over a memorial service in their home on the first-year anniversary of their loved one's death. This memorial service includes singing, scripture reading, prayers, and a sermon. Services on subsequent anniversaries may also be requested.

LIBERIAN-AMERICAN WORSHIP PRACTICES

with Rev. Dr. Daniel Grimes Gueh

The Service of the Word

The Language of the Liturgy

While there are twenty-eight official tribal languages in Liberia, English is the common language of the country. In America, most of the worship service is conducted in English, although gospel songs may be sung in the language of *Bassa, Kpelle,* or *Kru.* The choir anthem may be sung in any African language, not just those found in Liberia. While the sermon is preached in English, when the need arises, the sermon may also be translated into one of the four most common tribal languages represented in the congregation: *Bassa, Kpelle, Kru,* or *Kissi* (sometimes spelled Kisi).

The Liturgical Space

The sanctuary space may have symbols of the Liberian culture present. The most common symbols are the Liberian flag, drums and other instruments from the culture, and the pastor's stole made from *kente* cloth. Several members of the congregation wear African dress for worship.

Liturgical Time

Worship services last between two and three hours in Liberian-American churches.

Liturgical Garb

The pastor usually wears a pulpit robe in either white, gray, or black with stoles made from *kente* cloth.

Liturgical Seasons and Days

All the seasons of the church year are celebrated. During Holy Week there are services every evening. The Sunday after Thanksgiving is called Harvest Sunday and members of the congregation bring representations of their "first fruits": money, fruit, vegetables, canned goods, and boxed food. The food is then distributed to those in need.

On Mother's Day the women lead the service. On Father's Day the men lead the service, and on Children's Day (third Sunday in June), the children lead the service. A special service in the life of the community is the New Year's Eve Watch Night service. This service lasts about four hours and includes two sermons/speakers, much music, and lay testimony. Revival meetings may be held the two nights prior to the Watch Night service.

In addition, July 26 is honored as Liberian Independence Day. On or around American Memorial Day (last Monday in May), the Liberian-American church has a Day of Remembrance offering prayers for those who died in the Civil War in Liberia.

Beginning Our Praise to God

The opening Call to Worship based on various scripture passages, is printed in the bulletin and read responsively between the congregation and either the pastor or a lay liturgist.

Prayer Forms

Prayer forms in Liberian-American churches include: extemporaneous prayers by the pastor and lay worship leaders, a collect, bidding prayers, a pastoral prayer, which often includes themes of confession, and the Lord's Prayer. The Lord's Prayer may be recited in unison or chanted. Occasionally prayers of the people offered individually from the congregation are incorporated into the pastoral prayer. While the pastor is praying, members of the congregation call out words and phrases of affirmation.

At some point during the service the pastor offers an invitation for those who need prayer to come and kneel at the altar rail. As the people pray silently, the pastor may walk along the altar rail and lay hands on their heads or the pastor may stay in the pulpit and gesture in their direction. A general prayer is offered for all who are kneeling before they return to their seats.

During mid-week prayer meetings, another form of prayer (referred to as Pentecostal prayer) is used. Simultaneously, persons pray their individual prayers aloud in their native language. A cacophony of voices in various languages fills the room during this time of intercessory prayer. A flask of oil is present during the mid-week prayer meetings to use whenever the need arises for prayers for healing. The posture of prayer is sitting or kneeling.

Creeds

A creed is usually recited on Communion Sundays.

Music

Three to five hymns are sung each week in addition to several gospel songs. The hymns are taken from *The United Methodist Hymnal*. The gospel songs may be sung in one of the tribal languages. No hymnbook is used for these songs; the people know them by memory. The organ or piano (and occasionally drums) accompany the hymns. Drums, tambourines, guitars, shakers made from gourds known as *sasa*, and other instruments from Liberia are used to accompany the songs. When the choir sings these songs of praise, they may move out of the choir loft and dance up and down the aisles greeting people as they go. It is common for the congregation to join in the singing, clap, and move to the music while standing at their seat.

Clapping and saying "Amen" are all appropriate responses to soloists and choir anthems.

Offering

In Liberia, it is traditional for members of the congregation to "dance" their offerings to the altar. In America, however, this practice may be eliminated in order to save time. It is common for churches to collect two offerings every Sunday. The regular offering takes place early in the service. After the sermon, a benevolent offering is collected to assist in the emergency needs of the community. In addition, the children may take up a collection to support their activities and Sunday school.

Scripture Readings

An Old Testament and a New Testament passage is read each week by lay liturgists. The congregation stands for the reading of the Gospel lesson. In addition, a Psalm text may be read responsively between the worship leader and the congregation.

Preaching

Sermons usually last twenty to thirty minutes. The sermon is placed at the end of the service and is seen by the congregation to be the most important part of worship.

The pastor usually consults the lectionary in choosing texts for the basis of the sermon. Sermons tend to be topical in nature. Stories and illustrations are often taken from the history, folktales, and life context of Liberia as well as the issues facing Liberians in America today.

The congregation appreciates the use of humor in preaching. They also prefer the pastor to preach without any notes and to move out of the pulpit and into the congregation as a sign of being inspired by the Holy Spirit. A passionate, emotional tone of delivery is more acceptable than an intellectual approach.

Various forms of participatory preaching are practiced in the Liberian-American church. In affirmation of what the pastor is saying, people may shout out "Amen" or other phrases; individuals may stand and call out encouragement, then sit down; or persons may clap. Occasionally the pastor may ask the congregation to turn in the Bible to a particular text and read it aloud.

Passing of the Peace

The Passing of the Peace is practiced every week.

Benediction

At the end of worship, the congregation may join hands and raise them in a closing song. While still holding hands, the pastor pronounces the benediction. The congregation is standing with their eyes closed.

Sacramental Practices

Sacrament of Baptism

The most common age for baptism in Liberian-American churches is infancy. Occasionally adults request to be baptized. Baptisms take place whenever the need arises. Infants are baptized during Sunday morning worship through the method of sprinkling. Adults may be baptized in the church by sprinkling or at a lake, river, or ocean for immersion.

It is common for parents to choose several Christian godparents for their infant. The church provides sponsors from the congregation for adults who are baptized. The sponsors stand with the person being baptized and follow through on their Christian nurture during the months that follow.

Before the baptism, the pastor meets with the parents or adult being baptized at least once. The Sunday before the baptism, the parents of the infant or the adult being baptized testify to their faith during worship.

On the day of the baptism, the water is poured into a bowl before the service begins. During the baptism, an assistant pastor or a lay leader holds the bowl for the pastor. The baptismal liturgy is taken from *the United Methodist Hymnal* or *Book of Worship*.

The water is sprinkled on the person's head three times with the *traditional baptismal formula*. The pastor then walks the infant down the aisle of the church to introduce the newest member to the congregation. A baptismal certificate is given to the parents or the adult being baptized.

Confirmation

Confirmation classes are common in Liberian-American churches for youth ages ten and up. The preparation period usually lasts seven weeks and confirmation may take place on any Communion Sunday.

Sacrament of Holy Communion

"Holy Communion" is the most common term used to name this sacrament. It is celebrated on the first Sunday of every month after the sermon. The altar may be covered with a white cloth or African *kente* cloth.

Wafers and individual cups of grape juice are distributed to the congregation as they kneel at the altar rail. On Holy Thursday, a common loaf and one chalice are used instead. The elements are understood by the congregation to be symbols of Christ's real presence among us. They are covered until the appropriate time in the liturgy.

The liturgy used is usually the shortened version of the Great Thanksgiving with responses by the laity taken from The United Methodist Hymnal. The wafer is broken at the end of the Great Thanksgiving. Only clergy are permitted to consecrate the elements

171

but lay leaders may assist in leading other parts of the Great Thanksgiving. Laity participate in distributing the elements.

Clergy and lay assistants partake before the congregation communes. The elements are distributed with the words "This is the body and blood of our Lord Jesus Christ given for you."

Persons who are not baptized are discouraged from taking communion. However, if unbaptized individuals come forward, the sacrament is not withheld from them.

Rituals of Passage

Weddings

Several months before the wedding, Liberian-American couples participate in an engagement ritual at the bride's family's home. The groom's family is situated on one side of the room and the bride's family on the other side.

The pastor leads the ritual, which includes the reading of scripture, words about the significance of the engagement period, prayers for the couple, and a blessing of the engagement ring. Before the ceremony begins, the groom gives the ring to the pastor. After the pastor blesses the ring, the pastor gives the ring to the groom who then puts it on the ring finger of the bride's left hand. The bride offers her own words of acceptance and confirmation of the engagement. Following the ring ceremony, members of either family may speak words of advice and blessing to the couple. When the ritual is finished, food is served and a party ensues.

Between the engagement ritual and the wedding, the pastor meets with the couple twice. It is acceptable to marry persons who are divorced. Depending on the situation, more premarital counseling sessions may be recommended.

A week before the wedding, women family members and friends gather with the bride for a wedding shower. They offer her words of advice from their own experiences of married life, give gifts to the bride, and share food with one another.

The night before the wedding is known as the "bachelor eve." Male family members and friends gather with the groom for an evening of fun and laughter. The minister is often invited and if present, is expected to offer prayer for the groom's future life. The wedding usually takes place in the church.

The bride may be in a white wedding gown and the groom in a tuxedo, or they may choose to wear African dress. Bridesmaids, ushers, flower girl, and ring bearer serve as attendants to the bride and groom. The bride is escorted down the aisle by her father or closest male relative present. The "Wedding March" or traditional African drumming may accompany the procession.

The wedding ceremony includes scripture reading, music, a short sermon, prayers for the couple, the exchange of vows and rings, and the pronouncement that the couple is now husband and wife. Depending on the tribal tradition, the couple may share a *kola nut* before the pronouncement. The *kola nut* is very bitter but when one chews it and drinks water, it turns sweet. It symbolizes the reality of married life that can be both bitter and sweet.

Lighting the Unity Candle is becoming more common in Liberian-American weddings. When the Unity Candle is used, a representative of the bride's family and a representative of the groom's family light the outer candles.

In some weddings, the bride and groom pay respect to their parents. Often the bride pins a corsage on the groom's mother and the groom pins one on the bride's mother.

After the wedding, family and friends greet the couple in a receiving line at the place of the reception. After everyone is seated, the pastor offers a prayer before the meal is served. The reception includes words of blessing and hope for the couple, modern and traditional Liberian dancing, and the cutting of the wedding cake. Often the bride throws her bouquet over her shoulder to unmarried women and the groom throws the bride's garter over his shoulder to unmarried men.

Depending on the couple's tribal background, the sharing of the *kola nut* may take place at the reception. If the nut is shared at the reception, the couple eats the nut to further symbolize the experience of the bitter becoming sweet.

Funerals

Between the day of death and the day of the funeral (usually on Saturday), the pastor goes to the family's home every evening for an informal prayer service. Friends and family gather for prayer, singing, the reading of scripture, and a short meditation. Clergy from other churches may be invited to participate in the prayer services, *wake keeping*, and funeral service. The family decides who will preach the funeral sermon.

On Friday evening, people gather at the funeral home or the church for the *wake keeping*. The *wake keeping* begins with the viewing of the body. The casket is surrounded by flowers, candles, and a picture of the deceased. Occasionally, a Bible is placed in the casket with the body. The casket may remain open for the service.

During the *wake keeping*, scripture is read, a sermon is preached, prayers are offered, and songs are sung. Anyone present may stand and offer a tribute to the deceased. The service lasts until midnight. At the end, people approach the casket to pay their last respects. The family likewise, says their final farewell at the end of the *wake keeping*. After the wake, family and close friends go back to the family's home. Food is served, people share stories about the deceased, prayers are offered, and many traditional tribal songs are sung. This continues until the wee hours of the morning.

Before the funeral service, the pastor goes to the family's home and accompanies them to the funeral home. They then accompany the casket to the church. At the church, the pastor leads a procession from the hearse to the front of the church. Following the pastor are the pall bearers carrying the casket, then the family.

The funeral service consists of scripture reading, hymns, prayers, sermon, and many traditional songs. The family may choose one or two persons to read the obituary and pay tribute to the life of the deceased. The casket is closed during the service.

After the funeral, the pastor leads the procession out of the church, placing the casket in the hearse. A procession of cars follows the hearse to the cemetery. At the cemetery, the pastor leads the procession to the grave site. The grave site service is short with the singing of a hymn, a prayer, and the committal of the body to the earth. When the pastor says "ashes to ashes, dust to dust," the funeral director places a flower on the casket. After the service, everyone lays a flower on the casket.

The Liberian Christian tradition is to wait until the grave is filled in before people leave. In America, it seems more rushed. People may stay until the casket is lowered into the grave but leave before the dirt is filled in.

After the committal service, there is a *repast* at the church hall or the family's home. The minister is expected to offer the prayer before the food is served. Memorial services may be held in America for family who have died in Liberia.

There are no special services that mark the anniversary of someone's death. However, on the Sunday closest to the anniversary, family members often place flowers on the altar and a prayer of remembrance is offered during the worship service.

NATIVE AMERICAN WORSHIP PRACTICES

with Rev. Marvin B. Abrams

The Service of the Word

The Language of the Liturgy

While the members of some Native American churches are primarily of persons from one tribe who speak a common tribal language, most Native American churches are multitribal, including persons from many tribes within a single congregation. In these churches songs may be sung in various native languages and prayers may be offered by individuals in their native tongue. However, the major language of the liturgy is usually English. Occasionally, the sermon may be bilingual, using English and the most common native language represented in the congregation.

Because of the number of tribes (some 557) with a variety of language families, it is impossible to name the various words for God and Jesus. Since many of the languages do not have an exact translation for God, God is named in many ways: Great Spirit, Great Mystery of Life, Maker and Giver of Life, Manitou, and so on.

The Liturgical Space

Some churches have symbols from Native American cultures visible at every worship gathering: banners with images or symbols and elements of the earth (flowers, plants, trees). Others use particular symbols on certain Sundays or occasions: an eagle's feather and sage, cedar or sweet grass for blessings, Native American blankets draped on the altar, a prayer pipe (some call it a "peace pipe" but this is in error for it is used in prayer ceremonies), flags from various tribes represented in the congregation, or a circular object representing the Circle of Life, which is reminiscent of the Native American Medicine Wheel or Hoop.

Some Native American clergy prefer a worship design that creates a circle, with the communion table in the center. However, since many

Native American congregations share the facilities of another congregation, they usually do not have control over the architecture or worship space.

Liturgical Time

Most Sunday morning worship services last between one and one and a half hours. In some congregations, chronological time that is determined by the clock does not dictate when worship begins and ends. The service begins when it is the "right time"—when everyone has gathered and all is ready. Worship ends when the community feels that they have fully expressed their praise to God.

Liturgical Garb

Many Native American clergy do not wear any liturgical garb. Some choose to wear a robe or alb. On special occasions, clergy may wear traditional tribal dress. Several clergy wear stoles that are beaded in the Native American style.

In a few churches, acolytes and children's choirs wear traditional tribal dress.

Liturgical Seasons and Days

Some churches celebrate all the seasons of the liturgical year while others focus mainly on Christmas, Holy Week and Easter. Thanksgiving and the Celebration of the Christian Home (Mother's Day and Father's Day combined) are also frequently honored.

The second Sunday after Easter is Native American Awareness Sunday within The United Methodist Church. It is a day of celebration and festivities in most Native American churches.

Beginning Our Praise to God

In some churches, worship begins with singing several Native American songs of praise to God. The opening words or Call to Worship are often based on scripture verses.

On certain occasions, the Native American tradition of praying to the four directions (north, south, east, and west) or the seven directions (north, south, east, west, up toward the heavens, down toward the earth, and inward to our heart/soul) is observed.

177

There is a variety of understandings for these prayers. In praying to the four directions, the petitioner may ask God to care/heal/comfort members of the family living in that direction. Others may pray to the four directions but also pray to God and then to Mother Earth, thanking God for care and nurture. There may be the addition of the seventh direction, praying for inner strength, healing, or guidance.

Prayer Forms

Prayer forms in the Native American tradition include: the Lord's Prayer, extemporaneous prayers by the pastor and lay liturgists, pastoral prayer, prayer songs, and prayers of joys and concerns offered aloud by individuals within the congregation. Some churches also include a prayer of confession weekly or on communion Sundays.

Guided prayer sessions are a part of the prayer life of some churches with prayers offered in silence or corporately. During prayer meetings and in some worship services, a type of intercessory prayer is offered. The pastor or worship leader asks the congregation to focus on specific or general concerns of the community and the people pray their individual prayers aloud simultaneously. The posture of prayer may be sitting, standing, or kneeling.

In long-standing Native American churches, bulletins may not be used. Most newer congregations have bulletins that include the order of worship and occasionally printed corporate prayers.

Blessings

In many Native American churches, *smudging* is used for blessing and healing. This ritual is often used to bless persons but may also be used to bless homes. A large abalone shell is used to hold dried sweet grass, cedar, or sage. This is lit by fire and then blown out creating smoke. The smoke is a visible symbol of prayer. The pastor or worship leader uses a feather to brush the smoke toward the person. The person receiving the blessing or prayer for healing stands with palms open and assists in enveloping the smoke around him or her.

The sweet grass, cedar, or sage, abalone shell, and feather are symbols of the gifts of the earth given by our Creator God. The smoke is a visible and olfactory sign of God's presence and grace infusing our lives.

Creeds

Each church decides whether or not to include a creed in worship. For those churches who do recite a creed, a wide variety of creeds are used in addition to the Apostles' Creed.

Music

The United Methodist Hymnal, Voices (A United Methodist Native American hymnal and worship resource, published by Discipleship Resources), and songbooks that are collections of Native American songs developed by individual congregations and missionaries are used in worship. Three or four hymns in addition to several Native American songs may be sung each week. Tribal music may be lined out (someone sings a line, then the congregation repeats it, etc.).

The piano is the most common musical instrument used to accompany the hymns. Some churches may use an organ or guitar. Native American drums and flutes may also be played on certain occasions.

Though not traditional, some Native American churches include drama, liturgical dance, or cultural dance forms during worship for special occasions.

Responses to choir anthems and soloists vary. Some congregations prefer silence, others applaud as a sign of appreciation. Still others may say "Amen" in English or any one of the tribal languages.

Scripture Readings

The number of scripture passages read each Sunday varies from church to church. Some include an Old Testament and a New Testament reading, while others include all four lessons from the lectionary.

In most churches the pastor or lay liturgist reads the scripture texts. Occasionally the text is read collectively or read responsively (verse by verse) between the worship leader and the congregation. Most Psalm texts are read responsively.

Preaching

Sermons in Native American churches usually last between fifteen and thirty minutes. Sermon structure and style vary. Many pastors consult the lectionary each week, but the texts suggested in the lectionary are not always used.

179

Storytelling is expected, humor is appropriate, and leaving the sermon open ended is acceptable. Most clergy use stories and illustrations from Native American sources.

Various forms of participatory preaching are included in Native American churches. Some pastors ask a question during the sermon and persons within the congregation provide the answer. Other pastors may ask the congregation to turn to a particular text in the Bible and read it aloud. Occasionally pastors shorten their sermon and provide time during worship for members of the congregation to offer their insights and responses to the text or topic of the sermon. Some churches have a feedback time after the service where people discuss the text and/or theme of the sermon. Other churches discuss the texts for the sermon the week before during Bible study. The questions, concerns, insights and issues raised by the members are then incorporated into the sermon on Sunday.

In some congregations, skilled Native American storytellers find stories from various Native American tribes that apply to the text or theme of the sermon and tell these stories to the children before the sermon. These stories provide a cultural base for the lessons learned in scripture.

Passing of the Peace

Those churches that include the passing of the peace in their worship may have the congregation gather in a circle for this ritual.

Benediction

In the Native American tradition, anyone can offer the benediction. It is not reserved for ordained clergy only. Some may raise one or two hands in a gesture of blessing. Both the pastor and the congregation usually stand with their eyes open.

Pow-Wows

A pow-wow has social, cultural, and religious value among Native Americans. It demonstrates the traditional dances and songs of most of the pow-wow tribes in all parts of the United States. To some it may seem like entertainment. However, the drumming, singing, and dancing are reenactments of certain spiritual and symbolic aspects of Native American heritage. It instills a sense of cultural pride and a spirit of community.

The protocol of the pow-wow is very specific. The outside arena is set up in a circle with a central drum. To many, the drum is seen as the "heartbeat" of the people and as such, is looked upon with respect, humility, and dignity. Pastors may be asked to offer the opening prayer or invocation as the *pow-wow* begins.

Sacramental Practices

Sacrament of Baptism

Infants, youth, and adults are baptized within the Native American tradition whenever the need arises. While most baptisms take place during worship, some churches allow baptisms to take place anywhere, at any time. The pastor usually meets with the person (or parents) requesting baptism at least once in preparation for the sacrament.

If the family chooses godparents who are not Christian for their infant, the godparents are not involved in the baptismal counseling or the vow section of the liturgy. When Christian godparents are chosen, or when sponsors from the congregation are used for adults being baptized, the godparents and sponsors are sometimes involved in the baptismal liturgy.

No particular clothing is common for those involved in the baptismal ceremony. Some persons being baptized wear white, others may wear traditional tribal dress, and still others wear no special dress for the occasion.

Baptismal methods of sprinkling, pouring, and immersion are all practiced. When sprinkling or pouring is used, the water is often in a bowl or a large shell that is held by a lay leader rather than in a baptismal font. The water may be poured into the bowl or shell before the service begins or some churches pour the water from a pitcher during the liturgy. A few pastors dip an eagle's feather into the water and then shake/sprinkle the water onto the person's head.

The structure of the baptismal liturgy varies. Many clergy use no formal liturgy. The purpose of baptism, the questions asked of the candidate (or the parents), and prayers are all given extemporaneously. Others may use a printed liturgy throughout, while others ask a predetermined set of questions but lead the rest of the liturgy extemporaneously. Most include a blessing of the water during the liturgy.

181

The person is usually baptized with the *traditional baptismal formula*. Each pastor decides whether to sprinkle or pour the water on the person's head once or three times. Some clergy also make the sign of the cross on the person's forehead with the baptismal water.

When an infant is baptized, a tribal naming ceremony may also accompany the baptism. This naming ceremony may be done within worship simultaneously with baptism or it may take place outside the church on another day. If the tribal naming ceremony takes place within worship, an elder from the particular tribe may come in traditional dress and give the tribal name to the infant being baptized. The tribal name is explained and both the Christian and tribal names are used during the baptism.

Adults who are baptized may share their experience of conversion with the congregation before the baptism. he person being baptized is given a baptismal certificate and sometimes a Bible, rose, or other symbol to mark the occasion.

Occasionally, persons who were baptized as infants experience a conversion experience as an adult and request to be rebaptized. T

Confirmation

Confirmation varies within Native American churches. Some do not have confirmation at all. Others follow the confirmation format and style advocated by the denomination (around twelve weeks of preparation for youth ages twelve and above). Still others offer a time of preparation for youth and/or adults who wish to join the church or make a public proclamation of their faith, but the structure is unique to their context.

Sacrament of Holy Communion

A wide variety of terms are used to name this sacrament of the church: "Communion," "Holy Communion," "Lord's Supper," "Eucharist," and "Great Thanksgiving." Most celebrate communion once a month although some churches celebrate it quarterly. Liturgically, communion comes after the sermon in response to the word. In several Native American congregations, laity are permitted to assist in both the celebration of communion as well as the distribution of the elements.

182

Persons who are not baptized are often allowed to take communion although some clergy are criticized for this practice. In most churches parents decide when they feel their child is ready to commune.

The communion table may be covered by a Pendleton blanket with a Native American design, or other Native American weavings. The elements are usually covered until the appropriate time in the liturgy.

Most clergy use some shortened version of a formal Great Thanksgiving as the communion liturgy, including the *Words of Institution*. Some also include a consecration of the elements. Other clergy say the *Words of Institution* but offer words about the meaning of communion and pray extemporaneously with no other formal liturgy.

A loaf of bread and grape juice are the most common elements used. Some serve the grape juice in a chalice while other congregations use the individual cups. Occasionally unleavened bread or Native American fry bread is used.

The elements are distributed to the congregation in a variety of ways. Some kneel at the altar, others stand in a circle around the altar and pass the bread and the cup to one another, while still others receive the elements while sitting in the pew. When one cup is used, the method of partaking is *intinction*. Many clergy distribute the elements with the words "This is the body and blood of our Lord Jesus Christ." Others, however, use alternative language that is appropriate for the occasion or that is particular to an individual's needs.

In some Native American congregations, the elements remaining after communion are often given back to the earth. The bread is scattered to the birds, and the juice is poured back into the earth. In a few congregations, this action is ritualized. The people move outside and form a circle. The pastor commits the elements to care for the earth and calls on the people to likewise care for the earth and its peoples. The juice is then poured on the ground and the bread broken up and scattered for the birds.

Rituals of Passage

Give-Aways

In the Native American community, various rites of passage are marked by the practice of the "give-away." At baptism, birthdays, graduations, retirements, weddings, and funerals, instead of the person being honored receiving gifts (as in the Western tradition), the person gives gifts to others. People collect blankets and shawls as gifts (along with food) to be given away at these times of celebration and passage. These items are given to people as a symbol of honor and thanksgiving. Give-aways may take place at pow-wows, wedding receptions, the reception after a funeral, or at the mourning pow-wow which takes place on the first anniversary of someone's death. The appropriate times and events for give-aways are determined by the various tribal practices.

Weddings

Weddings may take place in the church, at someone's home, in a hotel, or a garden setting. Many ceremonies are held outdoors in the midst of God's creation. The pastor usually meets with the couple at least once in preparation for the ceremony. It is acceptable to marry persons who have been divorced.

There is no common dress for weddings. A white wedding gown and tuxedo, a white traditional buckskin dress, or many other combinations of modern and traditional clothing are all possible.

Bridesmaids, ushers, flower girl, and ring bearer serve as attendants for the bride and groom. Often the bride is escorted down the aisle by either her father (or father-figure) or by both parents. Occasionally, the groom or the bride's best friend serve as her escort. The processional music varies greatly. The "Wedding March," traditional drumming, classical music, recorded music, native songs, and Native American flutes are all common.

Smudging may be included in the wedding ceremony at the beginning to bless the space or at the end to bless the newly married couple. Sometimes a traditional blessing (which is different for each tribe) is given to the couple.

The ceremony includes singing of hymns and Native American songs, reading of scripture, prayers for the couple, the exchange of vows, and the pronouncement that the couple is now husband and wife. Usually rings are exchanged as well. When the Unity Candle is used, the bride and groom or people chosen by the couple light the outer candles. Some couples choose to pay respect to their parents by presenting them with roses or giving them kisses. After the pronouncement, a Native American blanket may be wrapped around the couple as a sign of their new union. Occasionally, leather thongs with feathers on them may also be wrapped around the wrists of the couple while they join hands.

After the wedding, the couple greet their guests formally at the back of the church (if held in the church) or at the wedding reception.

The reception may be held in the church hall, at a hotel, or other hall. The food may be an informal array of finger food or a formal catered meal. Clergy are often expected to attend the reception and offer the prayer before the meal.

Most receptions include words of blessing and hope for the couple, the bride throws her bouquet over her shoulder to unmarried women, the groom throws the bride's garter over his shoulder to unmarried men, and the couple cuts the wedding cake. Some receptions also include modern dancing, traditional dancing, and drumming. Occasionally, a money dance is included during which people place money in the clothing of the bride or groom in payment for a dance.

Funerals

Because there are literally hundreds of tribes in the United States with their own cultural practices surrounding funerals, the following descriptions are not in any way universal or exhaustive. Each pastor needs to find out from the individuals involved what is expected of the pastor and what tribal traditions the family wants to include.

Between death and the funeral service, there is often a viewing of the body. Sometimes this takes place at the funeral home on the evenings before the funeral. In other tribes, the open casket is at the family's home until the funeral service. Friends and extended family pay their respects to the family and view the body in the home. In some traditions, people keep a twenty-four hour vigil of the body. Members of the tribe often bring meals to the family during the days before the funeral.

Some tribes have a prayer service the night before the funeral. This may take place at the family's home, at the church, or at the funeral home. The prayer service often lasts about two hours and includes singing, prayers, scripture, a short meditation, and witnessing about the life of the deceased. Occasionally a choir sings or a group plays traditional music. The casket is open for viewing during this time. If someone of rank is present from the tribe, other tribal traditions may also take place on this occasion.

On the day of the funeral, the pastor is sometimes expected to pray with the family in their home and escort them to the place of the funeral. The funeral may take place at the church or at the funeral home. If the body has been at the home since death, there may be a procession from the family's home to the church for the funeral.

The family decides whether the casket is open or closed for the service. The practice varies from tribe to tribe. The body may be dressed in tribal clothes. The casket is surrounded by flowers and/or blankets, items of importance to the deceased, a picture of the deceased, and sometimes candles. Objects (e.g. a Bible, an eagle's feather) are occasionally placed in the coffin with the body. Shawls are often draped over the easels/flowerstands in place of flowers.

If the funeral service takes place in the church, there may be a procession of the casket from the back of the church to the front. The service lasts about an hour and includes singing, scripture reading, a sermon, and prayers. Often everyone present is given a chance to share memories of the deceased. Tribal religious leaders (non-Christian) may participate in some parts of the funeral.

After the funeral service, there may be a car procession to the cemetery and another procession from the hearse to the grave site. The grave site service is usually short with the reading of scripture, prayers, and a committal of the deceased to God (no sermon). Dirt or flowers may be placed on the casket during the service or immediately following. In some tribes, people remain at the grave site until the casket has been lowered and the grave is filled in.

After the service, there is often a meal at the church or at the family's home. In some tribal traditions, there is a service that marks the one-year anniversary of someone's death.

PAKISTANI-AMERICAN WORSHIP PRACTICES

with Rev. John N. David

The Service of the Word

The Language of the Liturgy

While there are several dialects spoken in Pakistan, *Urdu* is the common language of the country. Both *Punjabi* and *Urdu* are spoken by Christians in Pakistan and in the United States, but worship services in America are held in *Urdu*. Since *Urdu* is the common language, those who speak *Punjabi* also understand *Urdu*, but those whose native tongue is *Urdu* may not fully understand *Punjabi*.

In Pakistan as well as in the United States, there are no printed bulletins used in worship. Influenced by the Anglican Church of England during British occupation of India and Pakistan, the use of prayer books is more common than worship bulletins. Various liturgical elements from the prayer book of the Church of Pakistan (a union of Anglican, Methodist, Lutheran, and Presbyterian churches in Pakistan) are used in the United States.

The Liturgical Space

Since worship space is borrowed from other congregations, the sanctuary is devoid of any cultural symbols. The women in the congregation wear traditional Pakistani dress (*saris*) with shawls or scarfs covering their heads during worship. While the practice of women covering their head is common in Pakistani culture, Christians base this practice on the admonition from 1 Corinthians 11:5 and believe that when women cover their head, it is a sign of respect for the God they worship.

Liturgical Time

Weekly worship services last between one and one and a half hours.

187

Liturgical Garb

Most clergy wear a pulpit robe when leading worship.

Liturgical Seasons and Days

All the liturgical seasons of the year are celebrated. In addition, Christmas Eve, Mother's Day, Father's Day, and American Thanksgiving are also honored liturgically. On the Sunday closest to Pakistani Independence Day (August 14), special attention may be drawn to the Pakistani situation both in Pakistan and in the United States.

Holy Week receives special attention in Pakistani-American churches. Every night during Holy Week, the congregation gathers at different people's homes for worship. Shoes are left at the door, a white linen "sheet" is spread on the floor and the people sit for the worship services. On Holy Thursday (known in the Pakistani Christian community as the "Last Supper"), the people gather at the church for the sacrament of Holy Communion.

In Pakistan, after the Last Supper service, the people remove all the pews and benches, clean the mosaic floors and spread white linens on the floor in preparation for the three hour Good Friday service. In the United States, Pakistani-American congregations may join with other Christians for joint Good Friday services, or if possible, they remove the pews in the sanctuary, lay down white sheets and sit on the floor for their own Good Friday service. The Easter pageant that takes place between 3:30 a.m. and sunrise on Easter morning in Pakistan is not usually practiced in America.

Beginning Our Praise to God

Worship begins with an opening prayer, an opening hymn, and then a call to worship that is scripturally based and read responsively between the worship leader and the congregation.

Prayer Forms

Prayer forms in Pakistani-American churches include: the Lord's Prayer, extemporaneous prayers by the pastor and laypersons, corporate prayers of confession printed in the prayer book from the Church of Pakistan, and a pastoral prayer. In Pakistani-American churches there are no formal lay liturgists that assist in leading worship. At appropriate times in the liturgy, the pastor calls on someone from the congregation

188

to pray from their seat. After the sermon and before the pastoral prayer, people may come forward, kneel at the altar rail, and convey their individual prayer needs to the pastor. The pastor may include these prayer requests in the pastoral prayer. At the end of each prayer the congregation responds with a collective "Amen."

The posture of prayer is either sitting or kneeling.

Creeds

The Apostles' Creed is recited each week.

Music

Usually four hymns are sung during Sunday worship. The hymns come from the hymnal of the Church of Pakistan. Both the lyrics and the tunes are Pakistani in origin. The hymns are sung in unison by the congregation and are accompanied by the piano or organ. Tambourines and Pakistani drums called *tabla* may also be used for accompaniment, especially when Psalms are sung. There is no overt expression of response (e.g. clapping) to soloists or other musical offerings.

Scripture Readings

Three scripture readings are read each week: one from the Old Testament, one from the New Testament, and a Psalm text. The Bible translated into *Urdu* is the King James Version. The Psalm is read in unison by the congregation. The pastor reads either the Old Testament or New Testament lesson and without prior notice, calls on someone in the congregation to come to the lectern and read the other lesson. The lectionary is often consulted when choosing which texts to read each week. However, since sermons tend to be topical, the text chosen to support the topic of the sermon takes precedence over the lectionary lessons.

Preaching

While sermons last forty-five to sixty minutes in Pakistan, in America people prefer the pastor to preach between fifteen and thirty minutes. The sermon is in the middle of the service and is seen by the congregation to be the most important part of the liturgy.

Most often, the pastor chooses a topic first, then finds scripture to support the topic. Several scripture passages may be drawn upon during

189

the sermon. The tone of the delivery is usually pastoral although it may also be emotional or evangelical depending on the topic. The pastor draws upon Pakistani history and culture as well as personal experience and scripture for illustrations.

Humor is not appropriate in preaching in Pakistani-American churches. It is however, acceptable to end the sermon with a question. Tight conclusions are not expected. The congregation prefers the preacher to use some notes in the pulpit as a sign of being prepared.

No forms of participatory preaching are used in Pakistani-American churches although on occasion, the pastor may draw symbols on paper to support a point or illustration during the sermon.

Benediction

Only clergy are permitted to pronounce the benediction. The pastor stands in the front of the sanctuary with eyes closed and two hands raised in a gesture of blessing. The congregation, usually with eyes closed, stands to receive the benediction. After the benediction, the congregation is seated with heads bowed and eyes closed for a brief time of silent prayer.

Passing of the Peace

The ritual of Passing God's Peace to one another is common in Pakistani-American churches and takes place after the benediction. The women usually greet each other with the kiss of peace.

Blessings

Worship may also take place outside of church for a house blessing. When someone buys a new house, the congregation gathers at the home for worship. The house is blessed and the people celebrate with a feast.

Sacramental Practices

Sacrament of Baptism

Infancy is the most common age of baptism within Pakistani-American churches, although adolescents and adults occasionally request this sacrament. The baptisms take place during Sunday worship after the sermon unless there is an emergency situation whereby the pastor may baptize someone in the hospital. If an adolescent or adult is baptized, it is common for him or her to share their conversion experience with the congregation.

The baptism is scheduled upon request after two or three baptismal counseling sessions. If an infant is being baptized, the parents and godparents attend the counseling sessions. Godparents must be chosen from within the congregation. Often the person being baptized wears white clothing as a sign of purity.

Sprinkling is the only acceptable form of baptism. Immersion would never take place in Pakistani-American congregations. The water is poured into a bowl before the service begins. The baptismal liturgy comes from the Book of Worship of the Church of Pakistan and includes a blessing of the water, questions for the parents to answer, and prayers for the one being baptized.

During the baptism, a layperson holds the bowl of water while the pastor sprinkles water on the infant's head three times with the *traditional baptismal formula*. The pastor also makes the sign of the cross on the infant's forehead with the baptismal water.

A baptismal certificate is given to the parents and it is common for the parents to give a monetary gift to the church (although it is the parents' choice, not something that is required by the church).

Confirmation

Confirmation is common within Pakistani-American churches for youth in their early teenage years. The catechetical period is around four weeks and confirmation takes place on Easter Sunday.

Sacrament of Holy Communion

"Lord's Supper" and "Holy Communion" are the terms most often used in Pakistani-American churches. The sacrament is celebrated once a month after the sermon. The elements are covered until the appropriate time in the liturgy. The communion liturgy comes from the Book of Worship from the Church of Pakistan and includes a corporate confession, Great Prayer of Thanksgiving, consecration of the elements, and *Words of Institution*. The elements are blessed and then the bread is broken during the Institution. Only clergy are permitted to celebrate communion. Laity assist in the distribution of the elements.

The elements commonly used are individual cups of grape juice and either wafers or one loaf of bread. They are seen by the congregation to be the real presence of Jesus Christ within and among us. The people come forward and kneel at the altar rail to receive communion. The elements are distributed with the words "The body of Christ given for you. The blood of Christ shed for you." The pastor and lay servers partake after the congregation.

In Pakistan, children are not allowed to take communion until after they are confirmed. In America, it is more common for children to come forward and receive communion with their parents.

Rituals of Passage

Weddings

In the Pakistani tradition, preparations for a wedding begin with an engagement ritual that takes place at the bride's house. The pastor presides at the ritual and the liturgy is taken from the Book of Worship from the Church of Pakistan. The liturgical aspects of the engagement ritual include prayers, scripture reading, and words for the couple. During the ritual, the groom's family gives a ring and Pakistani dresses to the bride. The bride's family gives a watch and a suit to the groom. After the ritual, there is a party with food, music, and dancing.

Between the engagement ritual and the wedding, the pastor usually meets with the couple three times for premarital counseling. Under Pakistani law, it is almost impossible for Christians to get a divorce. Therefore, even in the United States, divorce is extremely rare in the Pakistani Christian community.

The night before the wedding there is an all night party called a *Hena* or *Menhdi*. *Hena* (a type of red dye) is painted on the palms of the bride's hands as decoration in preparation for the bridegroom. She is anointed with perfume and wears traditional Pakistani dress for the occasion. The *Hena* lasts all night long with singing and dancing, eating and drinking.

The wedding itself takes place in the church and is modeled on a Western-style wedding. Bridesmaids, ushers, flower girl, and ring bearer serve as attendants to the bride and groom. The groom and his attendants enter from the side of the sanctuary at the front. Following the bridesmaids, flower girl, and ring bearer, the bride processes down the aisle escorted by her father. The music that accompanies the procession is usually Western music. During the wedding however, Pakistani hymns are often sung.

The wedding ceremony is taken from the Book of Worship published by the Church of Pakistan and includes the reading of scripture, a sermon, prayers for the couple, and the exchange of vows and rings. The Unity Candle is also used in weddings in the United States. The outer candles are either lit by the mothers of the bride and groom or by the bride and groom themselves. After the benediction, the father of the bride stands and thanks the people for coming and invites them to the reception.

The reception includes a full meal, toasting the couple with words of blessing and hope, music, traditional Pakistani music and dancing, as well as modern dancing. The pastor is expected to attend the reception and pray before the meal is served. The bride and groom dance the first dance together. After the couple cuts the cake, the guests come forward and greet the entire bridal party along with the parents of the bride and groom, in a formal receiving line. The bride throws her bouquet over her shoulder to unmarried women and the groom throws the bride's garter over his shoulder to unmarried men.

After the reception, the couple goes to the bride's family's home. The bride pays respect to her parents with words of thanksgiving and farewell. The bride and groom then go to the groom's parent's home where they most often will live.

Funerals

Immediately after someone dies, friends and family gather at the family's home. Every evening until the night before the day of burial, there is a prayer meeting at the family's home. In Pakistan, the body would be present at the home for the prayer meetings. In the United States, however, the body stays at the funeral home during these services. Each prayer meeting includes prayer, scripture reading, a sermon, and hymns. These services last about one hour but the guests often stay several hours to be present with the family. Family and friends bring food into the home three times a day to care for the grieving family.

The night before the burial, family and friends gather at the funeral home for a memorial service. The casket is open all evening for viewing the body. In addition to prayers, hymns, scripture reading and a sermon, one person gives a eulogy about the person who died. The memorial service lasts about an hour.

On the day of burial, the pastor is expected to pray with the family at the their home and escort them to the funeral home for the funeral service. This service lasts about a half an hour. The closed casket is surrounded by flowers, candles, and sometimes a picture of the deceased. Scripture is read and prayers are offered but there is no sermon or testimony about the person who died during the funeral service.

After the funeral, there is a procession of cars to the cemetery. At the cemetery, the pastor leads the procession to the grave site. Following the pastor are the pallbearers carrying the casket, then honorary pallbearers (if chosen by the family), then the family and friends. Burial is always practiced among Pakistani Christians. Cremation is viewed as a Hindu practice and not acceptable for Christians.

The committal service includes one hymn, scripture reading, and prayer. During the service, the casket is lowered into the grave. Once in place, everyone throws either dirt or flowers into the grave. The people stay until the grave is completely filled in. Once the body is buried, the large bouquets and wreaths of flowers are placed on the mound of dirt. The pastor then says the closing prayer.

After the committal service, there is a reception at the family's home. The food is provided by extended family and friends. At the close of the reception, the pastor offers the final prayer.

If the deceased was an active member of the Pakistani-American community, clergy from other churches may be asked to participate in the prayer meetings, memorial service, or funeral service.

Upon request from the family, on the Sunday closest to the yearly anniversary of death, prayers and hymns are offered during worship in honor of the deceased. Memorial services may be held for family who died in Pakistan.

SAMOAN-AMERICAN WORSHIP PRACTICES

with Rev. Pita Lauti

The Service of the Word

The Language of the Liturgy

People in Samoan-American congregations may come from the country of Western Samoa or the territory of American Samoa. Both are islands in the South Pacific and they share a common language called Samoan.

While there are not as yet English language congregations within Samoan-American churches, some aspects of worship may be done in English and an English summary of the sermon is often provided for the 1.5 and second generations in the congregation.

The Liturgical Space

In Samoa, worship space is often circular. Samoan-American congregations are usually forced to adapt to the rectangular architecture of American churches.

Numerous flowers are always present in Samoan-American worship spaces. Lace and other cloth may be draped over the altar rail or used as altar cloth and pulpit frontals. At certain times, fine mats or *tapa cloth* (made from bark with symbols painted on it) may be placed on the floor of the chancel area. These treasured items of the culture are reserved for special occasions. Fine mats and *tapa cloth* are especially used for weddings and funerals.

Liturgical Time

Worship services in Samoan-American churches last between one and two hours.

Liturgical Garb

In Samoa, clergy wear white every Sunday. In America, it is common for clergy to wear a black robe on three Sundays of the month

195

and a white robe or white alb on the first Sunday of the month when communion is celebrated. In place of a robe, male clergy may wear a white shirt, suit coat, and *lavalava*, which is a wrap around, knee-length skirt common in the Pacific Islands (or a *ie faitaga* which is a *lavalava* with pockets). The suit coat and *lavalava/ie faitaga* are usually white on Communion Sundays and gray, navy blue or black on the other Sundays of the month.

Liturgical Seasons and Days

In Samoa, churches only celebrate Christmas and Easter. The other liturgical seasons receive little or no attention. However, in the United States, many Samoan churches are beginning to recognize Advent, Christmas, Epiphany, Lent, Easter, and Pentecost in their worship. Holy Thursday and Good Friday Services are also common.

In addition, Mother's Day, Father's Day, Student Graduations, and American Thanksgiving are also recognized liturgically.

White Sunday is celebrated the second Sunday of October. The children wear white clothing and leis. Tapa cloth may cover the floor or walls of the stage or chancel area. The prayers, scripture readings, and other elements of the service are led by the children and youth. The younger children prepare songs to sing for the congregation. The youth may prepare a drama that depicts a biblical story or various episodes in the life of a biblical character. In addition, children from various families in the church make an "offering" to the church in the form of songs accompanied by hand motions, reciting scripture verses, or a short skit on a biblical text. As the children from a particular family make their "offering," the parents or other family members walk forward and place money in an offering plate. It is expected that every family in the church that has children will prepare something to offer on White Sunday.

Beginning Our Praise to God

The Call to Worship, printed in the bulletin, is usually based on the Psalms and is read responsively between the pastor and the congregation. In many Samoan-American churches, the pastor takes full responsibility for leading the service. However, some Samoan-American congregations now use lay liturgists to assist them in worship.

SAMOAN-AMERICAN WORSHIP PRACTICES

Prayer Forms

Prayer forms in Samoan-American churches include: an invocation or opening prayer, a pastoral prayer followed by the Lord's Prayer, extemporaneous prayers by the pastor and lay liturgist (if used), and occasionally, a corporate prayer of confession. If a corporate confession is not used, themes of confession are often included in the pastoral prayer. In a few churches, people may offer their individual prayers of joys and concerns aloud.

Before the sermon, the pastor may kneel at the altar and pray silently, or pray aloud from the pulpit. In most Samoan-American congregations, the people kneel for the pastoral prayer. The posture of other prayers during worship is either sitting or standing.

Creeds

Most Samoan-American congregations recite the Apostles' Creed weekly.

Music

There are two hymnals common among Samoan-American congregations. *Tusi Pese* is the Samoan hymnal published in Samoa. There is also a Samoan Methodist hymnal published in America. Many of the hymns are the same. Usually, four hymns are sung each week in worship, accompanied by the organ or piano. Most hymns are sung in harmony. The use of traditional Samoan instruments or modern American instruments (guitar, drums) in worship is rare. In addition to hymns, other songs of praise may also be sung during worship.

The response to soloists and choir anthems is silence. Some in the congregation may quietly say "Amen." If the pastor claps, the congregation may do likewise.

Scripture Readings

In most Samoan-American congregations, two scripture texts are read, although some churches may choose to read only one. One is chosen from the Old Testament and one from the New Testament. These texts are often selected after consulting the lectionary. Both texts are usually read responsively, verse by verse, between the pastor (occasionally a lay liturgist) and the congregation.

Preaching

Usually a sermon lasts between fifteen and thirty minutes although some may be longer. Whether the sermon is placed in the middle of the service or at the end, it is seen by the congregation to be the most important part of worship. While much of Samoan-American preaching is topical, other methods are being used by some pastors. Most Samoan-American preaching includes illustrations and stories from Samoan history, folktales, and life experiences. Humor is also very common.

While some within the congregation still expect the sermon to have a tight conclusion, others are comfortable with a sermon that is open ended. Some laity believe that preaching without notes is a sign of being inspired by the Holy Spirit. The people expect the pastor to preach behind the pulpit and have good eye contact with the congregation. Moving out among the people is not appropriate in Samoan-American churches.

Samoan-American pastors utilize a variety of ways to include the congregation in their preaching. In some churches, Bible study groups discuss the texts for the upcoming sermon, giving the pastor input from a variety of people before the sermon is designed. In other congregations, there is a "talk-back" time after the service to discuss the text and sermon topic. During the sermon, a pastor may ask the congregation to turn to a particular scripture passage and read it aloud. Occasionally, pastors may write the main points or ideas of the sermon on newsprint for the congregation.

Passing of the Peace

This ritual is not traditional within Samoan-American congregations. It is still not well received by many. However, some Samoan-American congregations have begun to introduce this ritual into their liturgy.

Benediction

It is generally assumed that only clergy are authorized to give the benediction. However, in some congregations lay leaders are also permitted this privilege. In pronouncing the benediction, many clergy raise one or both hands in a gesture of blessing. Usually, both the pastor and the congregation stand with eyes closed during the benediction.

Sacramental Practices

Sacrament of Baptism

Baptism in the Samoan-American community almost always takes place in the context of Sunday worship. Most often, the person being baptized is an infant, although occasionally youth and adults may be baptized. Parents requesting baptism for their infant often meet with the pastor in preparation for the event. Youth requesting baptism often go through a period of preparation that lasts several weeks. Occasionally, persons baptized as infants, request to be rebaptized as adults. This poses a theological quandary for many Samoan-American clergy.

Some churches baptize the infants on White Sunday when the children of the church lead the service. Others offer baptism whenever the parents request it.

It is expected that the person being baptized will wear white as a sign of purity. Though not traditional, godparents are becoming more common in the Samoan-American community. Most churches prefer that parents choose Christians to be the godparents.

The liturgy surrounding baptism in Samoan-American congregations is varied. Some pastors use a formal liturgy from the Samoan hymnal that includes words about baptism, prayers, and questions to ask the parents, youth, or adult being baptized. Others use questions from a liturgical resource, but offer words about baptism and pray extemporaneously. Still others use the preprinted prayers but create their own questions to ask .

Sprinkling is the only method practiced in the Samoan church. It is not appropriate to baptize someone by immersion. Before the service, water is poured into either a baptismal font or a bowl. During the baptism, the water is sprinkled on the person's head three times while the pastor recites the *traditional baptismal formula*. Some may also make the sign of the cross on the person's forehead with the baptismal water.

A baptismal certificate and sometimes a Bible is given to the one being baptized. It is common in the Samoan Christian community for the family (or adult being baptized) to give money to the church in thanksgiving of the baptism. Sometimes food and money are also given to the pastor. After the baptism, a feast is held to honor the one baptized.

199

Confirmation

In some congregations, confirmation classes are offered for youth who were baptized as infants.

Sacrament of Holy Communion

While Holy Communion may be the most common way to refer to this sacrament, Communion, Lord's Supper, and Eucharist are also used. Holy Communion is celebrated on the first Sunday of every month after the sermon. Sometimes a Samoan cloth covers the altar. The elements traditionally used are small cubes of bread and individual cups of grape juice. Occasionally one loaf and one cup is used. On rare occasions, coconut and coconut juice, staple food and drink in Samoa, are used in place of the bread and grape juice. What the elements represent varies among the Samoan people. Some believe in the doctrine of *transubstantiation* or the doctrine of *consubstantiation*. Others believe that the bread and grape juice are symbols of Christ's presence and grace in our lives. The elements are covered until the appropriate time in the liturgy.

In most congregations, only clergy are authorized to celebrate communion. Some churches however, permit lay leaders to participate in the communion liturgy. It is common in many congregations for licensed lay speakers or other lay leaders to assist in the distribution of the elements.

The structure of the liturgy varies in Samoan-American communion services. Some pastors use a formal Great Prayer of Thanksgiving (long or short version) including responses by the laity. Others offer prayers and words of communion extemporaneously. Almost always, some version of the *Words of Institution* are included, at which time the bread is broken. Many pastors also include some form of consecration or blessing of the elements. The pastor and lay servers usually partake of communion before the congregation receives.

Distribution of the elements takes place in a variety of ways. The most common method is for the congregation to kneel at the altar and partake of the cubes of bread and individual cups of juice. When one loaf and one cup are used, the people commune by *intinction*, kneeling at the altar. Occasionally, the elements are passed to the people in the pews. The elements are distributed with the words "This is the body and blood of our Lord Jesus Christ given for you."

SAMOAN-AMERICAN WORSHIP PRACTICES

Although a few churches prefer that children wait until after confirmation to take communion, most Samoan-American churches allow children to partake whenever the parents feel they are ready. Those who are not baptized are welcome to the table.

Rituals of Passage

Weddings

The Samoan tradition does not have strong prewedding rituals. Most traditional rituals around weddings take place after the wedding ceremony. The bride's minister officiates at the wedding. This role is an important one since many Samoan-American ministers from other churches and denominations are invited to attend the wedding and reception. When gifts are given to the ministers at the reception, the officiating minister is given special consideration.

While premarital counseling is not traditional in the Samoan community, many pastors in the United States prefer to meet with the couple several times in preparation for the wedding. The wedding usually takes place in a church although in some communities, a garden setting may also be an appropriate context for the ceremony. *Tapa cloth* and fine mats are placed on the floor of the chancel area. They may also be draped over the altar, the altar rail, the pulpit, and the lecturn.

The bride is dressed in a white wedding gown and the groom in a tuxedo. There are often numerous attendants at Samoan-American weddings: several bridesmaids and ushers, flower girls, and ring bearers. In most weddings, the bridesmaids and ushers wear leis around their necks.

Before the ceremony begins, the altar candles are usually lit by the older children serving as attendants, or by the mothers of the bride and groom. Occasionally, the candles are lit by acolytes. The Unity Candle is seldom used, but if a couple requests it, either the pastor, the mothers, or the best man and maid of honor light the outer candles.

The groom and ushers enter from the side at the front of the sanctuary before the procession begins. The bridesmaids, flower girls, and ring bearers lead the procession, followed by the bride escorted by her father. The processional music may be either "The Wedding March," other Western-style music, or Samoan music.

201

The wedding proceeds with the reading of scripture, a sermon about love and marriage, the proclamation of vows, the exchange of rings, and the blessing of the couple in prayer. After the couple is pronounced "husband and wife," some families choose to include a ritual where the mother (or sister) of the bride places a lei on her daughter, followed by the mother of the groom placing a lei around her son's neck.

At the end of the service, it is tradition for the chief of the bride's family to stand and thank the officiating minister for performing the ceremony, thank the people for coming, and invite everyone to greet the newly married couple at the reception.

In Samoa, there are two receptions after a wedding: one at the bride's family's home, and one at the groom's. In America, there is only one reception which is usually held at a hotel banquet room, a hall, or a club. All the ministers are present for the reception and seated at special places of honor. The officiating minister sits at the bride and groom's table and is expected to pray before the meal and at the close of the reception. Samoan-American wedding receptions include feasting and dancing. At some point in the reception, the bride often throws her bouquet over her shoulder to unmarried women and the groom throws the bride's garter over his shoulder to unmarried men.

The dancing usually begins with the Bride's Dance. During the Bride's Dance, the bride and groom, bridesmaids and ushers dance. Friends and family of the bride come onto the dance floor and put dollar bills in the bride's clothing or place it on her body. These persons then begin dancing themselves. Someone picks up all the money and gives it to the parents of the bride.

The groom's family then declares a particular song to be the Groom's Dance and the groom's family participates in the same ritual. The money collected goes to the groom's parents. The money given to the bride's parents and the groom's parents assists them in the gift-giving time at the end of the day.

The Chief of the Day (from the bride's family), who functions as a Master of Ceremonies, declares the beginning of the official bride's dance called the "Newlywed Dance" and the process is repeated. In the same fashion as in the Bride's Dance, people come forward and put dollar bills on the bride. Because this dance is sanctioned by the Chief, more people participate and more money is given.

The meal is then served. After the meal, the bride's sisters and female cousins may do a traditional dance for the guests, followed by a traditional dance by the groom's brothers and male cousins. During these dances, people also put dollar bills in the clothes or on their body. The money is given to the newlywed couple.

After the traditional dances, the Chief often gives a speech addressing the many ministers present, the other chiefs, and any other dignitaries. The Chief then instructs the families of the bride and groom to present *sua* to the ministers. *Sua* is the ritual of presenting gifts to the ministers in order of their rank within the community. The officiating minister is presented with gifts first: roast pig (sometimes beef), many fine mats, tapa cloth, and an envelope containing a sizable amount of money. The other ministers also receive meat, fine mats, tapa cloth and money with the amount varing according to each person's rank. The process of giving *sua* can take some time as gifts are given to each minister first by the bride's family, then by the groom's family.

After the presentation of *sua*, the bride and groom cut the wedding cake and feed each other. The cake is then distributed in the appropriate order: the officiating minister first, then the bride and groom, the elder ministers present, the other ministers, the family of the bride, the family of the groom, the chiefs, other dignitaries, and finally the guests.

The Chief gives the last speech and thanks everyone for their participation in the festivities and the officiating minister closes with prayer. Once this has taken place, the ministers may leave. Other people may stay longer.

After the reception, another ritual may be held at a designated place (usually in the backyard of either the bride's parents' home, or the groom's parents' home). The bride's family presents many fine mats (sometimes up to two thousand) to the groom's family. These mats are made by the family, bought, or given to the family by extended family members and friends. The value and quality of these fine mats varies. The most valuable is a "named" mat that has been in the family for a long time and reserved especially for this particular daughter's wedding. This "named" mat may be worth up to $1,000. In addition, there may be twenty to thirty extra fine mats, each worth hundreds of dollars each. There may also be hundreds of regular fine mats. As each mat is given to the groom's family, the groom's family is expected to calculate the value of the mat, giving the total dollar amount back to the bride's family at the conclusion of the giving.

Thank you gifts in the form of food, fine mats, or occasionally money, are given to those who gave money, fine mats, or food for the ceremony.

Funerals

There are three funeral services in the Samoan tradition: one on Saturday, one on Sunday, and the final one on Monday, which is the day of burial. The funerals may take place the first weekend after a death, or they may be postponed for several weeks until family can arrive from either American Samoa or Western Samoa.

Before the funeral services, viewing of the body takes place during the day at the funeral home. The body is often dressed in Samoan clothing and surrounded by many flowers, candles, pictures of the deceased, fine mats, *tapa cloth*, and *falaie*. *Falaie* are mats similar to fine mats but with bright colored yarn placed as a fringe around the mat. The bottom of the mat may also be decorated with the colorful yarn depicting religious symbols or Samoan words. In addition, many of the deceased's possessions are placed in the casket, including one's Bible, and things the person wrote or made. These items are buried with the body.

Prayer meetings may take place every evening until the first funeral. Family and friends gather at the family's home for prayer, singing, scripture reading, and a short sermon. The church choir may also be present to sing an anthem or two. Alternatively, the family may request that only the pastor and his or her spouse visit them to conduct the prayer meeting. If the funerals are postponed, these services may be held every evening for several weeks or only once or twice a week until the time of the funerals. The prayer meetings usually last thirty minutes. Food is served after each prayer meeting.

The first funeral takes place on a Saturday and is called the Family Service. It may take place at the church, the funeral home, or the family's home. There is a viewing of the body before and after the service, but the casket is closed during worship. This service is primarily for the immediate and extended family members. It lasts about an hour and the sermon often focuses on the life of the deceased.

The second funeral service takes place on Sunday afternoon at the church. This service often lasts several hours. Again, there is a viewing of the body before and after the funeral, but the casket is closed for the service. Samoan-American ministers from other churches and denominations come and bring their choirs as well. There are often two or three sermons preached by different ministers, along with scripture reading, music by the choirs, prayers, and congregational singing. In addition, one or two people chosen by the family give testimony about the deceased. The sermons for this service tend to focus on God's comfort for those family and friends who are grieving the loss of their loved one.

The third funeral service takes place on Monday. Before this service begins, the chiefs decide whether the family of the person who died, or the family of the surviving spouse (or, in the case of a child's death, the family of the mother or the family of the father) has the honor of rubbing oil on the face of the deceased as the last act before burial. Once this ritual is completed, the final funeral service begins. Again, there is a viewing of the body before and after, but the casket is closed during worship. This service lasts approximately thirty minutes. The sermon often reiterates the themes preached in the first two funeral sermons and ends with God's gift of eternal life.

After the final funeral service, there is sometimes a car procession to the cemetery. Once at the cemetery, there may be a procession from the hearse to the grave site. If so, the pastor leads the procession, followed by the pallbearers carrying the casket, then the family and guests. Since cremation is not acceptable in the Samoan culture, burying the body in the ground is the most common form of disposing the body.

The committal service includes prayers, the reading of scripture, and sometimes singing and/or a sermon. While a few clergy throw dirt on the casket, in most Samoan-American services, everyone places a flower on the casket at the point in the liturgy where "ashes to ashes, dust to dust" is recited.

After the committal service, there is a reception at the church or at the family's home. The ritual of *sua* (discussed in the wedding section) is often practiced at the reception after the funeral as well. The ministers present are seated in the same format as at the wedding, and each is given meat, fine mats, tapa cloth, and money according to rank. These gifts are presented by both the family of the deceased's and the family of the surviving spouse (or in the case of a child's death, the family of the child's mother and the family of the child's father). In addition, both families give fine mats to the chiefs. After the *sua*, the chiefs give speeches to honor the deceased. Thank you gifts of food, fine mats, and occasionally money are given to those friends and relatives who gave money, food, and fine mats for the reception.

While the funeral arrangements in the death of an elderly parent are often made by the adult children, the reception is the responsibility of the extended family of the one who died and the extended family of the surviving spouse.

205

On the first anniversary of a person's death, a memorial service is held at the grave site. A *faleula* ("House of Leis") is constructed over the grave. This *faleula* is a wooden canopy frame covered with leis. During the service, memories of the deceased are shared, prayers are offered, scripture is read, and a couple of hymns are sung.

TONGAN-AMERICAN WORSHIP PRACTICES

with Rev. Matini Niponi Finau

The Service of the Word

The Language of the Liturgy

The language of the liturgy in Tongan-American congregations is Tongan. However, when children are specifically addressed during worship, English may be used.

The Liturgical Space

The worship space may have many Tongan images present. Some churches have the Tongan flag opposite the American flag. Other churches hang banners with Tongan language and images on them. The altar cloth and other paraments may be made from Tongan cloth. *Tapa cloth*, made from bark with symbols painted on it, may be "wallpapered" to the wall in the foyer or placed on the floor in the chancel area.

Liturgical Time

Sunday worship services in Tongan-American churches often last one and a half to two hours. Once the service begins, the doors to the sanctuary are closed. Latecomers have to wait until the first hymn to enter.

Liturgical Garb

Most clergy wear black robes three Sundays of the month and a white robe on Communion Sunday. In place of the robe, male clergy may wear a white shirt, suit coat, and *tupenu*, a wrap-around, knee-length skirt common in the Pacific Islands. The *tupenu* worn on Communion Sundays is white. On the other Sundays of the month, the *tupenu* is usually gray, navy blue, or black. Men may also wear a *ta'ovala* over the *tupenu*. The *ta'ovala* is a decorative open-weave skirt woven from *patanus* leaves. It is tied around the waist and may be dyed various colors. Female clergy may wear a *kiekie* over their clothes. A *kiekie* is similar to the *ta'ovala* worn by the men, but if dyed, it is more colorful than the *ta'ovala*. The *ta'ovala* and *kiekie* are worn for celebratory occasions.

Liturgical Seasons and Days

Most Tongan-American churches celebrate all the seasons of the church year. However, in some churches, Epiphany and Pentecost receive little or no attention. Services are also held on Good Friday and sometimes on Holy Thursday. American Thanksgiving is not celebrated liturgically.

The first week of January is Thanksgiving Prayer Week in the Tongan tradition. Services are held every morning and evening. Each service is thematically based and includes scripture reading, singing, and praying, but no preaching. It is a time for laypeople to offer their testimonies of faith.

The first Sunday of May is called *Fakame* or Children's Day. In the past, everyone wore white on this day, but today most wear new clothes, but not always white. Tapa cloth may cover the floor or walls of the stage or chancel area. The prayers, scripture readings, and other elements of the service are led by children and youth. The younger children prepare songs to sing for the congregation and the youth prepare songs or a scripture drama. In addition, children from various families in the church make an "offering" in the form of songs accompanied by hand motions, reciting scripture verses, or a short skit on a biblical text. It is expected that every family in the church that has children will prepare something to offer on *Fakame*.

The second Sunday of May is Mother's Day, and the third Sunday of May is Father's Day. In most Tongan United Methodist churches, the second Sunday in September is Women's Day. This is a day that honors the significance of women's role in the family, in the Tongan-American culture, and in the church community. All the Tongan-American churches in the various United Methodist conferences gather together for worship. During the service, there is a roll call of all the women from the various churches.

Beginning Our Praise to God

The Call to Worship is often scripturally based but may also follow the theme of the day. It is read responsively between the lay liturgist and the congregation.

Prayer Forms

Prayer forms in Tongan-American churches include: the Lord's Prayer, extemporaneous prayers by the pastor, a separate corporate prayer of confession, or a pastoral prayer that includes a confession. The Lord's Prayer is often sung to a Tongan tune by the entire congregation. As the pastor processes in, he or she may kneel next to the pulpit and pray until the processional music is ended.

On Communion Sundays, there is a prayer in chanting form. The pastor sings a line, and the congregation responds (not with the same words or tune as the pastor). This goes back and forth throughout the prayer.

The posture of prayer varies. Sitting is common, but kneeling is also appropriate, especially for the prayer of confession. People may stand for other prayers.

Creeds

The Apostles' Creed may be recited during worship, but it is not a weekly occurrence in most Tongan-American churches.

Music

Music in the Tongan tradition is unique. No instruments are used to accompany any singing. On very rare occasions, a piano or organ may be used in the United States. On special cultural occasions, Tongan drums and the *lali* are played. The *lali* is a hollowed-out wooden log that is hit with a mallet. Before the Europeans arrived in Tonga, the *lali* was used to call people to worship or to community gatherings. All songs are sung in various harmonies *a capella*.

Instead of an organ or piano prelude, someone in the congregation starts to sing and the rest of the congregation joins in. As the congregation sings, the minister and lay liturgists process down the aisle.

Three to four hymns are usually sung each week in addition to songs that rise spontaneously from individual members of the congregation. This spontaneous singing often takes place as the offering is being collected, when the communion elements are being uncovered, and during the distribution of the elements. The hymnbook most commonly used is the Wesleyan Tongan Methodist Hymnal. Only the lyrics are included in the hymnal. When hymns are sung in Tongan-American worship, a lay liturgist reads each verse in a poetic fashion before the congregation sings it. The choir leader or music director sounds a note on a pitch pipe so the congregation or choir begins on the same note.

Silence is the most common response to soloists and choir anthems. However, clapping or saying "Amen" is acceptable in some congregations.

Scripture Readings

Usually two to three scriptures passages are read each week in worship. Many congregations also read a Psalm text in unison from the Bible, or responsively from the Psalter in the back of the Tongan hymnal. The scripture passages are read by a lay liturgist and the congregation reads along in their own Bibles. Occasionally, a text is read responsively, verse by verse, between the liturgist and the congregation.

Preaching

Sermons in Tongan-American churches usually last fifteen to thirty minutes. The sermon is seen as the most important part of the liturgy whether it is placed in the middle of the service or at the end. Most pastors consult the lectionary in selecting texts for weekly sermons. Stories and illustrations are often taken from Tongan resources containing the history, legends, and folktales of the Tongan people.

Sermon structure and style vary from pastor to pastor. While some in the congregation feel more comfortable when sermons have a tight conclusion, for others leaving a sermon open ended is also appropriate. The use of humor in preaching is likewise appreciated by some, but not all in the congregation. Many laity in Tongan-American churches believe that preaching without notes is a sign of being inspired by the Holy Spirit.

While participatory styles of preaching are usually not utilized during the delivery of the sermon, some Tongan-American congregations discuss the text for the sermon the week before during Bible study. The discussion is then reflected to some extent in the Sunday sermon.

Passing of the Peace

This ritual is not customary in Tonga but it is being introduced in some Tongan-American congregations.

210

Benediction

The benediction can be pronounced by laity as well as clergy. The Tongan tradition treats the gesture of blessing, with either one or two hands raised, as optional. Both the person giving the benediction and the congregation have their eyes closed for the benediction. To receive the benediction, the congregation may be sitting, standing, or kneeling.

Sacramental Practices

Sacrament of Baptism

Most parents or guardians in Tongan-American churches bring infants for baptism. Adult baptisms do occur, but they are rare. Baptism often takes place on Communion Sundays but may also be held at other times during worship.

Infants and adults being baptized are always dressed in white as a sign of purity. The use of godparents for infants is up to the parents. Parents may meet with the pastor once in preparation for the baptism.

The baptismal liturgy commonly used is found in the back of the Tongan hymnal. It includes words about baptism, prayers, and questions to ask the parents (or adult). Occasionally, pastors offer their own prayers extemporaneously.

Sprinkling is the most common form of baptism. Immersion is not a tradition in the Tongan community. The water is poured into either a baptismal font or a bowl before the service begins. If a bowl is used, a layperson holds the bowl for the pastor during the baptism. Usually water is sprinkled on the infant's head three times (occasionally once), as the pastor recites the *traditional baptismal formula*. Some pastors also make the sign of the cross on the infant's forehead with the baptismal water.

A baptismal certificate is given to the parents of the infant, or the adult being baptized. While there are no expectations that the family (or adult) will give a gift to the church, some do.

After a baptism, the family holds a *fakaafe* (feast) for the entire congregation. There are many speeches given by various members of the community in honor of the one being baptized. Unlike other feasts in the Tongan community however, there is no dancing at the feast since dancing is not permitted on Sundays.

211

Confirmation

Confirmation has not historically been part of the Tongan tradition. Some Tongan-American churches however, offer confirmation classes for youth who were baptized as infants.

Sacrament of Holy Communion

The term most often used for Holy Communion is the *"Sakala-meniti"* or "Sacrament." The sacrament is usually held on the first Sunday of every month. Some congregations however, only celebrate the sacrament once a quarter and on special Sundays. It is traditional in Tongan-American churches for the women to wear long sleeves on Communion Sundays.

Only clergy are permitted to celebrate the sacrament, but laypersons assist in the distribution of the elements. The communion liturgy most often includes the *Words of Institution* and extemporaneous words and prayers by the pastor. Some pastors use prayers for communion from the Tongan hymnal. Consecrating or blessing the elements is not always included in Tongan communion liturgies. The bread is broken during the Institution.

When a prayer of confession is included, the pastor and lay servers kneel at the altar while the congregation kneels on the floor in front of the pew. The pastor and lay servers also kneel for prayer as they partake of the elements before they serve the congregation.

The most common elements used are small cubes of bread and individual cups of grape juice. Some churches however, use one loaf and one cup. The elements are understood by the congregation to be symbols of Christ's presence and grace. Most often, people come forward whenever they feel ready, although a few Tongan-American churches have adopted the use of ushers to direct the congregation to the altar rail. The people kneel at the altar rail and partake of the elements. When one loaf and one cup are used, the congregation partakes by *intinction.* The elements are distributed with the words "This is the body and blood of our Lord Jesus Christ." While kneeling at the altar, individuals may also be singing along with the congregation, or softly voicing their own prayers.

The children of the church often kneel at the altar rail as a group. When infants are brought by their parents, some pastors lay their hand on the child's head as a sign of blessing. Those who are not baptized are welcome at the table in Tongan-American churches.

Rituals of Passage

Weddings

In some Tongan communities, weddings are for the family only, although Tongan clergy from other churches and denominations may be invited. In other communities, friends and church members may also be invited to the wedding.

The night before the wedding, the groom goes to the bride's house where there is dancing and music until two or three in the morning. Traditionally, this ritual was a *faka lealea* or "watch night" to make sure no one took the bride before the wedding.

In some families, the bride has a farewell feast with all her relatives on the morning of the wedding. Her relatives give her gifts that are specifically for her, not her and her husband.

Weddings almost always take place in the church. The traditional color for weddings is white. Persons who are divorced can be married but sometimes it is frowned upon. Several premarital counseling sessions are common for all who wish to be married.

Tongan-American weddings have assimilated to Western customs over the years. The bride wears a white wedding gown and the groom wears a tuxedo. Bridesmaids, groomsmen, flower girl, and ring bearer are all common attendants in a wedding.

Before the wedding, the altar candles are lit by acolytes, or sometimes by the mothers of the bride and groom. Occasionally the Unity Candle is used. If so, the outer candles are lit either by the mothers of the bride and groom or by other representatives from each family.

The groom and groomsmen enter from the side at the front of the sanctuary. The bridesmaids and other attendants process down the aisle followed by the bride who is escorted by her father. The music accompanying the procession is either Western-style music, or Tongan music - sometimes Tongan hymns. During the wedding, Tongan music is used, occasionally accompanied by Tongan drums and other instruments.

Scripture is read, many songs are sung, a sermon is preached, vows are made, rings are exchanged, and the couple is blessed as they are pronounced husband and wife. In some weddings, the parents of the bride and groom give leis to each other after the pronouncement. The chief often thanks the people for coming and invites them to the *fakaafe*. At the end of the wedding, the bridal party may form a receiving line at the rear of the church to greet their guests.

After the wedding, the parents of the groom are responsible for the *fakaafe* (reception feast). The *fakaafe* usually takes place outside at someone's home. At the reception, all the ministers in attendance have special seats of honor. During the *fakaafe*, there are several speeches from both families. The chief often gives the last speech.

There is much dancing at the *fakaafe*. Arrangements are made with various persons to perform traditional dances for entertainment. The dancers put oil on their arms and legs before they dance. As they dance, many people come forward and stick dollar bills on their arms and legs, or into their clothing. As many of the bills fall to the ground, they are picked up and given to someone designated to collect the money. All the money received throughout the *fakaafe* is given to the couple.

There is also the tradition in Tongan wedding *fakaafes* called the "Bride's Dance" and the "Groom's Dance." When the Master of Ceremonies calls for the Bride's Dance, the family and friends of the bride dance, and the groom's family comes forward and places dollar bills in their clothes or on their body. During the Groom's Dance, the bride's family puts dollar bills on those dancing from the groom's family. The Bride's Dance and Groom's Dance can be called for several times during the *fakaafe*. Toward the end of the reception, there is a last Bride's Dance where anyone can dance and everyone comes forward to place bills on the dancers.

Meaofa is the practice of giving gifts to the ministers who are present at the wedding. Both families join together to provide the gifts of fine mats, food, cakes, and sometimes money to the Tongan clergy present from the various churches and denominations.

At the end of the reception, the bride's family presents to the bride gifts she will need in married life. Often these gifts are large items of furniture, appliances, or other household items. If the gifts are too large to bring out, the items are simply read to the couple. Among some families, after the *fakaafe* the bride is expected to confirm verbally to the groom's parents that she is a virgin.

Since weddings are almost always held on Saturday, the newlyweds are expected to come to church the next day, which is called "First Sunday." On their first Sunday in church as a married couple, they are given special recognition and a blessing during worship. After First Sunday, there is another *fakaafe* for the entire church that includes speeches but no dancing (since it is held on Sunday). After the *fakaafe*, the couple leaves for their honeymoon.

Funerals

The tradition in the Tongan community is for burial to take place the day after death. This is still practiced in America but the funeral may also be postponed to allow more time to notify the community which is more spread out in America and to allow time for family to arrive from Tonga. The all night service of *Awakening* may take place the night of death or a week later.

Traditionally, the pastor goes to the family's home and prays with them immediately after death. When the word has spread through the community, people begin to gather at the family's home. Once the body has arrived at the church from the hospital or funeral home, everyone gathers at the church for the *Awakening*. The casket is placed in the front of the sanctuary parallel with the altar. It is open throughout the *Awakening* surrounded by flowers, leis, fine mats, tapa cloth, a picture of the deceased, and items of importance to the deceased. (When the body is not present for the *Awakening*, it is called a memorial service.)

The *Awakening* is an all night vigil and worship service. Clergy from other churches and denominations, their choirs, and people throughout the Tongan-American community come to the church throughout the night. Scriptures are read, many prayers are offered, sermons are given, choirs sing, and family and good friends share testimony about the life of the one who died. In between these various aspects, throughout the night, the congregation sings a capella with full harmonies.

The family (sometimes assisted by relatives and friends) prepares food for everyone throughout the night. The guests often bring tapa cloth, fine mats, money, and flowers as gifts to the family.

The worship continues into the next day until the time of burial. When it is time to go to the cemetery, the family closes the casket and the pastor prays with them. Cars then process from the church to the cemetery for the funeral service. (Burial in the ground is the most common. Cremation is often frowned upon.) At the cemetery, the pastor leads a procession, followed by the pallbearers carrying the casket, then the honorary pallbearers (if the family desires), and finally the family. The family sits in chairs provided. The others may stand or sit on the ground.

215

The funeral service which takes place at the grave site lasts thirty to forty-five minutes with hymns, prayers, scripture reading, and a short sermon. The elements for the committal service may come from the liturgy found in the back of the Tongan hymnal. In many funerals, either the pastor, or someone from the family throws dirt on the grave.

In Tonga there is no reception on the day of the burial. The following day, the family expresses their appreciation by serving a meal for family and guests at the family's home. In America, some families provide plates of food for the guests to take home with them as they leave the cemetery.

Memorial services may be held for family who die in Tonga. On the first year anniversary of a person's death, the family often gives a sizable monetary gift to the church in memory of their loved one.

VIETNAMESE-AMERICAN WORSHIP PRACTICES

with Rev. Dr. Luat Trong Tran[1]

The Service of the Word

The Language of the Liturgy

The language used in worship services is Vietnamese.

The Liturgical Space

In most churches, the worship space is devoid of any cultural symbols.

Liturgical Time

Services in Vietnamese-American churches usually last between one and one and a half hours.

Liturgical Garb

Clergy wear a variety of liturgical garb including pulpit robes, albs, and regular street clothes with a clerical collar. For the celebration of Lunar New Year, clergy may also wear a Vietnamese dress in the form of a robe.

Liturgical Seasons and Days

While Christmas and Easter are the most celebrated days of the liturgical year, some Vietnamese-American churches also celebrate Advent, Epiphany, Lent, and Pentecost. The Lunar New Year may also be celebrated liturgically. It is a time of celebration and renewal. The Autumn Festival, which is usually held at the end of August during a full moon, is a special time for the children. There are food and candy, dancing and other festivities.

Beginning Our Praise to God

Many Vietnamese-American congregations open their worship services with a call to worship that is scripturally based (often on a Psalm text), and is either read by the worship leader or read responsively between the worship leader and the congregation.

Prayer Forms

Prayer forms in the Vietnamese-American tradition include the Lord's Prayer, a pastoral prayer, and extemporaneous prayers by the pastor or lay liturgist. Lay members, sitting in the congregation, may also stand in their place and pray. Some churches invite the people to offer up their individual joys and concerns before the congregation. These are then included in the pastoral prayer.

The posture for all prayer is standing (influenced by the Christian Missionary Alliance denomination, the first to missionize Vietnam and the strongest protestant denomination in that country).

At the end of every prayer offered during worship, the entire congregation says together: "In the name of Jesus Christ, Amen."

Creeds

Many Vietnamese-American congregations recite the Apostles' Creed at least every other week.

Music

The hymnal most commonly used is the Vietnamese Methodist Hymnal, which has its hymns in both Vietnamese and English. The piano is used to accompany the hymns each week. Some churches also use guitars in worship to accompany "praise music" in addition to hymns. Vietnamese folksongs accompanied by Vietnamese instruments may be played on special occasions but not during Sunday worship.

In Vietnamese-American churches, silence, clapping or saying "Amen" are all acceptable responses to soloists and choir anthems.

Scripture Readings

The number of scripture passages read during Sunday worship varies in Vietnamese-American congregations. Most churches read only one text although a few may read two or three texts.

The text used as the basis for the sermon is read by the lay liturgist or the pastor. If other scripture passages are read, they may be read responsively (verse by verse) between the liturgist and the congregation. Members of the congregation bring their own Bible to church so they can participate.

Preaching

Many Vietnamese-American pastors preach thirty to forty-five minutes. Pastors educated in America often limit their sermons to twenty to thirty minutes. The sermon is at the end of the worship service and has traditionally been the most important part of the service. Today, however, some are moving to an understanding of the liturgy being of equal importance to the sermon.

The lectionary is often consulted, but is not always used as the basis for scripture choice from week to week. Expository and topical preaching in a three-point structure is the most common, although Vietnamese-American preachers are beginning to utilize other forms and structures. It is assumed by most members of the congregation that every sermon will have a tight conclusion.

Storytelling is expected in Vietnamese-American preaching, and though humor is used, it is not always appreciated. Stories and illustrations often come from the history and folktales of Vietnam as well as the experiences the people had when they lived in Vietnam and the issues they face in the United States today.

The Vietnamese-American community does not have many expectations about whether the preacher uses notes in the pulpit. Some people believe that the use of notes or a manuscript shows that the preacher is prepared.

Some participatory styles of preaching are found in Vietnamese-American churches. The pastor may ask the congregation to turn in their Bibles to a particular passage and read it aloud, and/or the preacher intentionally asks the congregation a question which requires a verbal response. Some pastors may write the main points of the sermon on newsprint while preaching. A layperson may offer a prayer from his or her seat at the close of the sermon.

Passing of the Peace

Though not traditional, the ritual of passing God's peace to each other is common within Vietnamese-American worship.

219

Benediction

Only ordained clergy are permitted to pronounce the benediction in Vietnamese-American congregations. If more than one clergyperson is present, it is often the eldest who has the privilege of giving the benediction. The pastor stands in the front of the sanctuary with eyes closed, raising both hands in a gesture of blessing. The congregation stands with eyes closed to receive the benediction.

Sacramental Practices

Sacrament of Baptism

The most common age of baptism in the Vietnamese Christian community is between sixteen and twenty. This is a result of the influence of the Christian Missionary Alliance denomination, which only practices adult baptism through immersion. While adult baptism is still the most common, some churches in the United States today also baptize infants.

When infants are baptized, the parents occasionally ask persons to be godparents for their child, but it is not common. Before adults or infants are baptized, most pastors meet with the persons involved at least once to make sure they understand the commitment they will be asked to make at the baptism.

Since most United Methodist churches do not have baptisteries, congregations meet at a separate time in order to borrow another church's baptistery for baptism by immersion. Adults may also be baptized in church by the method of sprinkling or by pouring. In the case of infants, baptism takes place in church through the method of sprinkling.

Since infant baptism was not practiced in Vietnam, baptismal fonts are not found in Vietnamese churches. Today in the United States, many congregations pour water into a bowl and place it on the altar on Sundays when there is a baptism.

Where baptism takes place in the liturgy varies from congregation to congregation. Some have baptism at the beginning of the service, while others have it during the "Proclamation" section of the service, and still others celebrate baptism after the sermon in response to the Word of God.

220

The baptismal liturgy varies from a formal liturgy to combined formal and extemporaneous liturgy, to entirely extemporaneous liturgy. When adults are baptized, they may share their faith journey as a part of the liturgy as well. Laypeople from the congregation may serve as sponsors for adults being baptized.

The person is baptized with the *traditional baptismal formula*. When baptizing in church, the water is sprinkled or poured on the person's head once. Some pastors also make the sign of the cross on the person's forehead with the baptismal water. Those being baptized often wear white clothing as a sign of purity.

A baptismal certificate is given to each person being baptized and some churches also give the person a cross pin or some other symbol to honor the occasion. The person being baptized is not expected to give anything to the church.

Confirmation

Since infant baptism is not a common Vietnamese practice, confirmation is not a necessary ritual of adolescence. However, in congregations that have been baptizing infants for a decade or more, confirmation is becoming a time of training in the Christian life, as well a ritual of public confession of faith in Jesus Christ. In smaller churches, individuals baptized as infants may join confirmation classes that are sponsored by the district.

Sacrament of Holy Communion

Both "Lord's Supper" and "Holy Communion" are names used for this sacrament. It takes place once a month in Sunday worship after the sermon. The elements are placed on the altar or on a separate communion table that is used only on Communion Sundays. The communion liturgy often varies according to whether one's theological training took place in Vietnam or in the United States. Some pastors use a full Great Thanksgiving with responses by the laity. Others use a shortened version of a Great Thanksgiving, while still others offer prayer and speak extemporaneously about the sacrament.

Most pastors use some version of the *Words of Institution* as well as a consecration over the elements. Some, however, bless the elements before the *Words of Institution*, while others bless the elements afterwards. Most pastors break the bread during the Institution, although a few may break the bread at the end of the Great Thanksgiving.

221

While small cubes of bread and individual cups of grape juice are the traditional elements of Vietnam, many churches today use one loaf and individual cups. The elements are usually passed to the people in the pews. On occasion, the people kneel at the altar rail to partake. The elements are given with the words "This is the body and blood of our Lord Jesus Christ given for you."

When the elements are passed to the people in the pews, the pastor and lay servers partake simultaneously with the congregation. When the elements are distributed in another fashion, it is customary for the clergy and lay servers to partake after the congregation has received.

While the tradition in Vietnam is to only allow the baptized to take communion, most Vietnamese-American congregations do not turn unbaptized children away. However, many Vietnamese-American parents choose not to bring their unbaptized children forward for communion. However, as more generations are born in the United States, more infants will be baptized, and more children will be taking communion.

Rituals of Passage

Weddings[2]

Wedding preparations in the Vietnamese Christian tradition officially begin with an engagement ritual, which is followed by a party. The engagement ritual takes place at the bride's parents' home. A table is placed vertically in the center of a room, with the bride's family lined up on the right side. At the appropriate time, the groom's family processes into the bride's house, carrying trays covered in red cloth. Red is a traditional color for weddings, symbolizing happiness and new life. The trays are placed on the table as the groom's family takes their places on the left side of the table. The groom, dressed in a dark suit and tie, stands at the head of the table next to the minister. The bride is not visible.

After the minister offers some words of greeting and purpose of the gathering, the people sing a hymn, followed by a prayer. In response to every prayer offered, people respond "In the name of Jesus Christ, Amen."

Traditionally, the father of the groom, then the father of the bride speaks. The minister confirms the joining of the two families and invites the mother to present the bride. As the bride enters, everyone claps. Dressed in traditional Vietnamese clothing, the bride stands next to the minister with her family. The minister speaks about the meaning of marriage and the permission granted by both families for the union to take place. The bride now moves beside the groom on the left side of the table. The minister motions for everyone to be seated, except for the bride and groom.

The parents of the groom and the groom remove the red cloths from the trays on the table revealing the traditional gifts of fruit, bottles of alcoholic beverages (usually nonalcoholic in Christian contexts), a roast pig, cans of tea, boxes of rice cakes, and jewelry for the bride.

Scripture is read by the minister and a sermon is preached. After the sermon, the groom unwraps the boxes of jewelry: a pair of earrings, a bracelet, and a necklace. The mothers of the bride and groom place the jewelry on the bride. While the minister is confirming the engagement, the groom places the engagement ring on the bride's finger.

Everyone stands as the minister offers a prayer for the couple and the people respond "In the name of Jesus Christ, Amen." The people are seated as the father of the groom (or other representative of the family if the father is deceased or not present), then the father of the bride, introduce their respective relatives. The parents of both the bride and the groom stand and bow to the people present as they are introduced.

The minister offers some closing words then everyone stands and prays the Lord's Prayer together, followed by the singing of a doxology. The father of the bride thanks everyone for coming and invites them to the reception. The minister pronounces the benediction to which everyone responds "Amen." Food is served, and the engagement party continues.

Early in the morning on the day of the wedding, a similar ritual may take place at the bride's family's home. The minister is present to officiate this ritual as well. The bride's family is again lined up on the right as the groom's family processes in and takes their place on the left. The groom, who is now carrying a bouquet of flowers, takes his place beside the minister. In addition to the groom's family, the groomsmen also process in carrying flower nosegays. The bride and her bridesmaids are not present at this time. The gifts are brought by the groom's family covered with the red cloths and placed on the table.

The minister gives the greeting, reads scripture and prays, followed by the people's traditional response. The groom's mother unveils the gifts covered with red cloths (fruit, tea, and beverage) and then asks the bride's parents for permission to escort the bride to the church for the wedding.

The father of the bride speaks, and then the minister announces the bride who enters in a white wedding gown and veil followed by her bridesmaids dressed in traditional Vietnamese gowns called *ao dai*. None of the women are carrying flowers. Everyone claps as they enter. The bride joins the groom behind the table. A short sermon is preached. The mother of the bride then speaks to her daughter, and her parents and/or siblings present her with their wedding gifts.

The minister announces that it is time for the wedding ceremonies to proceed. The groom and groomsmen give their flowers to the bride and her bridesmaids. The mother of the groom unwraps a necklace and puts it on the bride. The minister offers a prayer for the couple then pronounces the benediction with the people responding "Amen." The father of the bride thanks the people for coming and invites them to the wedding at the church. Food is served as various relatives give their wedding gifts to the couple.

The groom's family escorts the bride to the church for the wedding. In Vietnam, the traditional procession at a wedding includes the bride and groom coming down the aisle together followed by their parents, grandparents, siblings, and cousins. The bridesmaids and groomsmen either process down the aisle following the cousins, or, enter from the side at the front of the sanctuary. While traditional processions are still practiced in the United States today, many choose a more Western-style of procession where the groom and groomsmen enter from the side and the bridesmaids process down the aisle followed by the bride, who is escorted by her father. The bridal party usually processes to western style music, although Vietnamese songs are often sung during the wedding ceremony.

If the Unity Candle is used (as is often the case), the mothers of the bride and groom light the outer candles before the procession begins. In addition to the Unity Candle, the liturgy includes a greeting, reading of scripture, a sermon, music, and prayers for the couple as well as the exchange of vows and rings. Though not customary, there may also be a time in the liturgy where the minister asks the parents of the bride and groom for their blessing of this union or a time when the couple pays respect to their parents.

At the end of the liturgy, but before the benediction, the father of the bride, followed by the father of the groom, offers words of congratulations to the couple and words of appreciation to the people present and invites them to the reception. The minister closes with the benediction to which the entire congregation responds "Amen."

Following the wedding, a reception meal is usually given at a restaurant. The bride changes from her wedding gown into other formal attire for the reception (often Vietnamese in style). Sometimes she changes clothes more than once.

At the reception, music is played (no dancing), and various people sing songs to the couple. The couple may even sing songs to each other. Moving from table to table, the couple greet their guests and receive envelopes of money given as wedding presents. Other gifts are usually placed on a table at the entrance to the reception. The couple cuts the wedding cake and feeds each other. It is expected that the minister will attend the reception and offer prayer before the meal is served.

Funerals

In Vietnamese-American churches, prayer meetings are held between the day of death and the day of burial. Among some congregations, one prayer meeting is the norm while among others, three services are held. Most prayer meetings take place at the funeral home. Occasionally, the prayer meeting is held at the family's home or the church. Wherever it is held, the content of the prayer meeting(s) is similar. The casket is open for a viewing of the body, which is dressed in special clothes. A Bible and additional clothes or items important to the deceased are often placed in the casket as well. Surrounding the casket are flowers, candles, and picture(s) of the deceased.

During the prayer meeting, scripture is read, the minister offers a short sermon, prayers are offered for the family, and people are given an opportunity to share their memories of the deceased. At the end of the prayer meeting (the first if there is more than one), there is a ritual known as the *Distribution of the Mourning Signs* or the *Distribution of the Mourning Bands*. Strips of white cloth are distributed to the spouse, children, and close relatives. The spouse and eldest son wrap the cloth around their foreheads. Other children and close relatives wrap them around their upper arm. The family may choose to wear a piece of rectangular cloth pinned to their shirt or lapel. In Vietnam, the mourning bands are supposed to be worn for three years. Here in the United States, however, that is not practiced.

225

The morning of the funeral, some families may request the minister to pray with them at their home. The funeral usually takes place at the funeral home although some may choose to have the service at the church. Family and friends often come dressed in white since that is the major color of funerals in Vietnam. Because black is more customary in the United States, black may also be worn as a sign of mourning. Vietnamese-American clergy from other churches and denominations are often invited to participate in the funeral.

Some prefer that the casket be open throughout the funeral while in other cases it is customary to have the casket closed. The casket is already in place as the people gather. The funeral service includes scripture reading, a sermon, prayers for the family, singing, and words of comfort for the congregation. While everyone has a chance to share testimonies about the person who died at the prayer meeting(s), there may also be a time in the funeral service for everyone, or a select few, to witness to the life of the deceased. If family members were not present at the first prayer meeting, *distribution of the mourning signs* may also take place at the funeral.

If the casket is closed throughout the funeral, at the end of the funeral the family comes forward and opens the casket. The congregation files past the casket on the way out. The funeral service often lasts forty-five minutes to one and a half hours.

After the funeral service, if the body is to be buried, there is a car procession from the funeral to the cemetery. Burial is the most common practice but a person may choose to be cremated. Cremation, however, is frowned upon by some as a Buddhist practice. At the cemetery, there is a procession from the hearse to the grave site. The pastor leads the procession, followed by the pallbearers who carry the casket, then the family and friends.

The grave site service includes prayers and scripture readings and, in some cases, a sermon. During the liturgy, often dirt and flowers are placed on the casket by everyone. Occasionally, the use of dirt is limited to the pastor, or the pastor and the family.

After the committal service, the people wait as the casket is lowered into the grave. As the cemetery workers fill in the grave, some families and guests may assist them by shoveling dirt or throwing flowers onto the casket. Once the grave is filled in, snacks and drink are served to the guests at the grave site. People may stay and eat or take the food with them as they leave. Special worship services are held on the yearly anniversary to mark the death of the loved one. Memorial services are often held in the United States for family who have died in Vietnam.

Notes

1. Special thanks go to Rev. Cam Phu Nguyen for providing much information that influenced the design of the questionnaire for Vietnamese pastors.

2. Special thanks to Hao Hong Nguyen and Ahn Tran Nguyen for allowing me to participate in their wedding rituals.

APPENDIX A

Words for "God," "Jesus Christ," and "Church"
in the various languages used in worship in
The United Methodist Church

Culture/Country	Language	"God"	"Jesus Christ"
Cambodia	Cambodian	Preah	Yesu Crist
China/Hong Kong	Chinese	Shangti or Shen	Yesu Gidou
Fiji	Fijian	Kalou	Jisu Karisito
Formosa/Taiwan	Fukienese	Siong Te	Iaso Kitok
Ghana	Twi	Nyankopɔn	Awurade Asɛm
	Fanti	Nyankopɔn	Iesu Christo
	Ga	Nyɔmmɔ	Yesu Christo
Haiti	Creole	Die	Jezu Kri
	French	Dieu	Jesus Christ
Hispanic/Latino	Spanish	Dios	Jesucristo
Hmong/Laos	Hmong	Vaaj Tswv	Tswv Yexus
India	Gujarati	Prabhu	Isu Khrist
	Hindi	Parmeshvar	Yeshu Masih
	Malayalam	Dheivam	Yeshu Khristu
	Tamil	Kadavul	Yesu Khristu
	Telugu	Devudu	Yesu Chreestu
India/Pakistan	Urdu	Khuda	Yesu Masih
Japan	Japanese	Kami	Iesu Kirisuto
Korea	Korean	Hananim	Yesu Kristo
Laos	Lao	Phrachao	Phra Jesu Cris
Liberia	Bassa	Gèdèpɔ̀ɔ̀	Ɉ̀ɪzè Kɛ́dɛ́ɛ́r

228

Culture/Country	Language	"God"	"Jesus Christ"
Liberia	Kissi	Mɛlɛka	Chriisu Kiliti
	Kpelle	Nan-Yala	Yesi Chili
	Kru	Nyansua	Yesu-Christi
Philippines	Tagalog	Dios or Diyos	Hesu-Kristo
	Ilocano	Apo Dios	Hesu-Kristo
	Pampango	Guinu	Hesu-Kristo
Samoa	Samoan	Atua	Iesu Keriso
Tonga	Tongan	'Otuo	Sisu Kalaisi
Vietnam	Vietnamese	Duc Chua Troi	Duc Chua Giexu Christ

Language	"Church"	"Church" as a building	"Church" as a community of the faithful
Cambodian	Preah Vihea		
Chinese		Li Bye Tang	Giao Hui
Fijian	Lotu	Vale Ni Lotu	Lotu
Fukienese		Lei Paitung	Kauhoe
Twi	Asɔre		
Fanti	Asɔre		
Ga	Sɔlemɔ		
Creole	Eglize		
French	Iglise		
Spanish	Iglesia		
Hmong	Church		
Gujarati	Mundli		
Hindi		Girja	Kalisiya
Malayalam	Sabha		
Tamil	Sabai		

Language	"Church"	"Church" as a building	"Church" as a community of the faithful
Telugu	Church		
Urdu		Girja	Kalisiya
Japanese	Kyokai		
Korean	Kyo Hoe		
Lao	Veehan		
Bassa	Cɔɔcì	Cɔɔcì-Gbo	Cɔɔcì-Nyɔ
Kissi	Church		
Kpelle		Yala-Polon	Yala-bala
Kru	Chuche		
Tagalog	Iglesiya		
Ilocano	Simbaan		
Pampango		Capilla	Pisamban
Samoan		Tapua'i	Lotu
Tongan		Falle Lotu	Siasi
Vietnamese		Nha Tho	Hoi Thanh

APPENDIX B

Calendars

Multicultural Calendar

January 1	New Year's Day
January 1	Haitian Independence Day
January 1–7	Prayer Week in Tongan-American churches
January 6	"El Dia de los Reyes" - the Day of the Kings in some Hispanic-American churches
January 19	Martin Luther King Day
February	Chinese New Year, Lunar New Year for the Korean-American, Formosan-American, and Vietnamese-American communities
February	Black History Month
February 14	Valentine's Day in the Euro-American community
February 19	Day of Remembrance within the Japanese community that recalls the day Japanese-Americans were sent to concentration camps.
March 1	Independence Uprising Movement in the Korean-American community
March 3	Girl's Day or Doll's Day in Japanese-American churches
March 6	Ghana's Independence Day
Second Sunday after Easter	Native American Awareness Sunday
April 13th or 14	Cambodian and Lao New Year
May: First Sunday	Children's Day in Tongan-American churches
May 5	Children's Day in Japanese-American churches

231

May: Second Sunday	Mother's Day in the Euro-American community
May 19	Malcolm X Day in the African-American community
May: Last Monday	Memorial Day (a day to honor those who died in war) in the Euro-American community
May: Last Sunday	Day of Remembrance in the Liberian-American community for those who died in the Liberian Civil War
June 12	Philippines' Independence Day
June: Third Sunday	Children's Day in Liberian-American churches
June: Third Sunday	Father's Day in the Euro-American community
June 19	Juneteenth. Freedom from slavery for African-Americans
July 4	Independence Day for the United States of America
July 26	Liberia's Independence Day
August 14	Pakistan's Independence Day
August 15	India's Independence Day
August 15	Korea's Independence Day
August: end of month during a full moon	Autumn Festival for children in the Vietnamese-American community
September: First Monday	Labor Day in the Euro-American community
September: Second Sunday	Women's Day in Tongan-American churches
October	Children's Sabbath in some African-American churches
October: Second Sunday	White Sunday in Samoan-American churches where the children take full responsibility for the service dressed in white with white flower leis on their heads

October 10	Fiji's Independence Day from Great Britain
November: Third Sunday	a service of Thanksgiving is celebrated in Korean-American churches
November: Last Thursday	American Thanksgiving
November: Last Thursday	Umoja Karamu - the Unity Feast. Substituted for American Thanksgiving in some African-American churches
December 17–24	"Las Posadas" in some Hispanic-American churches. It is a time of preparation for the coming of the Christ child.
December 26 -January 1	Kwanza in the African-American community
December 31	New Year's Eve Watch Night Services are held in many churches of various cultures

Liturgical Calendar

Advent	Begins four Sundays before Christmas
Christmas	December 25 - January 5
Day of the Epiphany	January 6
Season after Epiphany or Ordinary Time	January 7 - Shrove Tuesday (the day before Ash Wednesday)
Ash Wednesday	Forty-sixth day before Easter (Forty days of Lent plus six Sundays)
Lent	Begins on Ash Wednesday and ends on Easter Saturday
Easter Day	The first Sunday on or after the first full moon on or after the Spring Equinox.
Easter Season	Begins on Easter Sunday and ends 49 days later on the day before Pentecost
Day of Pentecost	The fiftieth day after Easter
Season after Pentecost or Ordinary Time	Begins the day after Pentecost and continues until the day before the first Sunday of Advent

233

GLOSSARY

Akan: One of the language systems of Ghana.

Akasaa: A gourd wrapped in beads that is used as a musical instrument in Ghanaian-American worship services.

Akwapim: One of the linguistic subgroups of the *Akan* language system of Ghana.

Ang Imnaryong Christiano: The name of the *Tagalog* hymnal used in many Filipino-American congregations.

Anke: An African symbol representing life sometimes worn as a necklace by African-American clergy in place of a cross.

Ao Dai: The traditional Vietnamese gown worn by the bride and bridesmaids in a wedding.

Arras: Gold colored novelty coins presented to Hispanic-American couples during their wedding ceremony.

Asanti: One of the linguistic subgroups of the *Akan* language system of Ghana.

Awakening: The name of the all night funeral celebration in Tongan-American churches.

Banduria: A Filipino instrument (similar to a mandolin) that is sometimes played in worship.

Banzai: A toast given at Japanese wedding receptions.

Barat: The name of the groom's entourage which includes his family and some friends in Indian-American weddings.

Barong: Ceremonial garb worn by Filipino men which may also be worn by clergy instead of a clerical robe, or by grooms in Filipino-American weddings.

Bassa: One of the common languages spoken in Liberian-American churches.

Bikabika: An all night worship service that precedes a funeral in the Fijian-American community. Literally translated it means "mourners."

Butubutu: A practice in the Fijian culture where the pastor stands on a pile of *fine mats* and *tapa cloths* during baptisms, weddings, and funerals.

Cantonese: The traditional dialect spoken in Hong Kong.

Chants D'Esperance: The name of the ecumenical Haitian hymnbook that includes hymns in both *Creole* and French.

Cloth Money: Money given to the family of the deceased at or before the memorial/funeral service in Chinese-American communities to assist the family in buying the white cloth for the service. Sometimes also called "white money."

Conga drums: Traditional drums from Ghana.

Consubstantiation: The belief that the communion elements are simultaneously the body and blood of Jesus as well as bread and wine/juice.

Contemporary Worship: More informal services in Euro-American churches that utilize many praise songs accompanied by instruments other than an organ or piano. The designers of contemporary worship do not assume the people present are familiar with biblical and traditional religious language.

Coritos: Short songs that are sung repeatedly in Hispanic-American churches.

Cov Ntseeg Yesxus Phoo Nkauj: The name of the Hmong hymnal.

Creole: The native language of Haiti.

Dance of Life: A dance form used in worship in Ghanaian-American churches.

Distribution of the Mourning Signs (Bands): A funeral practice within the Vietnamese Christian community.

El dia de los Reyes: "The day of the kings" which takes place on the day of Epiphany in the Hispanic tradition.

Fakaafe: A party or feast in the Tongan-American culture.

Falaie: Mats similar to the *fine mats* of Samoa but with bright colored yarn placed as a fringe around the mat. The bottom of the falaie may also be decorated with the colorful yarn depicting religious symbols or Samoan words.

Faleula: A house of leis built over the grave on the first year anniversary of death in the Samoan culture.

Fanti: One of the linguistic subgroups of the *Akan* language system of Ghana.

Flower Money: Money given to the family of the deceased in Chinese and Formosan churches It is given at or before the memorial/funeral service to assist them in buying flowers for the service.

Fritwa: A cone-shaped, metal musical instrument from Ghana.

Frutweaa: A metal musical instrument from Ghana.

Fukienese: The language of people of Taiwan and the Fukien (now Fujian) area of China who form the Formosan-American church.

Furoshiki: A square white cloth that covers the box containing the ashes of someone cremated in the Japanese tradition.

Ga: One of the languages of Ghana.

Gloria a Dios: "Glory to God" in Spanish.

Grambuba: African dress sometimes worn by African-American clergy to lead worship.

Gujarati: One of the native languages of people from India.

Hena: A red dye that is painted on the palms of the bride in the Pakistani culture in preparation for the bridegroom at an all night party which takes place the night before the wedding. It is also the word for this all night party.

Hikidemo: The practice in the Japanese community where the newly married couple sends thank you gifts to those who gave them wedding presents.

Hindi: One of the 2 national languages of India.

Hmoob Dawb: One of the Hmong dialects spoken by the "White Hmong."

Hmoob Ntsaub: One of the Hmong dialects spoken by the "Blue Hmong."

Ie Faitaga: A *tupenu* with pockets.

Ike Bana: A particular style of flower arrangement in the Japanese culture.

Ilocano: One of the languages spoken in the Philippines.

Imani: The seventh of the Seven Principles of *Kwanzaa*. It means Faith.

Intinction: A method of taking communion where the person dips a piece of bread into a chalice and partakes of both elements simultaneously.

Ipkwonsik: The name of the worship service that takes place at the funeral home the night before the funeral in the Korean-American church.

Ipkyosik: The name of the ceremony where a person 18 years of age makes a public renewal of one's baptismal vows and joins a Korean church.

Kava: The national drink of Fiji shared in wedding ceremonies.

Kente Cloth: Cloth made in Africa that is used to make clergy stoles, clothing, and vestments often worn by persons in the Ghanaian-American, Liberian-American, and African-American worship contexts.

Khloy: A Cambodian bamboo flute played in worship on special occasions.

Kiekie: The open-weave, skirt-like garment worn by women around their waist over their regular dress in the Tongan-American culture.

Kikombe Cha Umoja: The Unity Cup that holds the *libation* for the ritual of *Kwanzaa*.

Kinara: The candlestick holder that is used in the ritual of *Kwanzaa*.

Kissi: One of the common languages spoken in Liberian-American churches.

Koden: The Japanese practice of giving money to the family at the time of a funeral.

Koka: A tree in Tonga. Dye is made from the bark of the tree to paint symbols on *tapa cloth*.

Kpelle: One of the common languages spoken in Liberian-American churches.

Kru: One of the common languages spoken in Liberian-American churches.

Kujichagulia: The second of the Seven Principles of *Kwanzaa*. It means Self-Determination.

Kumpadre/Kumadre: Male and female relatives and friends that are asked to be godparents or sponsors for various aspects of the celebrations surrounding baptisms and weddings in the Filipino-American culture.

Kuumba: The sixth of the Seven Principles of *Kwanzaa*. It means Creativity.

Kwanzaa: An African-American holiday celebrated between Dec. 26 and Jan. 1.

Lali: A hollowed out wooden instrument that is struck with a mallet used on special occasions in the Tongan culture.

Lao: The name of the language used in Laotian-American worship.

Las Posadas: A ritual that takes place in many Hispanic cultures for the nine nights before Christmas, including Christmas Eve.

Lavalava: A wrap around, knee-length skirt worn by some Samoan-American male clergy in leading worship.

Lazo: A rope that is made in the form of a lasso. It is placed around the couple in Hispanic-American weddings.

Libation: Water that is poured from a gourd into a plant as the names of ancestors are read in some African and African-American ceremonies.

Madrina: A godmother in Hispanic cultures.

Magiti: The wedding feast in the Fijian culture.

Mandarin: The old term for one of the main dialects of China. Now the dialect is referred to as *Putonghua*.

Meaofa: The Tongan tradition of giving gifts to the ministers present at wedding *fakaafes*.

Menhdi: Another word for the all night party that takes place the night before Pakistani-American weddings.

Mihindi: Corn that is used to represent the children during the ritual of *Kwanzaa*.

Mil Voces: The title of a Hispanic hymnal.

Mishuma: The seven candles used to mark the seven days of *Kwanzaa*.

Mitunda: The fruits that are placed on the *Mkeka* and used symbolically in the ritual of *Kwanzaa*.

Mkeka: A straw mat used in the ritual of *Kwanzaa*.

Mochuu: The Japanese mourning practice that lasts one year after a spouse has died.

Na I Vakayakavi ni Turaga: The phrase for "the Lord's Supper" in the Fijian language.

Naming: A time in the funeral or memorial service that gives an overview of the life of the deceased in Euro-American United Methodist churches.

Nguzo Saba: The Seven Principles of *Kwanzaa*.

Nia: The fifth of the Seven Principles of *Kwanzaa*. It means Purpose.

Nichigo or Nihongo: The Japanese term used to refer to Japanese language congregations.

Nori: A flat sheet of seaweed used to pick up rice when rice is used in place of bread during Holy Communion in English language ministries of the Japanese community.

Padrino: A godfather in Hispanic cultures.

Pak-Bi Seng-Si: The name of the *Fukienese* hymnal published by the Taiwanese Christian Church Council of North America.

Pamanhikan: A Filipino-American engagement ritual where the parents of the groom ask the parents of the bride for permission for the marriage to take place.

Pampango: One of the languages spoken in the Philippines.

Pantanus: The leaves of the Patanus tree are used to make the Tongan *kiekie* and *ta'ovala*.

Paudau: A colorful embroidered cloth from the Hmong culture.

Pey: A Cambodian reed instrument played in worship on special occasions.

Piñata: A paper mache figure covered with strips of colored tissue paper and filled with candy. The piñata is hung by a rope as blindfolded children try to hit it with a stick to break it open. A piñata is a part of many Hispanic-American festivities.

Pow-wow: A religious, social, and cultural celebration in the Native American community.

Punjabi: One of the dialects spoken in Pakistan among Pakistani Christians.

Putonghua: The new word that replaces *Mandarin* as the common language of China.

Quinceañera: The celebration of a girl's 15th birthday in Hispanic cultures.

Repast: A reception following a grave site service in the Liberian-American tradition.

Roqoroqo: A ceremony in the Fijian culture to honor newborn infants.

Sakalameniti: The Tongan word for Sacrament, referring to Holy Communion.

Sake: A rice wine from the Japanese culture.

Sambika: The name of one of the Japanese hymnals.

Santa Communion: "Holy Communion" in Spanish.

Santa Cena: "Holy Supper" in Spanish.

Sari: The traditional dress for women in the Indian and Pakistani cultures.

Sasa: Shaker instruments made from gourds used in Liberian-American worship.

Smudging: A method of blessing in many Native American tribes. The smoke from burned sweet grass, cedar, or sage is brushed with a feather towards the person or space to be blessed.

Sua: The practice of giving gifts to Samoan-American clergy from various churches and denominations at weddings and funerals.

Tabla: The name of a Pakistani drum.

Tagalog: The most common language used in the Philippines and in many Filipino-American churches.

Tambu Kaisi: The name of the best quality mats from Fiji.

Ta'ovala: An open-weave skirt-like adornment worn by men in the Tongan-American culture over their *tupenu* on special occasions.

Tapa Cloth: A cloth made from bark with symbols painted on it in the Tongan, Samoan, and Fijian cultures.

Tapete: White embroidered cloth from the Philippines that is sometimes used as an altar cloth.

Toasting: After someone stands and offers words of blessing or hope for the couple in Euro-American weddings, everyone raises his or her glass as a gesture of honor and well wishing.

Tong Song Kido: A form of prayer in the Korean-American church where everyone prays their individual prayers simultaneously aloud.

Traditional Baptismal Formula: "I baptize you in the name of the Father, Son, and Holy Spirit."

Transubstantiation: The doctrine that the communion elements are literally the body and blood of Jesus— not bread and wine/juice.

Tro: A Cambodian stringed instrument played with a bow used in worship on special occasions.

Tupenu: A wrap-around, knee-length skirt sometimes worn by male clergy to lead worship in Tongan-American churches.

Tusi Pese: The name of the Samoan hymnal published in Samoa.

Twi: One of the linguistic subgroups of the *Akan* language system of Ghana.

Ujamaa: The fourth of the Seven Principles of *Kwanzaa*. It means Familyhood and Cooperative Economics.

Ujima: The third of the Seven Principles of *Kwanzaa*. It means Collective Work and Responsibility.

Umoja: The first of the Seven Principles of *Kwanzaa*. It means Unity.

Umoja Karamu: A Unity Feast that is sometimes celebrated in the African-American community in place of American Thanksgiving.

Urdu: The official language of Pakistan and one of the native languages of people from India.

Vaajtswv Fxujlug Cog Tseg Kws Cawm Taubneeg Txujsa: The name of the Hmong Bible. It means "God's Word Promised for the Salvation of Humankind."

Vidai: The name of the leave-taking ceremony that takes place the day after the wedding in the Indian (India) tradition where the bride goes home with the groom and his family.

Viewing: A time between someone's death and the funeral service where family and friends pay their last respects to the deceased and offer condolences to the family in the Euro-American culture.

Vola Ni Sere: The name of the Fijian Methodist Hymnal.

Wake: A worship service that takes place the night before the funeral in African-American churches.

Wake keeping: A worship service that takes place the night before the funeral in Liberian-American churches.

Witness: A time in the funeral or memorial service where family members and friends share their memories of the deceased in the Euro-American culture.

Words of Institution: (based on the last supper narratives from Matthew 26:26–28; Mark 14:22–24; Luke 22:19–20; and 1 Corinthians 11:23–25).

Zawadi: Gifts that are given to children during the ritual of *Kwanzaa*.

CONSULTANTS AND EDITORS

During the data gathering and writing stages of this book, the consultants and editors were pastors of the following churches:

Rev. Marvin B. Abrams
> Pastor of the Native American United Methodist Church in Anaheim, CA.

Rev. Samuel Acquaah Arhin
> Pastor of Ghana Wesley United Methodist Church in Brooklyn, NY.

Rev. Sony Augustin
> Pastor of Premier Eglise United Methodist Church in Brooklyn, NY.

Rev. Yvonne Williams Boyd
> Pastor of an African-American congregation, West Altadena United Methodist Church in Altadena, CA.

Dr. Seog Wan Cho
> Pastor of the Korean Central United Methodist Church in Los Angeles, CA.

Rev. Samuel Chow
> Pastor of the Chinese United Methodist Church in the Chinatown area of Los Angeles, CA.

Rev. John N. David
> Local pastor for the Pakistani congregation of the Geneva Avenue United Methodist Church in San Francisco, CA.

Rev. Dr. Ronald Dunk
> Pastor of the Pitman United Methodist Church in Pitman, NJ.

Rev. Myriam Escorcia
> Pastor of a Hispanic congregation, Trinity United Methodist Church in Whittier, CA.

Rev. Matini Niponi Finau
> Pastor of a Tongan congregation, the Tala-Fungani United Methodist Church in Long Beach, CA.

Rev. Dr. Daniel Grimes Gueh
Pastor of the African United Methodist Church in Trenton, NJ.

Rev. Keith P. Inouye
Pastor of a second and third generation Japanese congregation at the North Gardena United Methodist Church in Torrance, CA.

Rev. Dr. Winson Josiah
Pastor of an Indian congregation, Christ United Methodist Church in Brooklyn, NY.

Saimone Kete
Local pastor in training with the Fijian ministry of the Shoreline United Methodist Church in Seattle, WA.

Rev. Mamie Ko
Pastor of the English speaking congregation of the Chinese United Methodist Church in the Chinatown area of Los Angeles, CA.

Rev. Dr. John C. Kounthapanya
Pastor of the Laotian congregation at the Tecumseh United Methodist Church in Tecumseh, NE.

Rev. Dr. Richard Yasuhiko Kuyama
Pastor of a first generation Japanese congregation at West Los Angeles United Methodist Church in Los Angeles, CA.

Pitou Lao
Lay pastor of the Cambodian ministry at First United Methodist Church in Santa Ana, CA.

Rev. Pita Lauti
Pastor of the Samoan congregation at Silverado United Methodist Church in Long Beach, CA.

Rev. Dr. David Marcelo
Pastor of the Filipino congregation at Wilshire United Methodist Church in Los Angeles, CA.

Rev. Cam Phu Nguyen
Pastor of the Vietnamese congregation at Granada Park United Methodist Church in Alhambra, CA.

Rev. M. Andrew Robinson-Gaither
Pastor of an African-American congregation, Faith United Methodist Church in Los Angeles, CA.

Rev. Dr. Luat Trong Tran
Pastor of the West Anaheim Vietnamese United Methodist Church in Anaheim, CA.

Rev. Frank Yang
Pastor of the Formosan congregation at Park Presidio United Methodist Church in San Francisco, CA.

Rev. Kham Dy Yang
Pastor of the Hmong Community United Methodist Church in St. Paul, MN.